International Human Rights

Dilemmas in World Politics

Series Editor: Jennifer Sterling-Folker, University of Connecticut

Why is it difficult to achieve the universal protection of human rights? How can democratization be achieved so that it is equitable and lasting? Why does agreement on global environmental protection seem so elusive? How does the concept of gender play a role in the shocking inequalities of women throughout the globe? Why do horrific events such as genocide or ethnic conflicts recur or persist? These are the sorts of questions that confront policy makers and students of contemporary international politics alike. They are dilemmas because they are enduring problems in world affairs that are difficult to resolve.

These are the types of dilemmas at the heart of the Dilemmas in World Politics series. Each book in the series addresses a challenge or problem in world politics that is topical, recurrent, and not easily solved. Each is structured to cover the historical and theoretical aspects of the dilemma, as well as the policy alternatives for and future direction of the problem. The books are designed as supplements to introductory and intermediate courses in international relations. The books in the Dilemmas in World Politics series encourage students to engage in informed discussion of current policy issues.

BOOKS IN THIS SERIES

International Human Rights, Fourth Edition
Jack Donnelly

The United Nations in the 21st Century, Fourth Edition
Karen A. Mingst and Margaret P. Karns

Global Environmental Politics, Fifth Edition
Pamela S. Chasek, David L. Downie, and Janet Welsh Brown

Global Gender Issues in the New Millennium, Third Edition
V. Spike Peterson and Anne Sisson Runyan

United States Foreign Policy in the 21st Century: Gulliver's Travails
J. Martin Rochester

Democracy and Democratization in a Changing World, Third Edition
Georg Sørensen

Southern Africa in World Politics
Janice Love

Ethnic Conflict in World Politics, Second Edition
Barbara Harff and Ted Robert Gurr

Dilemmas of International Trade, Second Edition
Bruce E. Moon

Humanitarian Challenges and Intervention, Second Edition
Thomas G. Weiss and Cindy Collins

The European Union: Dilemmas of Regional Integration
James A. Caporaso

International Futures, Third Edition
Barry B. Hughes

Revolution and Transition in East-Central Europe, Second Edition
David S. Mason

One Land, Two Peoples, Second Edition
Deborah Gerner

Dilemmas of Development Assistance
Sarah J. Tisch and Michael B. Wallace

East Asian Dynamism, Second Edition
Steven Chan

International Human Rights

FOURTH EDITION

JACK DONNELLY

University of Denver

Westview Press
A Member of the Perseus Books Group

Westview Press was founded in 1975 in Boulder, Colorado, by notable publisher and intellectual Fred Praeger. Westview Press continues to publish scholarly titles and high-quality undergraduate- and graduate-level textbooks in core social science disciplines. With books developed, written, and edited with the needs of serious nonfiction readers, professors, and students in mind, Westview Press honors its long history of publishing books that matter.

Find us on the World Wide Web at www.westviewpress.com.
Every effort has been made to secure required permissions for all text, images, maps, and other art reprinted in this volume.

Westview Press books are available at special discounts for bulk purchases in the United States by corporations, institutions, and other organizations. For more information, please contact the Special Markets Department at the Perseus Books Group, 2300 Chestnut Street, Suite 200, Philadelphia, PA 19103, or call (800) 810-4145, ext. 5000, or e-mail special.markets@perseusbooks.com.

Designed by Linda Mark

Library of Congress Cataloging-in-Publication Data

Donnelly, Jack.
    International human rights / Jack Donnelly.—4th ed.
       p. cm.
    Includes bibliographical references and index.
    ISBN 978-0-8133-4501-7 (pbk. : alk. paper)—ISBN 978-0-8133-4502-4 (e-book)
    1. Human rights. 2. International relations. I. Title.
JC571.D753 2013
341.4'8—dc23
                                                                          2012017026

10 9 8 7 6 5 4 3 2

Contents

LIST OF CASE STUDIES

LIST OF PROBLEMS

TABLES AND BOXES

Tables

Boxes

Acronyms

AI	Amnesty International
ANC	African National Congress
APDH	Permanent Assembly for Human Rights
ASEAN	Association of Southeast Asian Nations
AU	African Union
CCP	Chinese Communist Party
CELS	Center for Legal and Social Studies
CIA	Central Intelligence Agency
CONADEP	Argentine National Commission on Disappeared Persons, the Sabato Commission
HRW	Human Rights Watch
IACHR	Inter-American Commission on Human Rights
ICC	International Criminal Court
JNA	Yugoslav National Army
MFN	most favored nation
MNC	multinational corporation
NGO	Nongovernmental organization
NSM 39	National Security Memorandum 39
OAS	Organization of American States
OHCHR	Office of the High Commissioner for Human Rights
OSCE	Organization for Security and Co-operation in Europe
SERPAJ	Service for Peace and Justice
UN	United Nations
UNAMIR	United Nations Assistance Mission in Rwanda
UNESCO	United Nations Educational, Scientific, and Cultural Organization
UNPA	United Nations Protected Area
UNPROFOR	United Nations Protection Force in the former Yugoslavia

Acknowledgments

I began working on the first edition of this book two decades ago. Over that time, I have had the help of literally dozens of friends, colleagues, students, research assistants, and editors. Any list would be both too long, losing the individuals in a stream of names, and too short, for I am sure that I would neglect mentioning at least a few people who contributed to the book. Thus, let me simply say: Thanks to all of you. (You know who you are.)

Introduction

A Note to the Reader

This is a book about the international relations of human rights since the end of World War II; that is, the ways in which states and other international actors have addressed human rights. The topic, although broad, is narrower than some readers might expect.

Life, liberty, security, subsistence, and other things to which we have human rights may be denied by an extensive array of individuals and organizations. "Human rights," however, are usually taken to have a special reference to the ways in which states treat their own citizens. For example, domestically, we distinguish muggings and private assaults, which are not typically considered human rights violations, from police brutality and torture, which are. Internationally, we distinguish terrorism, war, and war crimes from human rights abuses, even though all lead to denials of life and security. Although the boundaries are not always clear, the distinction is part of our ordinary language and focuses our attention on an important set of political problems.

No single book can cover all aspects of the politics of human rights. My concern is *international* human rights policies, a vital and now well-established area of policy and inquiry. This does not imply that international action is the principal determinant of whether human rights are respected or violated. In fact, much of this book demonstrates the limits of international action. And one of its distinctive features, as opposed to most other discussions of international human rights, is its substantial attention to the domestic politics of human rights. Chapter 4 provides a relatively detailed look at human rights violations in the Southern Cone of South America in the 1970s and 1980s. Later chapters provide briefer domestic case studies of South Africa, Central America, China, and the former Yugoslavia.

Another distinctive feature of this book, along with the other volumes in the Dilemmas in World Politics series, is a relatively extensive emphasis on theory, which provides the heart of Part 1. Chapter 2 addresses philosophical issues of the nature, substance, and source of human rights; the place of human rights in the contemporary international society of states; and the theoretical challenges posed to the very enterprise of international human rights policy by arguments of radical cultural relativism and political realism (realpolitik, or "power politics"). Chapter 3 explores the important theoretical issue of the universality (and relativity) of human rights.

Part 2 looks at multilateral, bilateral, and transnational action, both separately and comparatively, with an emphasis on cold war–era case studies. In earlier editions, this material was covered in two very long chapters. In this edition it has been broken into seven short chapters. These smaller pieces, in addition to being easier to swallow and digest, encourage comparisons within and across types of action and historical cases. Separate chapters consider global multilateral mechanisms, regional mechanisms, American foreign policy, foreign policy action in general, and transnational advocacy, and two extremely short chapters compare multilateral mechanisms and comparatively assess the different means of international action.

Part 3 turns to issues and cases since the end of the cold war, with an emphasis on issues of ongoing contemporary concern. Chapter 12 examines international reactions to human rights violations in China, focusing on responses to the 1989 Tiananmen Square massacre but also considering contemporary initiatives now that China has become a great power. The remaining chapters consider humanitarian intervention against genocide, globalization, and the human rights consequences of "the war on terror."

I have tried to write a book that assumes little or no background knowledge. Most readers with an interest in the topic, regardless of age or experience, should find this book accessible. However, I have tried not to write a textbook, a term that has justly acquired pejorative overtones. I have taken care not to write "down," either in style or in substance. And although I have made an effort to retain some balance in the discussion, I have not expunged my own views and interpretations.

Textbook presentations of controversial issues—when they are not entirely avoided—tend to involve bland and noncommittal presentations of "the two sides" to an argument. By contrast, I often lay out and defend one interpretation and give little attention to alternative views. I have made great efforts to be accurate and fair, but there is no false pretense of "objectivity."

I thus draw the reader's attention to the discussion questions for each chapter. There is almost a short chapter's worth of material in these questions, which often frame alternative interpretations and highlight controversial claims in the main body of the text. They thus provide at least a partial corrective to any "imbalance" in the main text.

I also draw your attention to a new feature of this edition of the book: nine "problems" spread throughout the volume. (See "List of Problems" above.) Each is, in effect, a discussion question, followed by my own answer, followed by further questions or problems. They aim to provoke further thought and discussion and to illustrate ways in which readers may take the material presented here and go beyond it.

Another central feature of this volume is the extensive use of case studies. (See "List of Case Studies" above.) I have found that students, especially undergraduates, have some familiarity with recent cases but that those from earlier decades are largely unknown to them. They thus lack both context and points of comparison—which the case studies in this volume try to provide.

Each chapter—as well as each case study and each problem—can be read independently, in any order. Teachers and readers can thus easily customize this book. My only strong suggestion is that those without a background begin with Chapter 1. From then on, follow your interests—or the instructions of your teacher. And approach everything here with a critical mind.

My goal is to get you to think about why and how human rights are violated, what can (and cannot) be done about such violations through international action, why human rights remain such a small part of international relations, and what might be done about that. These are pressing political issues that merit, even demand, thought and attention. This book provides resources to help you think about them more broadly, more deeply, and more subtly—and thus to be a more informed, and perhaps even more effective, person and citizen.

PART ONE
Introduction and Theory

1

Human Rights as an Issue in World Politics

Most of us today take human rights to be a normal and "obvious" part of international relations. Such an understanding, however, goes back only to the end of World War II.

The recognition of certain limited religious rights for some Christian minorities in the Peace of Westphalia (1648), which brought the Thirty Years' War to an end, can be seen as an early precursor of the idea of international human rights. The 1815 Treaty of Vienna, which brought an end to the Revolutionary and Napoleonic Wars, included limited minority rights provisions. Nineteenth-century campaigns against the slave trade and slavery had clear overtones of what today we would call human rights advocacy. After World War I, workers' rights and minority rights were addressed by the newly created International Labor Organization and League of Nations. Nonetheless, prior to World War II there was near-universal agreement that human rights were *not* a legitimate concern of international relations. For example, the term *human rights* is not even mentioned in the Covenant of the League of Nations, which is usually seen as an expression of the "idealism" of the immediate post–World War I era.

The principle of sovereignty has been the organizing principle of international relations for the past three centuries. States, the leading actors in international relations, are seen as **sovereign,** that is, supreme authorities in their own territories, and thus subject to no higher political authority. The principal duty correlative to the right of sovereignty is **nonintervention,** the obligation not to interfere in matters essentially within the domestic jurisdiction of sovereign states. Human rights, which typically involve a state's treatment of its own citizens in its own territory, were seen as such a matter of protected domestic jurisdiction. A major purpose of this book is to chronicle a fundamental change over the past seventy years in the understanding of the range of state sovereignty.

1. THE EMERGENCE OF INTERNATIONAL
HUMAN RIGHTS NORMS

The beginnings of what became the contemporary human rights movement can be traced back to the era between the two world wars. For example, the International Law Commission adopted the Declaration of the International Rights of Man in 1929. British novelist and activist H. G. Wells in the 1930s cast much of his advocacy for social reform in terms of human rights. But such efforts represented only a tiny, radical fringe of civil society. Even those who believed that all human beings had an extensive set of equal and inalienable rights—a distinctly minority idea in an era that had little trouble justifying colonialism—did not suggest that other states had rights or obligations with respect to those rights. And not a single state endorsed the idea that governments had *international* human rights obligations to their own citizens.

As the Allied powers reflected on the nature of their struggle with Hitler's Germany—and on how to justify the war to their own citizens and the rest of the world—respect for human rights became an increasingly central theme. The January 1942 Declaration of the United Nations claimed that "complete victory over their enemies is essential to defend life, liberty, independence and religious freedom, and to preserve human rights and justice in their own lands as well as in other lands." From late 1942 on, human rights were a part of postwar planning of both the American and the British governments, the two leading Allied powers. But the real impetus for international action came in 1945 as Allied governments and publics began to reflect on the Holocaust, Germany's systematic mass murder of millions of innocent civilians.

Before the war, little was done to aid Jews trying to flee Germany and surrounding countries. Some who escaped were even denied refuge by Allied governments, including the United States. During the war, no effort was made to impede the functioning of the death camps. The Allies did not even target the railway lines that brought hundreds of thousands to the slaughter at Auschwitz and other death camps. The world watched—or, rather, turned a blind eye to—the genocidal massacre of six million Jews, a half-million Gypsies (Roma), and tens of thousands of communists, social democrats, homosexuals, church activists, and just ordinary decent people who refused complicity in the new politics and technology of barbarism. As the war came to an end, though, Allied leaders and citizens, previously preoccupied with military victory, finally began to confront this horror.

But shocking as the Nazi atrocities were, the international community lacked the legal and political language to condemn them. Massacring one's own citizens simply was not an established international legal offense. The German government may have been liable under the laws of war for its treatment of citizens in occupied territories, but in killing German nationals it was merely exercising its sovereign rights.

The Nuremberg War Crimes Trials, which began in 1945, introduced the novel charge of crimes against humanity. For the first time, officials were held legally ac-

BOX 1.1   Treaties as a Source of International Law

Lawmaking treaties such as the 1948 Genocide Convention and the 1966 International Human Rights Covenants typically are drafted by an international organization or conference and then presented to states for their consideration—or, as international lawyers put it, they are "opened for signature and ratification." Neither the drafting of a treaty nor its approval by the United Nations or another international organization gives it legal effect. For a treaty to be binding, it must be accepted by sovereign states. And it is binding only on those states that have formally and voluntarily accepted it.

Signing a treaty is a declaration by a state that it intends to be bound by the treaty. That obligation, however, only becomes effective after the treaty has been ratified or acceded to according to the constitutional procedures of that country. (In the United States, the president signs a treaty and then transmits it to the Senate for ratification, for which a two-thirds vote is required.) States that have ratified or acceded to a treaty are said to be parties to the treaty. Typically a specified number of states must become parties before the treaty becomes binding. When sufficient ratifications have been filed, the treaty is said to enter into force.

countable to the international community for offenses against individual citizens, not states, and individuals who in many cases were nationals, not foreigners.

Of even broader significance, though, was the incorporation of human rights into the United Nations (UN), also created in 1945. The Preamble of the UN Charter lists as two of the four principal objectives of the organization "to reaffirm faith in fundamental human rights, in the dignity and worth of the human person, in the equal rights of men and women and of nations large and small" and "to promote social progress and better standards of life in larger freedom." Likewise, Article 1 lists as one of the four purposes of the United Nations "to achieve international cooperation in solving international problems of an economic, social, cultural, or humanitarian character, and in promoting and encouraging respect for human rights and for fundamental freedoms for all without distinction as to race, sex, language, or religion."

These statements were in themselves revolutionary. Even more radical was the creation in 1946 of the Commission on Human Rights, which quickly began to give definition to these abstract statements of postwar optimism and goodwill.

The original commission was composed of eighteen elected members, generally representative of the (then fifty-one) members of the organization. Its first task, which it discharged with speed and skill, was to draft an authoritative statement of international human rights norms. The initial drafts were written by John Humphrey, a young Canadian member of the commission's staff, and René Cassin, the French member of the commission. There was widespread participation, though, by non-Western representatives. The eight-member drafting committee included P. C. Chang of China (the vice chair of the commission), Charles Malik of Lebanon (the rapporteur of the commission), and Hernan Santa Cruz of Chile. Each, along with the chair of both the commission and the drafting committee, Eleanor Roosevelt of the United States, played a major role in shaping the Declaration.

By the fall of 1948, after barely a year and a half of work, the commission had completed a brief statement of principles. It was adopted as the **Universal Declaration of Human Rights** by the United Nations General Assembly on December 10, 1948. (December 10 is thus celebrated globally as Human Rights Day.) The vote was forty-eight in favor, none opposed, and eight abstentions. (Saudi Arabia abstained principally because of provisions that allowed Muslims to change their religion. South Africa abstained because of the provisions on racial equality. The abstention of the six Soviet-bloc states [USSR, Byelorussian SSR, Czechoslovakia, Poland, Ukrainian SSR, and Yugoslavia] was ostensibly because the document was insufficiently detailed and far reaching.)

Although most of Africa, much of Asia, and parts of the Americas were still under colonial rule, the Universal Declaration of Human Rights had global endorsement. It received the votes of fourteen European and other Western states, nineteen states from Latin America, and fifteen from Africa and Asia. In other words, Western and Afro-Asian states made up equal percentages. And the countries that later achieved their independence were at least as enthusiastic in their embrace of the Declaration as those who voted for it in 1948. In Africa in particular, the Universal Declaration was liberally referenced and frequently quoted in independence-era constitutions.

Article 1 of the Universal Declaration states its foundation: "All human beings are born free and equal in dignity and rights. They are endowed with reason and conscience and should act towards one another in a spirit of brotherhood." The substantive bookend is Article 28: "Everyone is entitled to a social and international order in which the rights and freedoms set forth in this Declaration can be fully realized." In between, Articles 2–27 lay out a comprehensive set of rights that have come to define what we mean by internationally recognized human rights. Article 2 recognizes the right to nondiscrimination. An extensive series of **civil and political rights** are recognized in Articles 3–21, including rights to life, liberty, and security of person; an array of legal protections and civil liberties; and the right to political participation. Articles 16–18 and 22–27 recognize a wide range of **economic, social, and cultural rights,** including rights to an adequate standard of living, social security, work, rest and leisure, family, education, and participation in the cultural life of the community.[1]

Even today the Universal Declaration provides the most authoritative statement of international human rights norms. This vital document is reprinted in the Appendix. Its main provisions are summarized in Table 1.1.

2. FROM COLD WAR TO COVENANTS

Technically, the Universal Declaration of Human Rights is not, in itself, legally binding. (The Declaration describes itself as "a common standard of achievement

TABLE 1.1 Internationally Recognized Human Rights

The International Bill of Human Rights recognizes the rights to:

Equality of rights without discrimination (Dl, D2, E2, E3, C2, C3)
Life (D3, C6)
Liberty and security of person (D3, C9)
Protection against slavery (D4, C8)
Protection against torture and cruel and inhuman punishment (D5, C7)
Recognition as a person before the law (D6, C16)
Equal protection of the law (D7, C14, C26)
Access to legal remedies for rights violations (D8, C2)
Protection against arbitrary arrest or detention (D9, C9)
Hearing before an independent and impartial judiciary (DID, C14)
Presumption of innocence (Dll, C14)
Protection against ex post facto laws (Dll, CIS)
Protection of privacy, family, and home (D12, C17)
Freedom of movement and residence (D13, C12)
Seek asylum from persecution (D14)
Nationality (D15)
Marry and found a family (D16, E10, C23)
Own property (D17)
Freedom of thought, conscience, and religion (D18, C18)
Freedom of opinion, expression, and the press (D19, C19)
Freedom of assembly and association (D20, C21, C22)
Political participation (D21, C25)
Social security (D22, E9)
Work, under favorable conditions (D23, E6, E7)
Free trade unions (D23, E8, C22)
Rest and leisure (D24, E7)
Food, clothing, and housing (D25, Ell)
Health care and social services (D25, E12)
Special protections for children (D25, E10, C24)
Education (D26, E13, E14)
Participation in cultural life (D27, E15)
A social and international order needed to realize rights (D28)
Self-determination (El, Cl)
Humane treatment when detained or imprisoned (CIO)
Protection against debtor's prison (Cll)
Protection against arbitrary expulsion of aliens (C13)
Protection against advocacy of racial or religious hatred (C20)
Protection of minority culture (C27)

Note: This list includes all rights that are enumerated in two of the three documents of the International Bill of Human Rights or have a full article in one document. The source of each right is indicated in parentheses, by document and article number. D = Universal Declaration of Human Rights. E = International Covenant on Economic, Social, and Cultural Rights. C = International Covenant on Civil and Political Rights.

for all peoples and all nations.") The commission, having completed its work on the Universal Declaration, thus immediately began drafting a treaty to give binding international legal force to international human rights norms. By 1952 a near-final working draft had been negotiated. But the rise of the **cold war**, the ideological and geopolitical struggle between the United States and the Soviet Union, brought this initial progress to a halt.

In the United States, a coalition of cold warriors, isolationists, and racists (who did not want additional international scrutiny of legalized racial discrimination in the United States) forced President Eisenhower to agree not to support any human rights treaty that would emerge from the United Nations. Fearing that a treaty without US participation might weaken rather than strengthen the development of international human rights law, the commission tabled its draft. For the following decade, international discussions of human rights largely degenerated into a device to score ideological debating points, each side highlighting violations in the other but ignoring their own problems and preventing any progress on effective international action.

With the dismantling of Western colonial empires, however, the membership of the United Nations, and its political priorities, began to change. In the early 1960s, a coalition of Third World and Western states, with Soviet-bloc support, revived the commission's draft treaty. With modest revisions, it became the 1966 **International Human Rights Covenants**. (For largely technical and procedural reasons, what was originally intended to be a single covenant became two, the International Covenant on Economic, Social, and Cultural Rights and the International Covenant on Civil and Political Rights.) The International Human Rights Covenants make a few substantive revisions to the Universal Declaration of Human Rights, most notably adding a right of self-determination of peoples, but for the most part they follow and elaborate on the 1948 Declaration.

The UN charter's human rights provisions, the Universal Declaration, and the Covenants are often referred to collectively as the **International Bill of Human Rights**. They state the minimum social and political guarantees recognized by the international community as necessary for a life of dignity in the contemporary world. Table 1.1 summarizes their content.

3. THE 1970s: FROM STANDARD SETTING TO MONITORING

The comprehensiveness of the International Human Rights Covenants meant that further progress on international human rights would now depend primarily on implementing these standards—an area in which the United Nations had been, and still is, far less successful. The existence of international norms does not in itself give the United Nations, or anyone else, the authority to implement them, or even to inquire into how states implement (or do not implement) them. By ratifying the Covenants, states agree to follow international human rights standards. But as we will see in more detail in Chapter 5, they do not authorize international enforcement of these standards.

Nonetheless, the late 1960s saw a flurry of international initiatives to monitor national human rights practices. In 1967 Economic and Social Council Resolution 1235 authorized the Commission on Human Rights to discuss human rights violations in particular countries. In 1969 the racial discrimination convention came into force, requiring parties to file periodic reports on implementation. In 1970 Economic and Social Council Resolution 1503 authorized the Commission on Human Rights to conduct confidential investigations of complaints that suggested "a consistent pattern of gross and reliably attested violations of human rights and fundamental freedoms." Although all of these efforts were limited and largely symbolic, the UN was at last beginning to move, however tentatively, from merely setting standards to examining how states implemented those standards.

The United Nations operates under severe structural constraints. It is an **intergovernmental organization** (IGO), established by a multilateral treaty (the UN Charter) among sovereign states. Its members are sovereign states. Delegates to the United Nations represent states, not the international community, let alone individuals whose rights are violated. Like other IGOs, the UN has only those powers that

---

BOX 1.2   Sources of International Law

The two main sources of international law are treaties and custom. Other sources—for example, the writings of publicists, general principles of law recognized in the domestic law of most states, national and international judicial decisions, or *jus cogens* (overriding international norms, very much like the classical idea of the natural law)—are either of lesser importance or their status is a matter of controversy.

Treaties are essentially contractual agreements of states to accept certain specified obligations. The process by which treaties become binding is briefly discussed in Box 1.1.

Customary rules of international law are well-established state practices to which a sense of obligation has come to be attached. One classic example often used in teaching international law in the United States is the case of *The Scotia*. The US Supreme Court decided in 1871 that it had become a binding customary practice of the international law of the sea that ships show colored running lights in a pattern originally specified by Great Britain, and the Court awarded damages on the basis of this unwritten, customary law. In the area of human rights, a US District Court held in the 1980 case of *Filartiga v. Peña-Irala*, brought by the family of a Paraguayan torture victim, that torture was a violation of customary international law.

Some lawyers have argued that the Universal Declaration of Human Rights has, over time, become a part of customary international law, or at least strong evidence of custom. Even if this is true, the Universal Declaration per se does not establish international legal obligations. That task was reserved by its drafters for a later treaty, which was ultimately adopted by the UN General Assembly in 1966, and entered into force in 1976.

states—which are also the principal violators of human rights—give it. Thus, perhaps more surprising than the limits on its human rights monitoring powers is the fact that the UN acquired even these limited powers. Although of little comfort to victims, a balanced assessment of the human rights achievements of the UN and other intergovernmental organizations cannot ignore the limits imposed by state sovereignty.

Modest progress on monitoring continued in the 1970s. In response to the 1973 military coup in Chile (see Chapter 4), the UN created the Ad Hoc Working Group on the Situation of Human Rights in Chile. In 1976 the International Human Rights Covenants entered into force, leading to the creation of the **Human Rights Committee** (HRC), which is charged with monitoring implementation of the International Covenant on Civil and Political Rights.

Human rights were also explicitly and systematically introduced into the bilateral foreign policies of individual countries in the 1970s, beginning in the United States. Although practice fell short of rhetoric, these bilateral initiatives helped to open space for new ways of thinking about and acting on international human rights concerns, as we will see in some detail in Chapters 8 and 9.

The 1970s also saw substantial growth in the number and range of activities of human rights **nongovernmental organizations** (NGOs), private associations that engage in political activity. Such groups act as advocates for victims of human rights violations by publicizing violations and lobbying to alter the practices of states and international organizations. Best known is Amnesty International (AI), which received the Nobel Peace Prize in 1977 and has an international membership of more than a million people. Chapter 10 briefly examines transnational human rights advocacy.

4. THE 1980s: FURTHER GROWTH AND INSTITUTIONALIZATION

Multilateral, bilateral, and transnational nongovernmental human rights activity continued to increase, more or less steadily, through the 1980s. New treaties were introduced on discrimination against women (1979), torture (1984), and the rights of the child (1989). The Human Rights Committee began to review periodic reports submitted by states (see §5.3). In 1985 a parallel Committee on Economic, Social, and Cultural Rights was established. The Commission on Human Rights undertook "thematic" initiatives on disappearances, torture, and summary or arbitrary executions. And a larger and more diverse group of countries came under commission scrutiny.

The process of incorporating human rights into bilateral foreign policy also accelerated in the 1980s. The Netherlands, Norway, and Canada developed particularly prominent international human rights policies (see §8.5). The European Community (predecessor of the European Union [EU]) introduced human rights concerns into its external relations. A few Third World countries, such as Costa Rica, also emphasized human rights in their foreign policies.

The 1980s also saw a dramatic decline in the fortunes of repressive dictatorships. Throughout Latin America, military regimes that had appeared unshakable in the 1970s crumbled in the 1980s (see §4.5). By 1990 elected governments held office in every continental country in the Western Hemisphere (although the democratic and human rights credentials of some, such as Paraguay, were extremely suspect). In addition, there were peaceful transfers of power after elections in several countries in 1989, including Argentina, Brazil, El Salvador, and Uruguay.

In Asia the personalist dictatorship of Ferdinand Marcos was overthrown in the Philippines in 1986. South Korea's military dictatorship was replaced by an elected government in 1988. Taiwan ended four decades of imposed single-party rule. In Pakistan Benazir Bhutto was elected president in December 1988, ending a dozen years of military rule. Asia, however, also presented the most dramatic human rights setback of the decade—the June 1989 massacre in Beijing's Tiananmen Square (see Chapter 12).

The changes with the greatest international impact, however, occurred in Central and Eastern Europe. Soviet-imposed regimes in East Germany and Czechoslovakia crumbled in the fall of 1989 in the face of peaceful mass protests. In Hungary and Poland, where liberalization had begun earlier in the decade, Communist Party dictatorships also peacefully withdrew from power. Even Romania and Bulgaria ousted their old communist governments (although their new governments included numerous former communists with tenuous democratic credentials). And in the USSR, where glasnost (openness) and perestroika (restructuring) had created the international political space for these changes, the Communist Party fell from power after the abortive military coup of August 1991. The Soviet Union itself was dissolved four months later.

5. THE 1990s: CONSOLIDATING PROGRESS AND ACTING AGAINST GENOCIDE

The 1990s was a decade of gradual, but generally positive, change in most regions—punctuated by striking examples of the most retrograde barbarism (see Chapter 13). In Latin America and Central and Eastern Europe, the progress of the 1980s was largely maintained. In many cases, such as El Salvador and Hungary, liberalization substantially deepened. In a few countries, such as the Czech Republic, Argentina, and Mexico, full democratization was achieved. In most of the former Soviet republics, however, the human rights situation even today is discouraging.

In sub-Saharan Africa, where one-party and no-party states remained the norm throughout the 1980s, political liberalization was widespread in the 1990s. Progress, however, was inconsistent, and often not very deep. Nonetheless, the November 1991 electoral defeat of Kenneth Kaunda, Zambia's president for the first twenty-five years of its independence, was an important democratic first for the region. And the end of apartheid in South Africa, which held its first elections under the principle of universal suffrage in 1994, was a dramatic change indeed. More typical, though, was Nigeria, Africa's most populous country, where the military annulled the results of elections in 1992 and 1993 and General Sani Abacha exercised particularly harsh military rule over the country from 1993 until his death in 1998.

In Asia the picture in the 1990s was also mixed but more generally positive. South Korea and Taiwan consolidated democratic, rights-protective regimes. Cambodia, with a substantial assist from the United Nations, cast off Vietnamese occupation and freely elected a government that was by far the most liberal it had seen in decades. Tentative and partial liberalization occurred in Vietnam. Indonesia saw limited political reform with the expulsion of the Suharto regime in 1998. And India, for all its problems, remained the world's largest multiparty electoral democracy.

China, however, despite its substantial economic opening and political reform, remained a highly repressive, Stalinist-party state. Burma continued to repress its internal democracy movement and rebuff international pressures for liberalization. Afghanistan suffered under the theocratic brutality of Taliban rule from 1996 to 2001. North Korea consolidated its position as the world's most closed and politically backward state. And many Asian governments and elites began to argue that international human rights standards did not apply in their entirety in Asia (see Problem 6).

Sadly, though, the mixed picture in Africa and Asia was far more encouraging than that in the Middle East in the 1990s. Hafez al-Assad, Saddam Hussein, and Mu'ammar Gadhafi sustained their personalist dictatorships in Syria, Iraq, and Libya, respectively. Religious intolerance and the suppression of all dissent remained the norm in Iran. The Gulf states remained closed and undemocratic. Increasingly violent Islamic fundamentalist movements led to growing repression in Egypt and plunged Algeria into a shockingly brutal civil war. About the only examples of substantial progress were modest liberalization in the monarchies of Jordan, Morocco, and Kuwait.

A similar pattern of solidifying past gains coupled with modest progress in selected areas was apparent internationally. Perhaps most striking was the decisive rebuff of arguments by China and other countries at the World Human Rights Conference in Vienna in 1993 against the full implementation of internationally recognized human rights in the short and medium terms. The very decision to hold the world conference indicates the growing force of the idea of international human rights. And the creation at the end of 1993 of a high commissioner for human rights proved to be an important step in expanding both the scope and the depth of multilateral monitoring (see §5.2). Such events, particularly when coupled with the changes in national practices already noted, signify a deepening penetration of the international consensus on human rights norms.

Human rights also became a more deeply entrenched and less controversial concern of bilateral foreign policy. National nongovernmental human rights organizations and advocates became a significant part of the political landscape in a growing number of countries in the Third World and former Soviet bloc. Transnational human rights NGOs also increased their prestige and influence.

In one area, however, the 1990s saw not incremental growth but unprecedented change, namely, the development of a practice of legitimate military intervention against genocide (see Chapter 13). This was a dramatic reversal of cold war–era (and earlier) practice.

The 1948 Genocide Convention, building on the Nuremberg charge of crimes against humanity, had made genocide an international crime. International practice during the cold war era, however, failed to turn that theory into practice. In places such as Burundi, East Pakistan (Bangladesh), Cambodia, and Uganda, **genocide** (killing large numbers of people because of their race, religion, ethnicity, or culture, with the aim of exterminating the group) and politicide (mass killing for other political purposes) were met by verbal expressions of concern but little concrete action—except by neighboring states such as India, Vietnam, and Tanzania with strong selfish interests in intervening.

The international tribunals for the former Yugoslavia and Rwanda, created in 1991 and 1994, respectively, revived the Nuremberg precedent—or, perhaps more accurately, began a process that transformed Nuremberg from an isolated exception into a precedent. The adoption of the Rome Statute in 1998 and the creation of the International Criminal Court (ICC) in 2002 mark an even deeper normative transformation. And the interventions in Kosovo and East Timor in 1999 consolidated an international practice of humanitarian intervention against genocide (see §§13.3–6).

6. INTERNATIONAL HUMAN RIGHTS AFTER 9/11

It is commonplace, especially in the United States, to claim that the attacks of September 11, 2001, "changed everything." This is, at best, a serious exaggeration. The human rights progress of the 1980s and 1990s has been maintained in most countries. In many it has been extended. In 2004 and 2005, Georgia's Orange Revolution, Ukraine's Pink Revolution, and the violently repressed protests in Uzbekistan indicate significant change along the borders of Russia. Iran's Green Revolution of 2009 expressed a new level of widespread popular discontent—which the ruling regime, however, continues to prove able to suppress. The Arab Spring of 2011, in which long-entrenched dictators were removed from Tunisia and Egypt (and in the autumn in Libya), brought major change to the one region that had largely avoided post–cold war progress. And in sub-Saharan Africa, steady if limited and often fitful progress has been the norm (although the Congo, Sudan, and Somalia continue to suffer under decades-long humanitarian crises).

The "war on terror," however, has often reduced international attention to human rights (see Chapter 15). In a number of countries, it has provided a widely accepted excuse for increased repression. And in some, including the United States, it has led to modest but significant restrictions on civil liberties. Furthermore, US abuses of (often illegally held) prisoners in Iraq, Afghanistan, and Guantánamo, as well as the kidnapping and international transport ("extraordinary rendition") of suspects, have provoked widespread national and international criticism.

Unlike during the cold war, though, human rights have not been forced into the background, let alone systematically co-opted and corrupted by a combination of national interests and overriding ideological concerns. After a decade of "the war on terror," even American willingness to accept human rights abuses in the name of antiterrorism may be declining.

This suggests that when we look back on the early years of the twenty-first century, the biggest change may lie in the accelerating and deepening impact of globalization. States are the central mechanism for implementing and enforcing internationally recognized human rights. Even if the threat to states posed by globalization is exaggerated, the relative capabilities of states are declining, especially when it comes to being able to extract revenues to support social welfare programs that realize economic and social rights. No alternative source of provision, however, seems to be emerging to fill the resulting gap. Therefore, as I suggest in more detail in Chapter 14, global markets are likely to be a bigger threat to human rights in the coming decades than either terrorists or the war against them.

7. THE GLOBAL HUMAN RIGHTS REGIME

Taken as a whole, we can say that in the decades since the end of World War II, a normatively robust global human rights regime has developed. (An **international regime** is conventionally defined as a set of principles, norms, rules, and decision-making procedures that states and other international actors accept as authoritative within an issue area.) States, however, have largely retained for themselves the responsibility—and the sovereign right—to implement these rights in their own territories.

Of the hundred or more treaties that address human rights issues, broadly understood, six are usually taken to provide the core of international human rights law: the two 1966 International Human Rights Covenants plus the 1965 Convention on the Elimination of All Forms of Racial Discrimination; the 1979 Convention on the Elimination of All Forms of Discrimination Against Women; the 1984 Convention Against Torture and Other Cruel, Inhuman, or Degrading Treatment or Punishment; and the 1989 Convention on the Rights of the Child.[2] As of December 2011, these six treaties had an average of 172 state parties—that is, states that had ratified, acceded, or succeeded to the treaties and thus were bound by them in international law. This represents an astonishing 88 percent ratification rate.[3] We have come a *very* long way from the early 1940s, when even genocide was not legally prohibited.

This extensive and substantively admirable body of international human rights law, however, is not matched by comparably strong international implementation procedures. As we will see in more detail in Chapters 5 and 6, states have largely reserved to themselves the right to interpret the meaning of their international human rights obligations and to implement them in their own territories. International law, in other words, has established a system of *national implementation of international human rights*. International human rights norms have been fully internationalized. Implementation of international human rights obligations, however, remains almost entirely national.

There is, of course, an immense amount of national and international human rights advocacy. States, international organizations, nongovernmental organizations, and private individuals advocate human rights every day in every country of the world. Their efforts, however, are focused ultimately on states, which still hold not only the duty but also the right to implement human rights in their own territories.

The shortcomings of this system of national implementation of international human rights are obvious and will be discussed in some detail in later chapters. Here, though, I want to emphasize the independent contribution of international human rights norms. International human rights law has been so widely endorsed because its normative force is seemingly inescapable in the contemporary world. Even states like North Korea and Belarus, which have never given any serious attention to implementing internationally recognized human rights, are parties to at least some core human rights treaties. And even cynical endorsements of these norms are of real practical significance for national and international human rights advocates.

Without an internationally agreed-upon list of human rights, national human rights advocates would be subject to charges of political or cultural bias, inauthenticity, and even treason. But when repressive governments today level such charges at their critics, those critics can reply that all they are doing is advocating rights that the government itself has repeatedly endorsed, including by accepting binding international legal obligations. This decisively shifts the burden of persuasion from the advocates of human rights to the governments that are violating those rights. Of course, might regularly triumphs over right, especially in the short run. But national human rights advocates are normatively supported and protected by international human rights norms. This makes a real practical difference in all but the most closed and repressive countries. And in countries with even merely not-too-bad human rights records, these protections are of immense day-to-day value to advocates and activists.

Similarly, when transnational human rights NGOs, foreign states, and regional and international organizations raise human rights issues, states cannot respond that it is none of their business. *All* states in the contemporary world have accepted that human rights are a legitimate subject of international relations—much as they hate to have their shortcomings brought to the attention of national and international audiences. And all states have agreed that the Universal Declaration of Human Rights and the International Human Rights Covenants provide an authoritative set of international human rights norms.

In what is ultimately a struggle of right against might—that is, the struggle for human rights against the power, prerogatives, and narrow interests of governments and states—agreed-upon terms of moral and legal reference are of immense importance. States and their governments cannot hide behind claims that their critics are using partisan or alien standards. They are forced to practice their depredations largely in the open. And the unmasking of vice for what it is often has surprising practical power, at least in the long run.

International human rights law has taken off the table debates over whether there really are human rights and what belongs on a list of human rights. The scarce resources of human rights advocates thus can be focused on the real work of implementing internationally recognized human rights.

For all its shortcomings, the body of international human rights law rooted in the Universal Declaration of Human Rights has both armed human rights advocates and disarmed their opponents, at least normatively. This fundamental redefinition of the terms of national and international political legitimacy is the principal legacy of the global human rights regime.

DISCUSSION QUESTIONS

1. Why should Americans be concerned with human rights practices abroad? Why should states or intergovernmental organizations be concerned? Anyone under thirty probably takes it for granted that states pursue human rights in their foreign policies. As we have seen, however, this is historically unusual. Whether you think the traditional practice of not pursuing international human rights objectives is good or bad, it is important to understand the logic underlying it. How can it be justified? Why do you think that people in the past were willing to treat human rights violations as a purely national concern?

2. Why have these traditional views changed over time? Consider the following possibilities:
    - Changing moral sensibilities. Are our moral views all that much different from those of other generations? (If so, what does that suggest about the universality of human rights?) Or is it that we now feel freer to act on these values? If so, why? Can changes in ideas, by themselves, have a significant impact on policy?
    - Changes in the character of international relations. Have peace and prosperity changed our views of human rights? Growing international interdependence? The end of the cold war? Decolonization? And then what about post-9/11 changes?
    - Changes in national human rights practices. Or is it that we are now doing better at home and thus want to project that progress abroad? Are we still doing better at home after 9/11?

3. How deeply have these changing views toward international human rights penetrated? We often talk about international human rights, but action regularly falls far short of rhetoric. Why? Is it due to a lack of real interest? Constraints on our ability to achieve our objectives? Competing objectives?

4. Should international agencies like the United Nations be involved in enforcing internationally recognized human rights? Why? What would be sacrificed by a greater international role? What would be gained? Can international organizations be trusted to make the sensitive political choices involved in human rights issues? Can *states* be trusted?

5. If you think that there should be a larger international role, why do you think that this has not come about? What would be required to overcome the existing impediments? How costly—economically, politically, and in human terms—would this be? Would these costs be worthwhile? Do you think that change is likely in the next few years? The next few decades? What factors would lead one to expect continuity? What factors suggest change?

6. What kind of actor is best suited to pursue international human rights: individuals, NGOs, states, or intergovernmental organizations? What are the strengths and weaknesses of each?

SUGGESTED READINGS

There are a number of good introductory overviews of international human rights. The best, in my view, is David P. Forsythe, *Human Rights in International Relations,* 3rd ed. (Cambridge: Cambridge University Press, 2012). Those with a somewhat more theoretical inclination might prefer Michael Freeman, *Human Rights: An Interdisciplinary Approach,* 2nd ed. (Cambridge: Polity Press, 2011). Micheline Ishay, *The History of Human Rights* (Berkeley and Los Angeles: University of California Press, 2008), and Paul Gordon Lauren, *The Evolution of International Human Rights: Visions Seen,* 3rd ed. (Philadelphia: University of Pennsylvania Press, 2011), are good places to start for those with a historical bent. David Weissbrodt and Connie de la Vega, *International Human Rights Law: An Introduction* (Philadelphia: University of Pennsylvania Press, 2007), offers an overview of contemporary international human rights law and practice that is generally accessible to those without a legal background. Henry J. Steiner, Philip Alston, and Ryan Goodman, *International Human Rights in Context: Law, Politics, Morals—Texts and Materials,* 3rd ed (Oxford: Oxford University Press, 2008), is a massive compendium of excerpts from a wide range of legal and nonlegal sources that although directed principally at law students contains much of interest to those with little or no interest in international law.

There are also several good general readers. First on my list is Patrick Hayden, ed., *The Philosophy of Human Rights* (St. Paul, MN: Paragon House, 2001). This huge and very reasonably priced volume includes an excellent selection of international documents, extensive excerpts from important historical and contemporary theorists, and excellent essays on a wide range of contemporary human rights issues. Micheline Ishay, *The Human Rights Reader,* 2nd ed. (New York: Routledge, 2007), and Jon E. Lewis, ed., *A Documentary History of Human Rights: A Record of the Events, Documents, and Speeches That Shaped Our World* (New York: Carroll & Graf, 2003), are complementary volumes that together provide good coverage of history and theory.

David P. Forsythe, ed., *Encyclopedia of Human Rights* (New York: Oxford University Press, 2009), is *the* general reference work. Attention should also be drawn to *Human Rights Quarterly.* This interdisciplinary journal is generally considered to be the best scholarly journal in the field, but its articles are typically quite accessible to the average reader.

The websites of Amnesty International (http://www.amnesty.org), Human Rights Watch (http://www.hrw.org), Minority Rights Group (http://www.minorityrights .org), and other NGOs have much useful current information on human rights situations in individual countries. The site of the Office of the High Commissioner for Human Rights (http://www.ohchr.org/english/) is a superb resource for international law and activities of the UN system.

On the Universal Declaration of Human Rights, Johannes Morsink, *The Universal Declaration of Human Rights: Origins, Drafting, and Intent* (Philadelphia: University of Pennsylvania Press, 1999), is the standard study, offering a theoretically informed history of the drafting of the Declaration and a thoughtful analysis of its content (although many readers will find the level of detail on drafting somewhat ponderous). Mary Ann Glendon, *A World Made New: Eleanor Roosevelt and the Universal Declaration of Human Rights* (New York: Random House, 2001), is excellent and immensely readable, although, as its title indicates, it is somewhat more limited in its scope. John P. Humphrey, *Human Rights and the United Nations: A Great Adventure* (Dobbs Ferry, NY: Transnational, 1984), is a memoir by the most senior human rights official in the early years of the United Nations Secretariat. On the role of the smaller states in the drafting process, see Susan Waltz, "Universalizing Human Rights: The Role of Small States in the Construction of the Universal Declaration of Human Rights," *Human Rights Quarterly* 23 (February 2001): 44–72, and Mary Ann Glendon, "The Forgotten Crucible: The Latin American Influence on the Universal Declaration of Human Rights Idea," *Harvard Human Rights Journal* 16 (2003): 27–39.

For critical perspectives on international human rights that see the entire enterprise as, at best, seriously distorted by hegemonic American dominance, see two books and one edited collection by Tony Evans: *U.S. Hegemony and the Project of Universal Human Rights* (Houndmills, UK: Macmillan Press, 1996); *The Politics of Human Rights: A Global Perspective,* 2nd ed. (London: Pluto Press, 2005); and *Human Rights Fifty Years On: A Reappraisal* (Manchester, UK: Manchester University Press, 1998). See also David Chandler, ed., *Rethinking Human Rights: Critical Approaches to International Relations* (Houndmills, UK: Palgrave Macmillan, 2002).

2

Theories of Human Rights

The preceding chapter reviewed major developments in the international politics of human rights over the past several decades. This chapter examines three sets of theoretical issues. Sections 1–6 consider philosophical theories of human rights. Sections 7 and 8 address the place of human rights in international society. Section 9 considers political realism, which challenges the very idea of international human rights policies. The following chapter extensively addresses the universality (and relativity) of human rights.

1. THE NATURE OF HUMAN RIGHTS

The term **human rights** indicates both their nature and their source: they are the *rights* that one has simply because one is *human*. They are held by all human beings, irrespective of any rights or duties they may (or may not) have as citizens, members of families, workers, or parts of any public or private organization or association.

If all human beings have human rights simply because they are human, then human rights are held equally by all.[1] Being human cannot be renounced, lost, or forfeited. Therefore, human rights are also inalienable. Even the cruelest torturer and the most debased victim are still human beings. In practice, not all people *enjoy* all their human rights, let alone enjoy them equally. Nonetheless, all human beings *have* the same human rights, which they hold equally and inalienably.

Right in English has two principal senses. We speak of some*thing being right;* that is, in accord with a standard of righteousness. We also speak of some*one having a right;* that is, being entitled to something. Although these two senses often overlap, here I will emphasize their divergences.

Not everything that *is* right is something to which anyone *has* a right. For example, it may be right (good, desirable) that everyone be loved. But no one has a right to be loved—and not just because some people are unlovable. Even the lovable have no right to be loved.

Conversely, many things to which people have rights are not right. For example, it may be wrong—that is, not right—that some people have immense wealth while others can barely survive. But, assuming no foul play, even the unjustly wealthy have a right to their property.

Rights create special relationships between people and things. "A has a right to x with respect to B." This paradigmatic statement of a right indicates that right-holders (A) stand in a special relationship to duty-bearers (B) with respect to the objects of their right (x). Conversely, with respect to x, B has special duties to A.

Theories of rights generally emphasize the entitlement of the right-holder or the special claims that having a right grounds. Both empower right-holders.

If A has a right to x, she is *entitled* to x. It is not merely good, desirable, or right that she have x. X belongs to her, in particular and in a special way. She suffers a special harm if denied x. It is not merely unjust (wrong). Her rights have been violated by depriving her of something to which she is entitled.

Having a right also makes available to the right-holder special claims and related practices that seek to guarantee her enjoyment of x. Rights claims ordinarily take prima facie priority over—"trump"—other types of claims. And when rights are violated, the remedial claims of right-holders also have a special force.

More precisely, rights have a *prima facie* priority. The right thing to do, *all things considered*, sometimes is to violate a right. But rights ordinarily trump other types of claims.

In fact, a principal purpose of rights is to take things out of the domain where decisions are appropriately based on calculations of what is right or good. Appeals to rights, as it were, (1) stop discussion, at least for the moment; (2) shift the burden of proof to those who would infringe a right; and (3) raise that burden of proof substantially. Only rarely, when something else of relatively great importance is at stake, is it right to override a right.

Human rights are a special type of rights. They are paramount moral rights. They are also recognized in international law. Most countries recognize many of these rights in their national legal systems as well. The same "thing"—for example, food or protection against discrimination—thus is often guaranteed by several different types of rights.

One "needs" *human* rights principally when they are not effectively guaranteed by national law and practice. If one can secure food or equal treatment through national legal processes, one is unlikely to advance human rights claims. One still has those human rights. But they are not likely to be used (as human rights). For example, in the United States both constitutional and statutory law prohibit racial discrimination. Discrimination based on sexual orientation, however, is not prohibited in most jurisdictions. Therefore, gay rights activists frequently claim a human right to nondiscrimination. Racial minorities, by contrast, usually claim legal and constitutional rights—"civil rights."

Human rights is the language of victims and the dispossessed. Human rights claims usually seek to alter legal or political practices. Claims of human rights thus aim to be self-liquidating. To assert one's human rights is to attempt to change political practices (and ultimately political structures) so that it will no longer be necessary to claim those rights (as human rights). For example, the struggle against apartheid in South Africa was a struggle to change South African laws and practices so that average South Africans could turn to the legislature, courts, or bureaucracy should they be denied, for example, equal protection of the laws or political participation.

Human rights thus provide a moral standard of national political legitimacy. They are also emerging as an international political standard of legitimacy. More precisely, the full legitimacy of regimes that grossly and systematically violate human rights is widely seen as compromised.

2. THE SOURCE OR JUSTIFICATION OF HUMAN RIGHTS

One common way to classify rights is according to the mechanism by which they are created. (This also typically sets the range of their operation.) Legal rights, for example, arise from, and operate within the domain of, the law. Constitutional rights arise from the constitution. Human rights, following this paradigm, arise from humanity.

Philosophically, it is not at all clear how humanity gives rise to rights. Nonetheless, international human rights law is clear and insistent that human rights are grounded in our shared humanity. The Universal Declaration of Human Rights refers to "the inherent dignity . . . of all members of the human family." The International Human Rights Covenants proclaim that "these rights derive from the inherent dignity of the human person." The Vienna Declaration, adopted at the conclusion of the 1993 World Human Rights Conference, likewise claims that "all human rights derive from the dignity and worth inherent in the human person."

Whatever the philosophical problems with such claims, I will take it for granted. This simply is how human rights are generally understood today. Humanity or inherent dignity is presented as a "natural" attribute of all human beings; it is a feature of our "nature" as human beings. (What we today call human rights were in the seventeenth, eighteenth, and nineteenth centuries usually called natural rights.)

The human nature that underlies human rights is sometimes explained in terms of (basic) human needs. But any list of needs that can plausibly claim to be empirically established provides an obviously inadequate list of rights: life, food, protection against cruel or inhuman treatment, and perhaps companionship. Science simply is incapable of providing the appropriate theory of human nature. (As we will see in §3.5, an anthropological approach that seeks to ground human rights on cross-cultural consensus faces similar problems.)

We have human rights not to what we need for survival but to what we need for a life of dignity. The human nature that is the source of human rights is a moral account of human possibility. It reflects what human beings might become, not what they "are" in some scientifically determinable sense or have been historically.

Human rights rest on an account of a life of dignity to which human beings are "by nature" suited. If the rights specified by the underlying theory of human nature are implemented and enforced, they should help to bring into being the envisioned type of person, who is worthy of such a life. The effective implementation of human rights thus resembles a self-fulfilling moral prophecy.

However we understand the source of human rights, though, in what follows I will simply assume that there are human rights. This theoretical evasion is justified by the fact that almost all states acknowledge the existence of human rights. It is further supported by an emerging international consensus, based on overlapping moral and religious theories, on human rights (see §3.3). The assumption that there are human rights thus is relatively unproblematic for our purposes here, namely, studying the international politics of human rights.

3. EQUAL CONCERN AND RESPECT

I will also take the list of rights in the Universal Declaration and the Covenants (see Table 1.1) as given and unproblematic. The principal justification for this is practical: to act internationally based on a different list would risk the charge of imposing one's own biased preferences instead of widely accepted international standards. This list, however, can also be derived from a plausible and attractive philosophical account, namely, the requirement that the state treat each person with equal concern and respect. Consider the Universal Declaration.

One must be recognized as a person (Article 6) in order to be treated with any sort of concern or respect. Personal rights to nationality and to recognition before the law, along with rights to life and to protection against slavery, torture, and other inhuman or degrading practices, can be seen as legal and political prerequisites to recognition and thus respect (Articles 3–5, 15). Rights to equal protection of the laws and protection against racial, sexual, and other forms of discrimination are essential to *equal* respect (Articles 1, 2, 7).

Equal respect for all persons is at most a hollow formality without the freedom to choose and act on one's own ideas of the good life. Freedoms of speech, conscience, religion, and association, along with the right to privacy, guarantee a private sphere of personal autonomy (Articles 12, 18–20). The rights to education and to participate in the cultural life of the community provide a social dimension to personal autonomy (Articles 26, 27). The rights to vote and to freedom of speech, press, assembly, and association guarantee political autonomy (Articles 18–21).

Rights to food, health care, and social insurance (Article 25) make equal concern and respect a practical reality rather than a mere formal possibility. The right to work is a right to economic participation very similar to the right to political participation (Article 23). A (limited) right to property also may be justified in such terms (Article 17).

Finally, the special threat to personal security and equality posed by the modern state requires legal rights to constrain the state and its functionaries. These include rights to be presumed innocent until proven guilty, due process, fair and public hearings before an independent tribunal, and protection from arbitrary arrest, detention, or exile (Articles 8–11). Anything less would allow the state to treat citizens with differential concern or respect.

The idea of equal concern and respect certainly is philosophically controversial. It does, however, have a certain inherent plausibility. It is closely related to the basic fact that human rights are equal and inalienable. And it offers an attractive application of the claim in the International Human Rights Covenants that the rights recognized "derive from the inherent dignity of the human person."

4. INTERDEPENDENT AND INDIVISIBLE HUMAN RIGHTS

All internationally recognized human rights are equally binding everywhere. Different states are not free to pick and choose. The Universal Declaration presents itself as "a common standard of achievement for all peoples and all nations." As the 1993 Vienna Declaration of the World Human Rights Conference puts it, "All human rights are universal, indivisible and interdependent and interrelated," and the goal of international human rights action is "universal respect for, and observance and protection of, all human rights and fundamental freedoms for all."

International human rights thus are regularly described as interdependent and indivisible. In principle, a life of dignity is not possible unless all internationally recognized human rights are respected. A bit more practically, we might say that any pattern of gross and persistent violation of any substantial set or subset of human rights is an intolerable deprivation.

A few philosophers, and a substantial segment of the political Right in the United States, have expressed skepticism about economic and social rights. Such skepticism, however, is largely baseless. It is sometimes suggested that economic and social rights are not as important as civil and political rights. In fact, though, a life of dignity, which is the goal of human rights, is no more possible without food, housing, health care, or education than it is without freedom of religion, protection from arbitrary arrest, or political participation.

It is also sometimes argued that economic and social rights are "positive rights" that require action and the expenditure of resources. Civil and political rights are by contrast held to be "negative rights" that require only abstention from violations. The implied moral distinction here is problematic. Is there really much difference between intentionally killing someone and intentionally leaving him to die? But even if we accept the moral distinction, many civil and political rights are in fact positive rights.

Consider the right to "a fair and public hearing by an independent and impartial tribunal" or the right to "periodic and genuine elections." Courts and elections are very positive, and expensive, endeavors. Furthermore, even some negative-seeming rights actually require substantial positive action if they are to be realized in practice. For example, real protection against torture requires extensive and expensive training and monitoring of police and prison personnel.

Finally, we should note that most critics of economic and social rights destroy their own arguments by defending a right to property. This is an *economic* right. Furthermore, standard defenses of a right to property support other economic and social rights. For example, the right to property allows economic participation in society and provides personal economic security. But so does the right to work.

There are, of course, differences between economic and social rights and civil and political rights. But there are no less important differences within each broad class of rights. And there are important similarities across these classes. For example, the (civil and political) right to life and the (economic and social) right to food can be seen as different means to protect the same value. Categorical distinctions, let alone blanket denials, simply do not withstand scrutiny.

Internationally recognized human rights represent a comprehensive vision of a set of goods, services, opportunities, and protections that are necessary in the contemporary world to provide the preconditions for a life of dignity. No systematic deviations are permitted from this list of interdependent and indivisible rights.

5. THE DUTY-BEARERS OF HUMAN RIGHTS

Rights have correlative duties. Extending a distinction originally drawn by Henry Shue, we can distinguish four types of duties: not to deprive, to protect from deprivation, to provide effective enjoyment, and to aid the deprived.[2] Furthermore—and of special relevance to us here—these different types of duties can be, and in practice have been, allocated to different actors.

We all have duties not to deprive. Every individual and all social actors are obligated to respect the human rights of every human being, in the sense of not depriving them of the enjoyment of those rights. In this sense, human rights not merely are held universally (by all human beings) but also apply universally (to all actors).

Logically, the duties to protect, provide, and aid the deprived might also apply universally. In fact, however, international human rights law allocates those duties almost exclusively to states. As we saw in the preceding chapter, the global human rights regime establishes a system of national implementation of international human rights.

Everyone—*all* social actors—is obliged not to violate human rights. Only states, though, are obliged to implement and enforce human rights, and then only for their citizens (and others under their jurisdiction). When one needs protection, provision, or aid, human rights authorize claims only against one's own state. Citizens of the United States, for example, cannot claim their human rights against Canada. Only the government of the United States has obligations to protect the human rights of Americans.

This link between human rights implementation and the state is so strong and central that we typically do not describe ordinary crimes as human rights violations even when they deprive people of the substance of their internationally recognized human rights. For example, if you are shot and killed by your neighbor, we don't say that she has violated your human right to life. We call it murder, an ordinary crime. If an on-duty uniformed policeman, however, breaks into your house and shoots and kills you, we do say that she has violated your human rights.

When states and their agents deprive people of the enjoyment of their human rights, they not only have failed to discharge the obligation not to deprive, which is shared by all social actors; they have also violated their obligations to protect or provide. And when the duty to aid the deprived is flouted as well, the violation is even more severe.

The above is actually an oversimplification. States in the first instance have duties to protect and provide. But they need not do so immediately through their own action. Rather, they are responsible for creating and maintaining an effective system of provision.

Consider health care. The United States has a complex, hybrid system. Most children get their health care through their families, most of whom purchase it (indirectly by buying insurance) with their own money (often with a financial contribution made by their employer). There is thus a substantial element of what might be called self-provisioning. Most elderly people, however, get most of their health care from the government. And many people too poor to purchase health care also receive coverage from the government.

In practice, this American system does not work particularly well. But in principle, there is no reason a mixed system of provision could not be made to work well. For example, in India, Israel, Singapore, and Taiwan, adult children have certain legal obligations to support their aged parents. Employer-provided housing has sometimes proved successful. Privately funded schools are an important part of the educational system of many countries. Churches and charities are an important part of the welfare systems of many states.

Turning to civil and political rights, in most countries legal services are obtained both by purchase on the market and through the state. Police protection is often substantially augmented by private security firms. Much of the burden of protecting property lies with property owners.

Different states may choose different mixes of public and private provision, for different rights and at different times. The state, however, has ultimate responsibility for the system of provision, based on its special duties to protect and provide internationally recognized human rights and to aid the deprived.

6. HUMAN RIGHTS AND RELATED PRACTICES

Human rights, as we have seen, are a particular type of social practice, founded on a particular conception of human dignity, implemented by particular kinds of mechanisms. They must not be confused with other values and practices.

Not all good things are human rights. People do not have a right to many good things: for example, love, charity, respect, talent, and beauty. Many things to which we do have rights arise not from mere humanity but from our actions (e.g., contractual rights) or from particular relationships in which we stand (e.g., the rights of members of families or the rights of citizens). And many actors other than individual human beings hold rights (e.g., states, corporations, and clubs).

Human rights do not even provide a comprehensive account of social justice. Justice is particular as well as universal. And it is not entirely a matter of rights.

Human rights are the minimum set of goods, services, opportunities, and protections that are widely recognized today as essential prerequisites for a life of dignity. No more. And no less.

7. SOVEREIGNTY, ANARCHY, AND INTERNATIONAL SOCIETY

I want to turn now from philosophy to a broad theoretical consideration of the place of human rights in international relations. The modern international system is often dated to 1648, when the Treaty of Westphalia ended the Thirty Years' War. As we saw in Chapter 1, though, human rights have been an issue in international relations for fewer than seventy years. The absence of human rights from the first three centuries of modern international relations was the direct result of an international order based on sovereign states.

To be **sovereign** is to be subject to no higher power. In early modern Europe, sovereignty was a personal attribute of rulers. In many other times and places, as in medieval Europe, no (earthly) power was considered to be sovereign. In contemporary international relations, sovereignty is an attribute of states.[3]

International relations is structured around the legal premise that states have exclusive jurisdiction over their territories, their occupants and resources, and the events that take place there. Practice regularly falls far short of precept, as usually is the case with legal and political principles. Nonetheless, the fundamental norms, rules, and practices of contemporary international relations rest on state sovereignty and the formal equality of (sovereign) states.

Nonintervention is the duty correlative to the right of sovereignty. Other states are obliged not to interfere with the internal actions of a sovereign state. Because human rights principally regulate the ways states treat their own citizens within their own territories, international human rights policies would seem to involve unjustifiable intervention.

A principal function of international law, however, is to overcome the initial presumption of sovereignty. International law, including international human rights law, is the record of restrictions on sovereignty accepted by states.

A **treaty** is a contract between states to accept mutual obligations—that is, restrictions on their sovereignty. For example, a treaty of alliance may oblige a state to aid an ally that is attacked. Such a state is no longer (legally) free to choose whether to go to war. Through the treaty, it has voluntarily relinquished some freedom of action. The same is true of international human rights treaties.

A system of sovereign states is, literally, anarchic—without *arkhē* (rule) or an *arkhos* (ruler)—a political arena without formal hierarchical relations of authority and subordination. But **anarchy**, the absence of hierarchical political rule, does not necessarily imply chaos, the absence of order. In addition to international law, states regulate their interaction through institutionalized practices such as diplomacy, balance of power, and recognition of spheres of influence. Although there is no international government, there is rule-governed social order. International relations take place within an anarchical **society of states**.[4]

The international society of states during the eighteenth, nineteenth, and early twentieth centuries gave punctilious respect to the sovereign prerogative of each state to treat its own citizens as it saw fit. Today, however, as we have seen, there is a substantial body of international human rights law. States have become increasingly vocal in expressing, and sometimes even acting on, their international human rights concerns. In addition, human rights NGOs, which seek to constrain the freedom of action of rights-violating states, have become more numerous and more active.

This reflects (and has helped to create) a transformed understanding of the place of individuals in international relations. States have traditionally been the sole subjects of international law, the only actors with international legal standing (the right to bring actions in international tribunals). The rights and interests of individuals were traditionally protected in international law only by states acting on their behalf. The International Bill of Human Rights does not empower individuals (or even other states) to act against states. Contemporary international human rights law, however, has given individuals, or at least their rights, a place in international relations.

It has also introduced a new conception of international legitimacy. Traditionally, a government was considered legitimate if it exercised authority over its territory and accepted the international legal obligations that it and its predecessors had contracted. What it did at home was largely irrelevant. Today, human rights provide a standard of moral legitimacy that has been (very incompletely) incorporated into the rules of the international society of states.

Consider the almost universal negative reaction to the Tiananmen Square massacre in 1989, when Chinese troops fired on unarmed demonstrators and brutally crushed China's emerging democracy movement. China's diplomatic isolation reflected this new human rights–based understanding of legitimacy. But, as we shall see in Chapter 12, that isolation lasted only a year or two. Even the strongest supporters of sanctions were not willing to allow Chinese brutality to interfere with long-term economic and security interests.

This tension is characteristic of the current state of international human rights. The future of international human rights activity can be seen as a struggle over balancing the competing claims of sovereignty and international human rights and the competing conceptions of legitimacy that they imply.

8. THREE MODELS OF INTERNATIONAL HUMAN RIGHTS

The universality of human rights fits uncomfortably with a political order structured around sovereign states. Universal moral rights seem better suited to a cosmopolitan conception of world politics, which sees individuals more as members of a global political community ("cosmopolis") than as citizens of states. Instead of thinking of international relations (the relations between nation-states), a cosmopolitan thinks of a global political process in which individuals and other nonstate actors are important direct participants. We thus have three competing theoretical models of the place of human rights in international relations, each with its own conception of the character of the international community.

The traditional **statist** model sees human rights as principally a matter of sovereign national jurisdiction. Statists readily admit that human rights are no longer the exclusive preserve of states and that the state is no longer the sole significant international actor (if it ever was). They nonetheless insist that human rights remain *primarily* a matter of sovereign national jurisdiction and (ought to continue to be) a largely peripheral concern of international (interstate) relations. For statists, there is no significant independent international community, let alone an international body with the right to act on behalf of human rights. We have an international system but not much of an international society.

A **cosmopolitan** model starts with individuals rather than states—which are often "the problem" for cosmopolitans. Cosmopolitans see the state challenged both from below, by individuals and NGOs, and from above, by the truly global community (not merely international organizations and other groupings of states). International action on behalf of human rights is relatively unproblematic in such a model. In fact, cosmopolitans largely reverse the burden of proof, requiring justification for nonintervention in the face of gross and persistent violations of human rights. International society, in other words, is seen as a global or world society.

The space toward the center of the continuum defined by statism and cosmopolitanism is occupied by what we can call **internationalist** models. "The international community," in an internationalist model, is essentially the society of states (supplemented by NGOs and individuals, to the extent that they have been formally or informally incorporated into international political processes). International human rights activity is permissible only to the extent authorized by the norms of the society of states. These norms, however, may vary considerably across particular international societies. (Consider, for example, the difference noted earlier between the late nineteenth and late twentieth centuries.) Therefore, we need to distinguish between strong internationalism and weak internationalism, based on the distance from the statist end of the spectrum.

Each of these three models can be read as making descriptive claims about the place that human rights do have in international relations or prescriptive claims about the place they ought to have. For example, a statist might argue (descriptively) that human rights are in fact peripheral in international relations or (prescriptively) that they ought to be peripheral, or both.

Cosmopolitanism, however, even in this era of globalization, has little descriptive power. States and their interests still dominate world politics. The international political power of individuals, NGOs, and other nonstate actors is real, and appears to be growing, but is still relatively small—and power is a relative notion. The global political community—world society as opposed to the international society of states—is at best rudimentary. The cosmopolitan model, if more than a prescription about what is desirable, predicts the direction of change in world politics.

If the world envisioned by cosmopolitans has yet to come into being, that envisioned by statists is at least in part a thing of the past. Although accurate even into the 1970s, the statist model of international human rights today is at best a crude first approximation. Furthermore, it misleadingly directs attention away from three decades of significant, cumulative change.

Some sort of internationalist model—or a very heavily hedged statism—provides the most accurate description of the place of human rights in contemporary international relations. I began to lay out the evidence for this claim in Chapter 1. The case studies discussed in Parts 2 and 3 indicate that a relatively weak internationalist model, with modest international societal constraints on state sovereignty, describes the nature of the contemporary international politics of human rights.

Current descriptive power, however, is no guarantee of future accuracy. And it does not mean that internationalism is the best, or even a good, way to treat human rights in international relations. Nonetheless, as later chapters show in some detail, the international human rights reality that we face today is one of considerable state sovereignty, with modest limits rooted principally in the international society of states.

9. REALISM AND HUMAN RIGHTS

Before leaving the discussion of theory, we need to consider two common theoretical challenges to even this limited concern with international human rights, namely, political **realism,** or **realpolitik** (power politics), and cultural relativism, considered in this section and the next chapter, respectively.

The theory of realpolitik is an old and well-established theory of international relations, typically traced back to figures such as Niccolò Machiavelli in the early sixteenth century and Thucydides, whose *History* chronicles the great wars between Athens and Sparta in the final decades of the fifth century BCE. Realism stresses "the primacy in all political life of power and security." Because men are egoistic and evil and because international anarchy requires states to rely on their own resources even for defense, realists argue that "universal moral principles cannot be applied to the actions of states."[5] To pursue a moral foreign policy would not only be foolishly unsuccessful but also leave one's country vulnerable to the power of self-interested states.

Realists argue that only considerations of the national interest should guide foreign policy. And the national interest, for the realist, must be defined in terms of power and security. For example, George Kennan, one of the architects of postwar US foreign policy and one of the most respected recent realist writers, argued that a government's "primary obligation is to the *interests* of the national society it represents . . . its military security, the integrity of its political life and the well-being of its people." He maintained, "The process of government . . . is a practical exercise and not a moral one." As for international human rights policies, "it is difficult to see any promise in an American policy which sets out to correct and improve the political habits of large parts of the world's population. Misgovernment . . . has been the common condition of most of mankind for centuries and millennia in the past. It is going to remain that condition for long into the future, no matter how valiantly Americans insist on tilting against the windmills."[6]

Such arguments do contain a kernel of truth. The demands of morality often do conflict with the national interest defined in terms of power. But *all* objectives of foreign policy, not just moral ones, may compete with the national interest thus defined. For example, arms races may contribute to the outbreak of war. Alliances may prove dangerously entangling. Realists, however, rightly refuse to conclude that we should eschew arms or allies. They should also abandon their categorical attacks on morality in foreign policy. A valuable caution against moralistic excess has been wildly exaggerated into a general principle of politics.

Realist arguments against morality in foreign policy also appeal to the special office of the statesman. For example, Herbert Butterfield argued that although a man may choose to sacrifice himself in the face of foreign invasion, he does not have a "right to offer the same sacrifice on behalf of all his fellow-citizens or to impose such self-abnegation on the rest of his society."[7] But nonmoral objectives as well may be pursued by statesmen with excessive zeal—and equally deadly consequences. In any case, most moral objectives can be pursued at a cost far less than national survival. This certainly is true of many international human rights goals.

In addition, there is no reason that a country cannot, if it wishes, include human rights or other moral concerns in its definition of the national interest. Security, independence, and prosperity may be unavoidable necessities of national political life. Governments, however, need not limit themselves to these necessities. Even if the primary obligation of governments must be to the national interest defined in terms of power, this need not be their sole, or even ultimate, obligation.

Finally, using the anarchic structure of international relations as a rationale will not rescue realist amoralism. For example, Robert Art and Kenneth Waltz claim that "states in anarchy cannot afford to be moral. The possibility of moral behavior rests upon the existence of an effective government that can deter and punish illegal actions."[8] But even if we set aside the confusion of morality and law, this logic is clearly faulty. Just as individuals may behave morally without government to enforce moral rules, so moral behavior is possible in international relations.

The costs of moral behavior are typically greater in an anarchic than a hierarchical system. Nonetheless, states often can act on moral concerns without harm, and sometimes with success. There may be good policy reasons to pursue amoral, or even immoral, policies *in particular instances*. There are, however, no good theoretical reasons for requiring amoral policies, or even accepting them as the norm.

PROBLEM 1: DEMOCRACY AND HUMAN RIGHTS

The Problem

Americans typically describe their form of government as a democracy committed to protecting basic human rights (especially those rights specified in the Constitution). Across the globe as well, the terms *democracy* and *human rights* are often used more or less interchangeably. The analysis offered in this chapter, which emphasizes the differences between human rights and other moral, legal, and social practices, challenges this understanding.

One standard conception of democracy is government of, by, and for the people. This fits with the etymology of the term, *dēmokratia,* the rule (*kratos*) of the people (*dēmos*). But the people can, and regularly do, choose to do some very nasty things to some segments of the national population, including systematically violating their human rights. Think about legalized racism, sexism, and religious discrimination in the United States (and most other democratic countries).

Human rights require that democratic governments, no less than other forms of government, respect human rights. They demand what we can call a rights-protective regime—which often requires acting in opposition to the will of the people. This is especially true when protecting rights involves substantial governmental expenditures or challenges traditional practices or prejudices.

How should we resolve the conflicts between democracy and human rights?

A Solution

Human rights set the boundaries of democratic decision making. A rights-protective regime will be democratic both for instrument reasons (other forms of government, such as theocracy, aristocracy, monarchy, and vanguard party dictatorship have all proved to be systematically incapable of providing sustained protection of human rights) and for intrinsic reasons (self-rule is an important part of the conception of human dignity underlying internationally recognized human rights). But democratic government is desirable only to the extent that the rule of the people realizes the rights of all citizens (and in particular guarantees every citizen equal concern and respect).

Political scientists often describe such governments as "liberal democracies." Democracy operates within the constraints of the "liberties" (human rights) of the citizenry, which provide the justification and standard of legitimacy for any government. (The language of *democratic rights-protective regime* is clearer and more accurate—*democracy* is the adjective, rather than the noun—but clumsy and unlikely to gain wide acceptance.)

Whatever the verbal formula, though, human rights trump democracy when they conflict. This is especially important when the democracy in question is (merely) an electoral democracy. Even when elections are free, fair, and open—and especially when they are not—"democratic" regimes may fall far short of the demands of human rights. (Freely) elected governments are, as a rule, better than unelected governments. But the demands of human rights are about ensuring that all governments provide all of their citizens (and others under their jurisdictions) all the goods, services, opportunities, and protections required by internationally recognized human rights.

Further Problems

How should we respond to foreign governments that claim, with some plausibility, that their actions reflect the will of the people?

How should we respond to our own government when it plausibly argues that the will of the people not merely justifies but demands infringements of internationally recognized human rights? Here I adopt the perspective of my own country, the United States. Suppose that the American people really do not want "Obamacare" and that, for all its problems, they prefer the health care system based on non-mandatory employer-provided insurance. Is this a case where human rights (see Article 25 of the Universal Declaration) ought to take priority over democracy?

If so, how do we deal with the fact that there seem to be no legal means to advance such human rights claims in the United States? Health care is not a constitutional right, so the courts do not provide a remedy in the absence of congressional legislation. And not only is the United States not a party to the International Covenant on Economic, Social, and Cultural Rights, but there is not any serious discussion of accepting even the weak international legal obligations it entails. What are human rights advocates to do when a national legal system is fundamentally incompatible with international human rights obligations?

Now realize that the conflict between democracy and human rights is only one of many such fundamental conflicts. Human rights and the demands of development often conflict in the short run. How should we deal with that conflict? With the conflicts between human rights and broader conceptions of social justice? Human rights and environmental protection? Human rights and the precepts of religion? (Does it matter if it is a majority or a minority religion?)

DISCUSSION QUESTIONS

1. Are there such things as human rights? Where do they come from? How would you go about trying to convince someone who answers these questions differently from you? Do you find my claim that human rights rest on a moral account of human possibility to be plausible? Persuasive? Satisfying? Why?

2. I emphasize differences between rights and other sorts of moral principles and practices. Do I overemphasize the differences? What are the ways in which rights are similar to considerations of righteousness?

3. Should we prefer to protect human rights when doing so conflicts with social utility? Should the rights of the individual or the few take priority over the happiness of the many? (Try thinking about different rights in answering this question.) In particular, should *governments* act on any principle other than social utility?

4. How do we determine what constitutes a justifiable list of human rights? How would you go about trying to convince someone who proposes a radically different list? Would it be easier or harder if the list were less radically different?

5. Consider the principle of equal concern and respect, which I draw on to justify the list of human rights in the International Bill of Human Rights.

Should this principle be preferred over others? What are some other plausible grounds that might underlie the list of internationally recognized human rights?

6. I assume that some sort of justification of human rights is possible. But doesn't it matter *why* people believe that there are human rights? For what purposes might it matter?

7. Why are many Americans reluctant to consider economic and social rights as fully legitimate human rights? Are the reasons philosophical? Are they a reflection of the generally poor performance of the United States on ensuring these rights? How different are such arguments from the old Soviet claims that civil and political rights are really not as important as economic, social, and cultural rights?

8. Is there a moral dimension to the "positive-negative" distinction? Is there really no difference between killing someone and failing to help someone who is dying? Does your answer differ when you move from personal behavior to the activities of governments?

9. What is the relation between philosophical theory and international human rights norms? Can we legitimately evade philosophical difficulties by pointing to international consensus? What are the costs of such a strategy? What are the costs of not following the consensus?

10. Should human rights function as an international standard of legitimacy? If so, what else, if anything, is required for international legitimacy? If a government meets all the other criteria but violates human rights, why should it be seen as *internationally* (rather than morally or nationally) illegitimate?

11. Sovereignty issues have impeded the acceptance of international human rights policies. Is that really such a bad thing? Do you want other countries and international organizations inquiring into the human rights practices of your country? International anarchy has its obvious drawbacks, but do you *really* want a higher political authority telling your country how to behave?

12. Which of the three models of international human rights—statist, cosmopolitan, or internationalist—do you find most attractive (issues of their current descriptive accuracy notwithstanding)? Why? What are the greatest strengths of your preferred model? Why might others find it defective?

13. Even if realists overstate their case, don't they have a legitimate one? How often do states have the political space and resources to be successful in pursuing international human rights concerns? Have the end of the cold war, globalization, or 9/11 made it harder or easier? (In answering this question, consider a range of different rights.)

14. How often do states use "realism" as an excuse for not doing what they know they ought to do but don't want to be bothered with? Imagine personal moral relations if "realist" arguments were allowed. Are the

differences between interpersonal and international relations really so great that we can allow radically different standards to apply? Conversely, are the similarities so great that we can apply the same standards without major modifications across the two realms?

SUGGESTED READINGS

Steven Lukes, "Five Fables About Human Rights," in *On Human Rights,* edited by Stephen Shute and Susan Hurley (New York: Basic Books, 1993) (available online at http://stevenlukes.com/wp-content/uploads/2009/05/five_fables.pdf), provides a brilliant brief discussion of the difference that having human rights makes. The chapters in Part 3 of Patrick Hayden, ed., *The Philosophy of Human Rights* (St. Paul, MN: Paragon House, 2001), are well worth consulting. I have found that students particularly enjoy Martha Nussbaum's "Capabilities and Human Rights," which argues for rooting human rights in a notion of human capabilities (rather than the broader and vaguer idea of human dignity). For an excellent book-length discussion that emphasizes the similarities between rights and other grounds of action (in contrast to my emphasis on the special features of rights), see James W. Nickel, *Making Sense of Human Rights: Philosophical Reflections on the Universal Declaration of Human Rights,* 2nd ed. (Berkeley and Los Angeles: University of California Press, 2006).

A powerful but brief and readily accessible version of the realist argument against pursuing moral issues, including human rights, in foreign policy is presented in George F. Kennan, "Morality and Foreign Policy," *Foreign Affairs* 63 (Winter 1985–1986): 205–218. A rather more nuanced version of a similar argument is provided in Chapter 4 of Hedley Bull, *The Anarchical Society,* 3rd ed. (New York: Columbia University Press, 2002). For a counterargument, see Chapter 6 of Jack Donnelly, *Realism and International Relations* (Cambridge: Cambridge University Press, 2000).

Henry Shue's *Basic Rights: Subsistence, Affluence, and U.S. Foreign Policy,* 2nd ed. (Princeton, NJ: Princeton University Press, 1996), provides a subtle and powerful argument for the equal and overriding priority of rights to security, subsistence, and liberty; an extended discussion of the duties that flow from these rights; and a sensitive (if now rather dated) application of these theoretical ideas to US foreign policy. A shorter version of the core of the argument is available in Shue's essay "Rights in the Light of Duties," in *Human Rights and U.S. Foreign Policy: Principles and Applications,* edited by Peter G. Brown and Douglas MacLean (Lexington, MA: Lexington Books, 1979). For attacks on the idea of economic and social rights, see Maurice Cranston, "Are There Any Human Rights?" *Daedalus* 112 (Fall 1983): 1–18, and Hugo Adam Bedau, "Human Rights and Foreign Assistance Programs," in the Brown and MacLean reader. Sandra Fredman, *Human Rights Transformed: Positive Rights and Positive Duties* (Oxford: Oxford University Press, 2008), is an interesting discussion of positive rights and duties. Daniel J. Whelan and Jack Donnelly,

"The West, Economic and Social Rights, and the Global Human Rights Regime: Setting the Record Straight," *Human Rights Quarterly* (2007): 908–949, provides a detailed empirical refutation of the often-encountered idea that the West resisted including economic and social rights in the Universal Declaration and the Covenants. Daniel J. Whelan, *Interdependent Human Rights: A History* (Philadelphia: University of Pennsylvania Press, 2010), traces the history of the ideas of interdependence and indivisibility in discussions in the United Nations.

3

The Relative Universality
of Human Rights

Human rights are understood today to be universal rights, held by every human being, everywhere in the world. The foundational international legal instrument is the *Universal* Declaration of Human Rights. The 1993 World Human Rights Conference, in the first operative paragraph of the Vienna Declaration and Programme of Action, insisted that "the universal nature of these rights and freedoms is beyond question." The universality of human rights is a central theme in diplomatic, political, popular, and academic discussions alike.

But if by human rights we mean equal and inalienable rights that hold against the state and society and that all human beings have simply because they are human, then almost all societies throughout almost all of their history not merely have had no idea (let alone practice) of human rights, but had it occurred to them, they would have rejected it. How can such historically particular ideas and practices reasonably purport to be universal? And how does this purported universality relate to the undeniable cultural, political, economic, and historical diversity of our contemporary world? The answer proposed here is that human rights are relatively universal, a notion that, although initially paradoxical, captures the essential universality *and* the essential particularity of internationally recognized human rights.

1. UNIVERSALITY AND RELATIVITY

Human rights are often presented as either universal or relative. In fact, though, they are both. And this duality is built into the very notion of universality.

The first definition of *universal* in the *Oxford English Dictionary* is "extending over, comprehending, or including the whole of something." *Universal,* in this sense, is "relative" to a particular class or group, the "something" that is encompassed. *Universal,* in this most basic sense, means "applies across all of a particular domain." For example, universal health care, universal primary education, and universal suffrage involve making health care, primary education, and voting rights available to all citizens, nationals, or residents of a country—not everyone on the globe (let alone anywhere in the universe). A "universal remote control" neither controls all possible entertainment devices nor works everywhere in the universe—only in the movie *Independence Day* are alien spaceships designed so that a Mac can be effortlessly plugged into its command console—but controls only those devices that are "standard" for "us" here and now. Most American "universal remotes" won't even work in Europe.

There is a second sense of *universal*: "Of or pertaining to the universe in general or all things in it; existing or occurring everywhere or in all things." In this sense, though, little if anything in the empirical world is universal. Thus, the *Oxford English Dictionary* goes on immediately to indicate that this sense is "chiefly poetic or rhetorical," to which we might add "or philosophical or theological." Human rights are definitely *not* universal in this "occurring everywhere" sense.

They are, however, universal in at least three important "across a class" senses. I label these international legal universality, overlapping consensus universality, and functional universality.

2. INTERNATIONAL LEGAL UNIVERSALITY

Human rights are universal in the sense that they have been accepted by almost all states as establishing obligations that are binding in international law. As we saw in Chapter 1, the six core international human rights treaties—the two Covenants plus the conventions on racial discrimination, women's rights, torture, and the rights of the child—have, on average, an 88 percent ratification rate. In this important sense, we can say that despite all the cultural, political, regional, and economic diversity in the contemporary world, there is near-universal agreement on both the existence and the substance of internationally recognized human rights.

International legal universality, however, is bounded. Although states have agreed that they have obligations with respect to these rights, there are no significant international enforcement mechanisms. International legal universality is a universality of possession. It does not entail universal implementation, enforcement, or enjoyment.

Furthermore, international legal universality depends on the contingent decisions of states, international organizations, transnational actors, and various national groups to treat the Universal Declaration and the Covenants as authoritative statements of internationally recognized human rights. International actors may in the future no longer accept or give as much weight to such principles. Today, however, the overwhelming evidence is that they have chosen, and are continuing to choose, human rights—making those rights, for us, today, effectively universal for the purposes of international law and politics.

3. OVERLAPPING CONSENSUS UNIVERSALITY

The second kind of universality I will discuss, overlapping consensus universality, relies on a useful distinction drawn by the American political philosopher John Rawls. Rawls identifies what he calls comprehensive doctrines: overarching or foundational philosophical, religious, or ideological perspectives or worldviews. He distinguishes these comprehensive doctrines from what he calls political conceptions of justice: narrower, "constitutional," accounts of the basic elements of political legitimacy, specified largely without reference to any particular comprehensive doctrine.

Proponents of very different, and even irreconcilable, comprehensive doctrines may reach an overlapping consensus on a political conception of justice. This consensus is only partial; it is overlapping, not complete. It is restricted to a political conception of justice. But it can be real and important.

Human rights can be readily grounded in a variety of moral theories. For example, they can be seen as encoded in the natural law, called for by divine commandment, political means to further human good or utility, or institutions designed to produce virtuous citizens. Since the end of World War II, and especially over the past two decades, more and more proponents of more and more comprehensive doctrines from more and more regions of the globe have come to see in human rights a political expression of their deepest values. Christians, Muslims, Jews, Buddhists, Confucians, and atheists; Kantians, utilitarians, neo-Aristotelians, Marxists, social constructivists, and postmoderns; and many others as well—all, for their own very different reasons—have come to participate in an overlapping consensus on the rights of the Universal Declaration.

We are quite familiar with this process within Western democracies. For example, neo-Thomists and utilitarians disagree about just about everything at the level of foundational moral theory. Thomists do not even consider utilitarianism to be a moral theory. Nonetheless, today most Thomists and most utilitarians, despite their irreconcilable differences at the level of comprehensive doctrines, endorse human rights as a political conception of justice. And much the same process is occurring today globally.

The implication of this argument is that human rights have no *single* philosophical or religious foundation. Rather, they have *multiple* foundations. And this multiplicity of foundations is essential to human rights (as we understand them).

Human rights *are* a (Rawlsian) *political* conception of justice. "Human rights" is a category of political, legal, and social theory—not moral theory. Human rights are not a moral "primitive" or foundation, an irreducible core that defines in the most basic possible sense what is right and wrong. They are one level removed from such foundations.

This remove, however, strengthens, rather than weakens, human rights—as they actually function in the world. Multiple foundations make human rights much more strongly rooted. They provide a wide-ranging, complex, interlocking mesh of roots that support and ground international human rights far more effectively than any single taproot could.

Overlapping consensus universality, besides its intrinsic interest and importance, also helps to explain international legal universality. The striking extent of the formal international legal endorsement of human rights reflects the fact that adherents of most leading comprehensive doctrines across the globe do in fact endorse internationally recognized human rights.

Again, we must carefully specify the limits of this universality. In particular, I am not arguing that all of the comprehensive doctrines that today endorse human rights have done so throughout all or even much of their history. Quite the contrary. Consider the West. The Greeks distinguished between civilized Hellenes (Greeks) and barbarians and among Greeks made a variety of categorical moral and political distinctions based largely on birth and virtue—both of which were understood in deeply inegalitarian ways. The Romans may have had a somewhat wider conception of who was capable of being civilized. For legal and political purposes, however, a sharp line was drawn between civilized and barbarian peoples. And both class distinctions and slavery were central to Roman society.

During the medieval era, Europeans drew a comparable distinction between Christians and heathens, practiced slavery and serfdom, and regularly ranked men by their birth (noble or common) or their work (ruling and fighting, praying, or working to provide sustenance for the community). And, of course, "men" meant adult males. "Everyone," in both the ancient and medieval worlds, "knew" that women of whatever status were not entitled to the same rights as men of similar status.

Therefore, if we date Western history to the Persian Wars, in the first half of the fifth century BCE, then the West, for its first two millennia, had neither the idea nor the practice of human rights (understood as equal and inalienable rights that all human beings have and may exercise against society and the state). And, as we will see below, we can't find much of an idea of human rights—or even a real hint of the practice—in early modern Europe either.

Much the same is true of all the great non-Western civilizations and almost all documented nonstate societies. The international overlapping consensus on human rights largely emerged after World War II. This does not make the contemporary consensus any less real or important. It does, however, point to its historical particularity.

4. FUNCTIONAL UNIVERSALITY

Overlapping consensus universality can itself be explained, in part, by global social changes over the past two centuries. These social changes provide the basis for what I call the functional universality of human rights. Human rights represent a set of "best practices" to respond to certain standard threats to human dignity posed by modern markets and modern states.

Natural or human rights ideas first developed in the modern West. Early inklings are clear in Britain by the 1640s. A full-fledged natural rights theory is evident in John Locke's *Second Treatise of Government,* published in 1689 in support of

Britain's so-called Glorious Revolution of 1688. The American and French Revolutions used these ideas as the basis for constructing new political orders.

The essential point, however, is the modernity, not the cultural "Westernness," of human rights ideas and practices. Nothing in classical or medieval culture made the West unusually conducive to the development of human rights ideas. Quite the contrary, in the thirteenth and fourteenth centuries, parts of the Islamic world, perhaps most notably Fatimid Spain, provided a much more tolerant cultural and religious environment that would on its face seem to have been more conducive to the development of human rights ideas and practices. The Catholic Counter-Reformation and the intolerance of most ruling Protestant regimes in the sixteenth and seventeenth centuries suggest that early modern Europe was in many ways a particularly *un*supportive cultural milieu for developing human rights ideas. The late sixteenth and early seventeenth centuries, it is important to remember, were an era of violent, often brutal, internecine and international religious warfare. No widely endorsed reading of Christian scriptures before the mid-seventeenth century supported the idea of a broad set of equal and inalienable individual rights held by all human beings—or even all Christians.

At the risk of gross oversimplification, I suggest that capitalist markets and absolutist states lie behind both the rise of human rights ideas and practices and the modernization of Western economies, societies, polities, and cultures. Ever more powerful (capitalist) markets and (sovereign, bureaucratic) states disrupted, destroyed, or radically transformed "traditional" communities and their systems of mutual support and obligation—with traumatic consequences. Rapidly expanding numbers of (relatively) separate families and individuals faced a growing range of increasingly unbuffered economic and political threats to their interests and quality of life. New kinds of what Henry Shue calls "standard threats" to human dignity provoked a variety of remedial responses.[1] By the late seventeenth century, claims of natural rights began to become a preferred mechanism for securing new visions of human dignity in these new social, economic, and political conditions.

At roughly the same time, the Protestant Reformation disrupted the unity of Christian Europe, often quite violently. By the middle of the seventeenth century, however, states, due more to exhaustion than conviction, began to stop fighting over religion. (The Westphalia settlement of 1648 is conventionally presented as the start of "modern" international relations.) Although full religious equality remained very far off, religious toleration for selected Christian sects became the European norm and provided an important foundation for broader ideas of human rights. If individual choice was permitted on the most important of all issues, the salvation of one's immortal soul, why not allow it on issues of lesser magnitude as well?

Add to this the growing possibilities for physical and social mobility and we have the crucible out of which contemporary human rights ideas and practices were formed. Privileged ruling groups faced a growing barrage of demands from an ever-widening range of dispossessed groups—first for relief from particular legal and political disabilities and eventually for full inclusion on the basis of equality. Such demands took many forms, including appeals to scripture, church, morality, tradition, justice, natural law, order, social utility, and national strength. Claims of equal and inalienable natural/human rights, however, became increasingly common.

These processes of threat and response occurred first in modern Europe. Modern markets and states, however, have spread to all corners of the globe, bringing with them roughly the same threats to human dignity. This has created a functional universality for human rights. Human rights represent the most effective response yet devised by human ingenuity to a wide range of threats to human dignity that have become nearly universal across the globe.

Although it was no coincidence that the idea and practice of human rights developed first in early modern Europe, this was, if not an accident, then an effect rather than a cause. Westerners, as we have already noted, had no special preexisting cultural proclivity to human rights. Rather, they had the (good or bad) fortune to be the first to experience the indignities of modern markets and states. These new forms of suffering and injustice called forth new remedies. One increasingly popular and effective response was claims of equal and inalienable individual human rights. And nothing better has yet been devised.

Human rights remain the only proven effective mechanism for ensuring human dignity in societies dominated by markets and states. The near-universal spread of the idea of human rights is rooted in the fact that they represent the record of a process of social learning about the most necessary protections needed as preconditions for a life of dignity in a world of modern markets and states.

Although this universality is rooted in a particular time and place—or, more precisely, in a particular kind of social structure—human rights are (relatively) universal for us, now. And by *us,* I mean virtually everyone on this planet. Almost all of us live in a world of modern markets and modern states, which need to be tamed by human rights if those powerful institutions are to be made compatible with a life of dignity for the average man and woman.

5. ANTHROPOLOGICAL OR HISTORICAL RELATIVITY

The arguments in the preceding sections clearly imply that human rights are *not* universal either historically or anthropologically. Although it is often claimed that most cultures and civilizations have long-standing indigenous ideas and practices of human rights, such arguments are entirely without empirical support. We have just seen that the idea and practice of human rights is historically relatively recent in the West. The same is true of other areas of the world.

As we saw in Chapter 2, rights—entitlements that ground claims with a special force—are one particular mechanism for realizing social and political values. Human rights—equal and inalienable entitlements held by all individuals that may be exercised against the state and society—are a very distinctive way to seek to realize social values such as justice and human flourishing. The literature on so-called non-Western conceptions of human rights regularly confuses values such as limited government or respect for personal dignity with the practice of equal and inalienable individual human rights to realize such values. For example, Dunstan Wai argues that traditional African beliefs and institutions "sustained the 'view that certain rights should be upheld against alleged necessities of state.'"[2] This confuses human rights with limited government. Government has been limited on a variety of grounds other than human rights, including divine commandment, tradition, legal rights, and extralegal checks such as a balance of power or the threat of popular revolt.

Similarly, Tai Hung-Chao, discussing traditional Chinese views, argues that "the concept of human rights concerns the relationship between the individual and the state; it involves the status, claims, and duties of the former in the jurisdiction of the latter. As such, it is a subject as old as politics."[3] Not all political relationships, however, are governed by, related to, or even consistent with human rights. What the state owes those it rules is indeed a perennial question of politics. Human rights provide one answer. Other answers include divine-right monarchy, the dictatorship of the proletariat, the principle of utility, aristocracy, theocracy, and democracy.

Much the same confusion is evident in the extensive literature claiming that "Islam has laid down some universal fundamental rights for humanity as a whole, which are to be observed and respected under all circumstances . . . fundamental rights for every man by virtue of his status as a human being."[4] For example, the scriptural passages that Khalid M. Ishaque argues establish a "right to protection of life" are in fact divine injunctions not to kill and to consider life inviolable.[5] The "right to justice" proves to be instead a duty of rulers to establish justice. The "right to freedom" is a duty not to enslave unjustly (not even a general duty not to enslave). "Economic rights" turn out to be duties to help to provide for the needy. And the purported "right to freedom of expression" is actually an obligation to speak the truth.

Even the claim that because "different civilizations or societies have different conceptions of human well-being . . . they have a different attitude toward human rights issues" is misleading.[6] Other societies may have (similar or different) attitudes toward issues that we consider today to be matters of human rights. But without a widely understood concept of human rights that is endorsed or advocated by some important segment of that society, it is hard to imagine that they could have *any* attitude toward human rights. And it is precisely the idea of equal and inalienable rights that one has simply because one is a human being that was missing in traditional Asian, African, Islamic, Latin American, and (as we saw above) Western societies. Although most arguments of anthropological universality are rooted in an admirable desire to show cultural sensitivity, respect, or tolerance, in fact they impose an alien analytical framework that misunderstands and misrepresents the foundations and functioning of those societies.

Just to be clear, I am *not* claiming that Islam, Confucianism, or traditional African ideas cannot support internationally recognized human rights. Quite the contrary, I argued in §3.3 that they not only logically can but in practice increasingly do. My point here is that Islamic, Confucian, and African societies—like Western societies—did not endorse human rights ideas or practices until rather recently.

6. CULTURAL RELATIVISM

We have already seen that human rights are historically relative to the modern era and that their foundations are relative to a number of comprehensive doctrines that participate in the contemporary overlapping consensus on internationally recognized human rights. Human rights, however, are *not* culturally relative in any strong sense of that term. Their justification is not based on any particular culture. Neither is their endorsement or practice tied to a particular culture or set of cultures.

In particular, there is nothing special about the West or Western culture that made the West particularly suited for human rights. For example, Christianity through the early modern period was harnessed to support forms of social and political life that were deeply hierarchical and organized people according to divisions—of religion, gender, race, and occupation—rather than drawing political attention to what bound all human beings (or even all Christian men). And although there have always been mass movements from below inspired by Christian ideas, such elements were effectively repressed in the name of Christianity throughout almost all of Christian history.

Nonetheless, when men and women faced new social conditions—when traditional hierarchies were destroyed and modern ones built—these Christian and other Western cultural resources increasingly came to be appropriated by new groups, in new ways, on behalf of the idea of universal human rights. Thus, today we are all familiar with biblical texts that point in a universalistic and egalitarian direction. And, I would argue, just as modernity and human rights transformed Western culture, so the same transformation not only can take place but is taking place throughout the non-Western world.

If the medieval Christian world of crusades, serfdom, and hereditary aristocracy could become today's world of liberal and social democratic welfare states, then it is hard to imagine a place where a similar transformation would be impossible. For example, Gandhi took Hinduism—on its face perhaps the least likely comprehensive doctrine to support human rights, given its traditional emphasis on qualitative caste differences and its denial of the moral significance of the category "human being"—and transformed it into a powerful force in support of human rights.

No particular culture or comprehensive doctrine is by nature either compatible or incompatible with human rights. It is a matter of what particular people and societies make of and do with their cultural resources. Cultures are immensely malleable, as are the political expressions of comprehensive doctrines. Most if not all cultures have in their past denied human rights, both in theory and in practice. But that stops none of them from today not merely endorsing human rights but also finding human rights to be a profound expression of their deepest cultural values.

Denying that human rights derive from or are defined by culture implies neither the irrelevance of culture to human rights nor cultural homogenization. Quite the contrary, an overlapping consensus approach emphasizes the importance of people using their own local cultural resources on behalf of their own human rights. The universality of human rights is fully compatible with a world of rich cultural diversity. Although the problems that human rights were designed to remedy are today universal—as is the now almost hegemonic global endorsement of that remedy—people, in the Western and non-Western worlds alike, come to universal human rights by a great variety of paths. And a central purpose of human rights is to protect the right of different individuals, groups, and peoples to make those choices of path.

7. UNIVERSAL RIGHTS, NOT IDENTICAL PRACTICES

Although culture is not particularly relevant to the definition of human rights, it may be central to their reception. Different places at different times will draw on different cultural resources to provide support for human rights. And the different cultural idioms within and by which human rights are justified and explicated are of immense local importance. Therefore, effective advocacy of human rights requires knowledge of and sensitivity to how human rights fit with local cultures—and histories, and economies, and ecologies, and social structures.

Culture is also important to the details of implementation. Elsewhere I have developed a three-tiered scheme for thinking about universality.[7] Human rights are relatively universal at the level of the *concept,* the broad formulations characteristic of the Universal Declaration such as the claims in Articles 3 and 22 that everyone has "the right to life, liberty and security of person" and "the right to social security." Particular rights concepts, however, usually have different defensible *conceptions,* introducing a very real element of relativity among universal human rights. Furthermore, any particular conception is likely to have many defensible *implementations.* At this level—for example, the design of electoral systems to realize the claim in Article 21 of the Universal Declaration that "everyone has the right to take part in the government of his country, directly or through freely chosen representatives"—the range of legitimate variation and relativity is substantial.

Functional and overlapping consensus universalities lie primarily at the level of human rights concepts; the arguments that support these kinds of universality usually operate at a high level of abstraction that rarely reaches very far into the level of conceptions, let alone implementations. The resulting, quite substantial, range of legitimate variability means that universal human rights do not require identical human rights practices. In fact, substantial second-order variations, by country, region, or other grouping, are fully compatible with the relative universality of internationally recognized human rights.

Striking legitimate variations exist even within regions. For example, conceptions and implementations of many economic and social rights differ dramatically between the United States and most of the countries of western Europe. Important variations exist even within Europe. For example, Robert Goodin and his colleagues demonstrate important systematic differences between the welfare states of Germany and the Netherlands.[8]

Even here, though, we should be careful not to overstate the significance of "culture"—which is not the only, or even obviously the most important, source of diversity in justifications and implementations of human rights. There are often immense philosophical and religious differences *within* a culture that are absolutely central to how human rights are understood and practiced. And historical, political, economic, and simply accidental factors are no less important than culture in explaining the different ways that societies implement human rights.

8. UNIVERSALISM WITHOUT IMPERIALISM

These brief arguments, although hardly conclusive, clearly illustrate that the universality of internationally recognized human rights does *not* require, or even encourage, global homogenization or the sacrifice of valued local practices. Certainly, nothing in this chapter implies or justifies cultural imperialism. Quite the contrary, (relatively) universal human rights protect people from imposed conceptions of the good life, whether those visions are imposed by local or foreign actors.

The underlying purpose of human rights is to allow human beings, individually and in groups that give meaning and value to their lives, to pursue their own vision of the good life. Such choices deserve our respect as long as they are consistent with comparable rights for others and reflect a plausible vision of human flourishing to which we can imagine a free people freely assenting. Understanding human rights as a political conception of justice supported by an overlapping consensus *requires* us to allow human beings, individually and collectively, considerable space to shape (relatively) universal rights to their particular purposes—within the constraints at the level of the concept established by functional, international legal, and overlapping consensus universalities.

The legacy of imperialism does demand that Westerners in particular show special caution and sensitivity when advancing arguments of universalism in the face of clashing cultural values. Caution, however, must not be confused with inaction. Even if we are not entitled to impose our values on others, they are our own values. They may demand that we act on them even in the absence of agreement by others, especially when that action does not involve force. If the practices of others are particularly objectionable, even strongly sanctioned traditions may deserve neither our respect nor our toleration.

Such concerns are especially relevant to American foreign policy, which has often and not unreasonably been accused of confusing American interests with universal values. Even if there is no longer an American consensus that "what's good for GM is good for America," it does appear that most Americans today subscribe to the view that what's good for the United States is good for the world.

The proper solution to the "false" universalism of a powerful actor mistaking its own interests for universal values, however, is not **relativism** but relative **universalism**. Without authoritative international standards, what is there to hold the United States (or any other power) accountable to? If international legal universality has no force, it is hard to find a ground for saying that human rights are not whatever the United States says they are. This is especially true in international relations, where normative disputes that cannot be resolved by rational persuasion tend to end up being resolved by political, economic, and cultural power—of which the United States today has more than anyone else.

Consensus is no philosophical guarantee of truth. Nonetheless, insisting that the universality of internationally recognized human rights lies in significant measure in international legal and overlapping consensus provides important protection against the arrogant "universalism" of the powerful. The relative universality of human rights, besides being "correct," can be a significant resource for calling the powerful, including the United States, to account—especially because the principal problem with American foreign policy is not where it does raise human rights concerns but where it does not, or where it allows them to be subordinated to other concerns.

Universal human rights are hardly a panacea for the world's problems. They do, however, fully deserve the prominence they have received in recent years. The world is a better place than it would have been without the spread of universal human rights ideas and practices. And for the foreseeable future, universal human rights are likely to remain a vital resource in national, international, and transnational struggles for social justice and human dignity.

9. THE RELATIVE UNIVERSALITY OF HUMAN RIGHTS

Are human rights universal? Yes and no; it depends on the sense of *universal*. Are human rights relative? Yes and no; it depends on the sense of *relative*.

Sometimes the relativity of particular human rights practices and justifications deserves emphasis. Other times, the universality of internationally recognized human rights deserves emphasis. But both relativity and universality are essential to international human rights. There is danger both in treating the universal as if it were relative and in falsely universalizing particular contingent practices.

Human rights empower free people to build for themselves lives of dignity, value, and meaning. To build such lives anywhere in the contemporary world requires internationally recognized universal human rights. But one of the central purposes of universal human rights is to protect the free decisions of free people to justify and implement those rights in ways rooted in their own histories and experiences.

It is an empirical, not a logical, matter whether the legitimate demands of universality and relativity conflict or coordinate. Perhaps the most striking fact about the universality of human rights in the contemporary world, however, is how infrequently there is a truly fundamental conflict. And when there is indeed a real conflict, it is almost always restricted to a particular right or even just one part of an internationally recognized human right.

When I have lectured overseas and the question of **cultural relativism** comes up, I have often asked my audience to name the rights in the Universal Declaration that their society, culture, or religion rejects. I have never found an audience that objected to more than parts of two or three rights. For example, many Muslims reject the provision of Article 18 that allows anyone to change their religion. (Islam is ordinarily interpreted to prohibit Muslims from renouncing their faith.) But this is only one relatively small part of the internationally recognized right to freedom of religion—a right that Muslims strongly endorse. (The other example that I have commonly encountered includes some of the details of Article 16, which deals with family rights. But again, the basic right to marry and found a family is always strongly endorsed by those who challenge details of the conception elaborated in the Universal Declaration.)[9]

It is common to talk about universality and relativity as the end points of a continuum. Until recently (including earlier editions of this book), I used this formulation myself, describing the position I have defended as a form of weak relativism. I now, though, think that a multidimensional conception of universality and relativity is preferable. For example, international legal, overlapping consensus, and functional universalities are probably better seen not as parts of a single entity called "universality" but as qualitatively different dimensions of the universality of internationally recognized human rights. This formulation encourages us to appreciate the multiple forms that both universality and relativity take—and the fact that in different contexts, different dimensions of both appropriately come to the fore.

However we conceptualize it, though, the universality of human rights is relative to the contemporary world. The particularities of implementation are relative to history, politics, and contingent decisions. But at the level of the concept as specified in the Universal Declaration, human rights are universal. The formulation *relatively universal* is thus apt. Relativity modifies—operates within the boundaries set by—the universality of the body of interdependent and indivisible internationally recognized human rights.

PROBLEM 2: HATE SPEECH

The Problem

Article 4(a) of the racial discrimination convention requires parties not just to prohibit violence and incitement to violence but also to "declare an offence punishable by law all dissemination of ideas based on racial superiority or hatred." This provision has been rejected by the United States, where the view that freedom of speech includes even "hate speech" is deeply embedded in constitutional history and jurisprudence. How ought Americans respond to this conflict? What is the appropriate response for outsiders?

A Solution

Dealing with cases of conflicts between internationally recognized human rights would be facilitated by some general principles. In addition to the distinction between concepts, conceptions, and implementations introduced above, I suggest the following.

1. Important differences in the character of the threats being faced are likely to justify variations. For example, countries with a recent history of violent ethnic conflict might reasonably choose to deal with issues of discrimination differently from other countries.
2. Variations that appeal to important principles or precepts in underlying comprehensive doctrines involved in the overlapping consensus deserve special consideration. The case of apostasy in Muslim countries, mentioned above, may fall under this principle.
3. Arguments claiming that a particular conception or implementation is, for cultural or historical reasons, deeply embedded within or of unusually great significance to some significant group in society deserve, on their face, sympathetic consideration.
4. Variations from international standards are likely to be more acceptable the lower the level of legal and political coercion used to support them (which suggests both a greater degree of popular support, or at least acquiescence, and relatively limited damage to those who suffer as a result of these practices).

How do these criteria apply to the case of hate speech in the United States? The first two are not particularly relevant, but the last two do seem to imply some toleration for this American peculiarity. Free speech has an especially important place historically among human and constitutional rights in the United States. And there is a long legal history of allowing even hate speech (or what used to be called "fighting words")—so long as it is restricted to speech that does not incite violence. Furthermore, even targets of hate speech are legally protected against not only violence but also incitement to violence. Many local and state jurisdictions have even increased the penalties for "hate crimes"; hate *speech,* in other words, has been very narrowly understood and has been protected only so long as it remains unconnected to other criminal activity. And part of the underlying justification for the American practice is that prohibiting speech because of its content harms those whose speech is prohibited and in effect involves state support for particular viewpoints.

It thus seems relatively unproblematic for Americans to support this particular deviation from international human rights norms—especially because in ratifying the racial discrimination convention, the United States, as was its legal right, explicitly included a "reservation" that it would not be bound by this provision.

What about foreigners? Although they ought to have some appreciation for American arguments, there is no compelling reason for them to accept those arguments. Verbal pressure to criminalize hate speech is entirely appropriate. And those with a particular concern for the suffering it creates or an especially strong commitment to the general cause of international human rights standards may rightly feel compelled to draw critical attention to this internationally deviant American practice and to press for its change.

Further Problems

Suppose that we are talking about hate speech in, say, Rwanda or Bosnia, less than two decades after genocide. Or Singapore, half a century after racial violence against Chinese helped to lead to its independence from Malaysia. These societies do in fact prohibit hate speech. But what if they were to move to allow it? This example points to a very general problem, namely, different human rights regularly conflict with one another. (It also suggests that one of the ways in which societies differ is in how they handle such conflicts.)

What are some of the more prominent examples of conflicting human rights that you are familiar with? What are the implications of such regular and important conflicts for our understanding of the universality and relativity of human rights? Do such conflicts, when combined with the forms of relativity already noted above, leave much *as a practical matter* to the universality of human rights? (Be careful to consider different types of countries in thinking about your answer.)

PROBLEM 3: DISCRIMINATION BASED ON SEXUAL ORIENTATION

The Problem

Many countries have in recent years taken more or less strenuous efforts to remedy discrimination based on sexual orientation or gender identity. In fact, LGBT (lesbian, gay, bisexual, and transgender) rights have been a major focus of human rights activism in most Western and many non-Western countries. But gender and sexual minorities are not explicitly protected in international human rights law. And many countries are strongly opposed to ending discrimination against them. How should international human rights advocates respond to the competing demands to become involved and to remain silent—because international human rights law itself is silent?

A Solution

Established nondiscrimination norms provide a strong prima facie case for international action on behalf of LGBT rights. Article 2 of the Universal Declaration reads, "Everyone is entitled to all the rights and freedoms set forth in this Declaration, without distinction of any kind, such as race, colour, sex, language, religion, political or other opinion, national or social origin, property, birth or other status." The language clearly says *everyone* is entitled to *all* human rights *without distinction of any kind*. And particular articles typically begin "Everyone is entitled . . . ," "Everyone has the right . . . ," or "No one shall be . . . " *Everyone*, it would seem, would include those with a minority gender identity.

But "without distinction of any kind" does not really mean what it seems to say. For example, children and the mentally incompetent are, appropriately, excluded from the exercise of many rights. Those incarcerated for crimes are not permitted full liberty of person (as guaranteed in Article 3). In many countries, those who have not registered to vote may not exercise the right to participate in government through elected representatives (Article 21). And certain felons do not have equal access to public service (Article 21).

Furthermore, the phrase *such as race . . .* has typically been taken as something like an authoritative list of impermissible grounds. More precisely, it is widely held that all countries are required to specify only these grounds as impermissible—although they are, of course, free to add additional grounds.

In addition, had the drafters of the Declaration (and the Covenants) been asked, they almost certainly would have said that sexual orientation was *not* an impermissible grounds for discrimination—and certainly the governments who voted for the Universal Declaration would have agreed. For example, when Article 16 states, "Men and women of full age, without any limitation due to race, nationality or religion, have the right to marry and to found a family," it was unquestionably assumed that this meant that men could marry women, and vice versa. Period.

Finally—and from my point of view decisively—international human rights law has been developed by consensus. In the 1940s, 1950s, and 1960s there was a clear and strong international consensus that discrimination based on sexual orientation was permissible. Such a consensus has collapsed over the past two decades. But there is nothing even close to a consensus on positive protections for gender or sexual minorities. Therefore, advocacy for LGBT rights is *not* advocacy for internationally recognized human rights.

This does not mean that *all* advocacy for protections for sexual minorities is problematic from the point of international human rights law. In many countries, LGBT people are subjected to private violence that is not prosecuted by the authorities—who sometimes even condone it. Such treatment is a clear violation of basic internationally recognized human rights. Denial of rights to vote, education, health care, or social security simply because one has a minority gender identity is similarly prohibited. Even accepting that homosexuality is a moral abomination, people cannot be denied the enjoyment of their human rights for private moral behavior. Compare blasphemy.

Where to draw the line between permissible and impermissible discrimination will be a matter of considerable controversy. But the criminalization of consenting same-sex sexual activity is clearly *not* prohibited. And this is a powerful wedge that could be used to justify further discrimination—although homophobic governments rarely bother to prosecute offenders (except for political purposes), and thus "justifiable" discrimination against convicted felons is actually more a theoretical than a practical problem.

Furthermore, there is no reason that advocates of LGBT rights—individuals, NGOs, states, and even regional organizations—should not campaign on their behalf. But they should be careful to differentiate these activities from the defense of internationally recognized human rights.

I am not comfortable with this "solution." But if we take seriously the commitment to international human rights law *as it is,* there seems to me no alternative.

And we must remind ourselves of the larger context. Advocates for LGBT rights want to expand international human rights protections. But once we open up the possibility of deviations from international standards, there will be a flood of demands for reducing existing protections—demands that advocates will be in a significantly weaker position to resist.

Further Problems

Can human rights advocates really allow systematic discrimination and suffering to be consistent with international human rights norms simply because a half century ago most people denied the full humanity of a particular group?

How are LGBT people different from the disabled, who obtained their own convention? But the disabled obtained that convention through the process of international consensus creation. What should LGBT people do while they wait for international consensus?

Do we really have a *human rights* issue here for which international human rights law provides no adequate solution?

DISCUSSION QUESTIONS

1. Make a list of all the arguments you can think of that can be made for cultural relativism. Which of these actually involve *cultural* factors, and which involve political, economic, or ideological factors? Are arguments of political relativism as persuasive as arguments of cultural relativism? Why? What about economic relativism? Is the distinction among culture, politics, and economics helpful or revealing? Why?

2. Suppose that there are indeed major cultural differences with respect to human rights in the world today. Should we take those into account? Why? Should we allow them to alter our international human rights policies and practices? If so, are we then acting on the basis of other people's values? If not, what right do we have to act on the basis of our values when dealing with others who do not share them?

3. *Are* human rights ideas truly universal? Are the differences between cultures and countries really primarily concerned with secondary human rights issues? Do recent changes in international relations have anything to tell us about the universality of human rights? Consider, for example, the fall of the communist bloc and democratization in much of the Third World. Then consider Islamic fundamentalism and the rise of nationalist ethnic hostilities.

4. Does the geographical and political relativity of human rights that arises from the system of national implementation fatally undermine the universality of human rights? How can we assert that human rights are in any significant sense universal when they are subject to such radically different national systems of implementation?

5. Why do so many people, in the West and non-West alike, insist that their cultures have had human rights ideas and practices at times when they clearly have not? How much of this can be attributed to the notion that the legitimacy of cultures is somehow dependent on their conformity with "modern" Western ideas?

6. What do you think of the argument that human rights ideas and practices are rooted in social structure rather than culture? What does this imply about the nature of culture?

7. How can we untangle the relative contributions of states and markets to the need for and rise of human rights? Would modern states have been possible without the rise of capitalist markets? Does the notion of functional universality have significant implications for the relationship between civil and political rights and economic, social, and cultural rights?

8. Is it really true that *nothing* except human rights has yet been devised that works tolerably well to protect individuals and communities against the standard threats posed by modern markets and states? List some of the leading alternatives and try to figure out why they have failed and what would have been needed to make them work. Does this suggest anything interesting about the nature of potential alternatives to human rights that might develop in the future?

9. What are some of the principal threats to human dignity that are *not* connected with markets and states? How important is their absence from the list of internationally recognized human rights? If they are very significant, how much does this undermine the claim for even the relative universality of human rights?

10. Is consensus morally important? Politically important? If so, why?

11. How much of the apparent appeal of human rights today is due to their inherent advantages? To the collapse of the leading alternatives? To the power and prestige of Western states that support them?

12. In assessing claims of relativism, how important is coercion? Isn't the "brainwashing" that goes with ordinary socialization just as coercive? Is the idea of voluntary consent just a myth? To the extent that it is, how can any system of values be justified?

13. Just how malleable is culture? Even if it is immensely malleable across extended periods of time, is it relatively static over a few decades? Isn't that the time frame of politics?

14. If practices are changing (or even just capable of change), should international human rights policy respect those practices or exert pressure to modify them so that they are more consistent with international human rights standards? What are the strengths and weaknesses of each approach?

15. Should the United States be held to the same standards as everyone else? If not, how can Americans justify holding others to human rights standards?

SUGGESTED READINGS

The literature on cultural relativism is immense. In my opinion, the best short overviews of the issue are provided by Ann-Belinda S. Preis, "Human Rights as Cultural Practice: An Anthropological Critique," *Human Rights Quarterly* 18 (May 1996): 286–315; Andrew J. Nathan, "Universalism: A Particularistic Account," in *Negotiating Culture and Human Rights,* edited by Lynda Bell, Andrew J. Nathan, and Ilan Peleg (New York: Columbia University Press, 2001); Abdullahi A. An Na'im, "Towards a Cross-Cultural Approach to Defining International Human Rights Standards," in *Human Rights in Cross-Cultural Perspectives,* edited by Abdullahi A. An Na'im (Philadelphia: University of Pennsylvania Press, 1992); and Onuma Yasuaki, "Toward an Intercivilizational Approach to Human Rights," in *The East Asian Challenge for Human Rights,* edited by Joanne Bauer and Daniel Bell (Cambridge: Cambridge University Press, 1999). See also Bhikhu Parekh, "Non-ethnocentric Universalism," in *Human Rights in Global Politics,* edited by Tim Dunne and Nicholas J. Wheeler (Cambridge: Cambridge University Press, 1999).

Two superb books that treat the complexities of rights and related ideas in Chinese philosophy and political practice are Stephen C. Angle, *Human Rights and Chinese Thought: A Cross-Cultural Inquiry* (Cambridge: Cambridge University Press, 2002), and Marina Svensson, *Debating Human Rights in China* (Lanham, MD: Rowman and Littlefield, 2003). Both are extremely sympathetic to the similarities and the differences between Chinese and Western ideas and their significant changes over time. Even for readers with no special interest in China, these books are well worth reading. They offer careful and detailed understandings of complex issues that are far too often handled in glib generalities. Ann Elizabeth Mayer, *Islam and Human Rights: Tradition and Politics,* 4th ed. (Boulder, CO: Westview Press, 2007), does much the same for the Islamic world.

Classic statements of a rather radical relativism are Adamantia Pollis and Peter Schwab, "Human Rights: A Western Construct with Limited Applicability," in *Human Rights: Cultural and Ideological Perspectives,* edited by Adamantia Pollis and Peter Schwab (New York: Praeger, 1979); and Alison Dundes Rentlen, "The Unanswered Challenge of Relativism and the Consequences for Human Rights," *Human Rights Quarterly* 7 (November 1985): 514–540. For a sharp response to such views, see Rhoda E. Howard, "Cultural Absolutism and the Nostalgia for Community," *Human Rights Quarterly* 15 (May 1993): 315–338.

The following are, in my view, the best arguments in support of indigenous non-Western conceptions of human rights: Adbul Aziz Said, "Precept and Practice of Human Rights in Islam," *Universal Human Rights [Human Rights Quarterly]* 1, no. 1 (1979): 63–80; Fouad Zakaria, "Human Rights in the Arab World: The Islamic Context," in *Philosophical Foundations of Human Rights* (Paris: UNESCO, 1986); Majid Khadduri, "Human Rights in Islam," *Annals* 243 (January 1946): 77–81; Dunstan M. Wai, "Human Rights in Sub-Saharan Africa," in *Human Rights: Cultural and Ideological Perspectives,* edited by Schwab and Pollis; Kwasi Wiredu, "An Akan Perspective on Human Rights," in *The Philosophy of Human Rights,* edited by Patrick Hayden (St.

Paul, MN: Paragon House, 2001); Timothy Fernyhough, "Human Rights and Pre-colonial Africa," in *Human Rights and Governance in Africa,* edited by Ronald Cohen, Goran Hyden, and Winston P. Nagan (Gainesville: University Press of Florida, 1993); Asmarom Legesse, "Human Rights in African Political Culture," in *The Moral Imperatives of Human Rights: A World Survey,* edited by Kenneth W. Thompson (Washington, DC: University Press of America, 1980); Yougindra Khushalani, "Human Rights in Asia and Africa," *Human Rights Law Journal* 4, no. 4 (1983): 403–442; Ralph Buultjens, "Human Rights in Indian Political Culture," in *Moral Imperatives of Human Rights,* edited by Kenneth W. Thompson; James C. Hsiung, "Human Rights in an East Asian Perspective," in *Human Rights in an East Asian Perspective,* edited by James C. Hsiung (New York: Paragon House, 1985); and Lo Chung-Sho, "Human Rights in the Chinese Tradition," in *Human Rights: Comments and Interpretations,* edited by UNESCO (New York: Columbia University Press, 1949).

Finally, I have written extensively on questions of universality and relativism. This chapter summarizes views that are developed in more detail in Part 2 of my *Universal Human Rights in Theory and Practice,* 2nd ed. (Ithaca, NY: Cornell University Press, 2003, 3rd ed. forthcoming in 2013).

4

The Domestic Politics of Human Rights:
Dirty Wars in the Southern Cone

Although this is a book about the international politics of human rights, in a world of sovereign states, national politics largely determines how human rights are protected or violated. National case studies can both illustrate this important point and provide concreteness to the notion of "human rights violations." This chapter looks in some detail at violations in the Southern Cone of South America—particularly Chile, Argentina, and Uruguay—in the 1970s and 1980s.

Some readers may consider this case study very far away, both in time and in space. Its inclusion, however, reflects this book's commitment to putting contemporary international politics of human rights in a broader historical perspective— a perspective that, beyond its intrinsic interest, is essential to understanding what has changed and what remains the same in both human rights violations and international responses. Contemporary international human rights policies and practices were significantly shaped by efforts of governments, NGOs, and regional and international organizations to deal with the violations in Chile, Argentina, and Uruguay in the 1970s and 1980s.

The same is true of the (much shorter) case studies of violations we will consider in later chapters. In Part 2, we will look at Central America and South Africa under apartheid, which were especially important in the development of American international human rights policy in the 1980s. And in Part 3 we will look at China, Bosnia, Rwanda, Kosovo, and East Timor in the 1990s, as well as Sudan up to the present day. Although these later chapters address national violations, their primary focus is on international responses. Here the emphasis is reversed. This chapter considers only national violations. We will look at international responses in §§6.5 and 8.3.

1. POLITICS BEFORE THE COUPS

In Chile, military rule had been rare since the mid-nineteenth century. After World War II, a stable three-party democratic system emerged. In 1970, Salvador

Allende became the world's first freely elected Marxist president. Allende dramatically intensified the economic and social reforms begun under his Christian Democratic predecessor, Eduardo Frei. Large agricultural estates were expropriated. Key private industries and banks were nationalized, including Chile's (largely US-owned) copper industry. Social services were expanded. These changes were both lavishly praised and reviled, both within Chile and abroad. The resulting ideological polarization helped to set the stage for a military coup in September 1973, which installed a repressive military regime that ruled until 1990.

In Uruguay, the military had not intervened in politics since the 1860s. Furthermore, beginning in the first two decades of the twentieth century, under President José Batlle y Ordóñez, Uruguay implemented a series of model social and political reforms that created a widely admired social democratic welfare state that provided education and health care for all.

The system, however, began to collapse in the late 1960s. Political stalemate between its two dominant parties weakened Uruguay's government. The economy faced high inflation and labor unrest. And the Tupamaros were waging a dramatic campaign of guerrilla terrorism. In response, some civil liberties were suspended in 1968, 1970, and 1971 and even more seriously restricted in 1972. In June 1973, President Bordaberry suspended most remaining constitutional rights, closed the National Assembly, and for three years provided a public face for the military government—until he too was forced from office.

Argentina has a more checkered political history. Following independence in 1821–1822, Argentine politics were noted for violent struggles among provincial bosses (*caudillos*) and for leadership in the capital, Buenos Aires. Later in the century, however, a less violent political order emerged. Argentina even experienced a period of democratic rule from 1916 until 1930.

After World War II, populist leader Juan Perón ruled Argentina as an elected president for a decade. In 1955, however, he was overthrown in a military coup. Civilian governments were also prevented from completing their terms in office by coups in 1966 and 1973. The military, however, was not able to impose its preferred candidates when the country returned to civilian rule. Marcelo Cavarozzi aptly characterized this alternation of ineffective civilian and military regimes as the "failure of 'semi-democracy.'"[1]

In the mid-1970s, an already unstable political situation was made much worse by the incompetence and corruption of the civilian government. Meanwhile, the Argentine state and society were under guerrilla attacks by the Montoneros and the Revolutionary Army of the People. The political Right, with the support of the military and security forces, responded with assassinations of leftist students, lawyers, journalists, and trade unionists, in addition to guerrillas. In October 1975, five months before the overthrow of the civilian government, Army Commander in Chief Jorge Rafaél Videla warned that "as many people will die in Argentina as is necessary to restore order."[2] The following year, Videla, who had become president, delivered on his promise of violence, if not order.

2. TORTURE AND DISAPPEARANCES

A distinguishing feature of repression in the Southern Cone was the extensive use of **disappearances**, that is, extrajudicial detentions, usually accompanied by torture, often followed by death.[3] The politics of disappearances were most highly developed in Argentina.

> Task forces of the armed services . . . were detailed to arrest suspected subversives without warrant; to avoid identification of the captors; to take the detainees to clandestine detention camps, generally within military or police facilities; and to disclaim any knowledge of the whereabouts of their prisoners. In those camps, prisoners were interrogated under the most severe forms of torture. . . . The camps were deliberately shielded from any judicial or administrative investigation so that the torturers could be free to use any methods, and to deny even the existence of their prisoners, without fear of punishment. . . . The overwhelming majority of those who entered the system of "disappearances" were never seen alive again.[4]

After the return of civilian government, the Argentine National Commission on Disappeared Persons (CONADEP, also known as the Sabato Commission) documented 8,960 disappearances, a figure that probably underestimates the total by one-third or more. The commission identified 340 clandestine detention and torture centers, involving about 700 military officers, organized in 5 zones, 35 subzones, and 210 areas. The kidnappers operated with such impunity that three-fifths took place in the home of the victim, with witnesses present during the abduction. The mere passing of an unmarked green four-door Ford Falcon, the car of choice of the arresting squads, was enough to spread terror.

The Navy Mechanics School (ESMA) in Buenos Aires was Argentina's most important clandestine detention center. Torture at ESMA became a routine, bureaucratic activity. A trip to ESMA typically began with "Caroline," a thick broom handle with two long wires running out the end. The victim was stripped and tied to a steel bed frame. "Caroline" was attached to a box on a table that supplied the current. Then the electricity was applied to the victim, who often was periodically doused with water to increase the effects. "It was unhurried and methodical. If the victim was a woman they went for the breasts, vagina, anus. If a man, they favored genitals, tongue, neck. . . . Sometimes victims twitched so uncontrollably that they shattered their own arms and legs. Patrick Rice, an Irish priest who had worked in the slums and was detained for several days, recalls watching his flesh sizzle. What he most remembers is the smell. It was like bacon."[5]

Children were tortured in front of their parents, and parents in front of their children. Some prisoners were kept in rooms no longer or wider than a single bed. And the torture continued for days, weeks, months, even years, until the victim was released or, more often, killed. The sadistic brutality did not always even end with the death of the victim. "One woman was sent the hands of her daughter in a shoe box." The body of another woman "was dumped in her parents' yard, naked but showing no outward signs of torture. Later the director of the funeral home called to inform her parents that the girl's vagina had been sewn up. Inside he had found a rat."[6]

Most bodies, however, were never recovered. At ESMA, which also served as a disposal site for other naval camps, corpses were initially buried under the sports field. When this was filled, the bodies were burned daily, at five-thirty in the afternoon, usually after having been cut up with a chain saw. Finally, those in charge of destroying the evidence of their crimes hit on the idea of aerial disposal at sea. Once they had mastered the currents—at first bodies washed up in Buenos Aires, then in Montevideo—there was no trace to be found. Other units encased their victims in cement and dumped them in the river. The army's preferred method seems to have been to drive the corpses to the cemetery and register them as "NN," Name Unknown.

Repression in Chile was very similar, although the number of deaths was much lower. The Uruguayan style, however, was significantly different. Almost all the disappeared reappeared, usually in prison, after having been severely tortured. Only forty-four Uruguayans who disappeared in Uruguay remained unaccounted for at the end of military rule. The per capita rate of permanent disappearances in Uruguay was only about one-fifth that of Chile and one-twentieth that of Argentina. But about sixty thousand people, roughly 2 percent of the population, were detained, giving Uruguay the highest per capita rate of political prisoners and torture victims in all of Latin America. Virtually everyone in the country knew someone who had been detained—an extraordinarily powerful technique of state terror.

Uruguay developed a grotesque division of labor between clandestine detention centers, which specialized in physical abuse, and official prisons, which specialized in psychological abuse. The prison regimen was carefully calculated to dehumanize and break people who had already suffered excruciating physical torture. Prisoners were never referred to by name, always by number or insulting epithet: "cockroach," "rat," "apesto" (diseased one). Peepholes and listening devices were common, and broken prisoners were used as informants. Cell mates were often chosen based on psychological profiles in order to cause one another the most annoyance. Even families were incorporated into the routine of torture. For example, children were sometimes permitted to visit their parents once a month, but only if the parent demonstrated no sign of affection.

Prisoners were allowed outside only one hour a day. When they were in their cells, they were often required to stand except during designated sleeping hours. Every aspect of existence was regulated by ominously arbitrary rules. Violations were typically punished by isolation in a windowless cell with a bare electric lightbulb that burned twenty-four hours a day. In the most extreme case, nine top Tupamaro leaders, following months of vicious physical torture, were kept in complete solitary confinement for more than a decade. One spent an extended period of his confinement at the bottom of a dry well. Mauricio Rosencof reported, "In over eleven and a half years, I didn't see the sun for more than eight hours altogether. I forgot colors—there were no colors."[7]

3. THE NATIONAL SECURITY DOCTRINE

Some of the brutality reflected simple sadism: "At ESMA the complete licence they [the torturers] had to do what they wanted with their prisoners seems to have acted on them like an addiction. Sometimes they would stay in the torture room for a full 24 hours, never taking time off or resting; or else they would go home, and then return a couple of hours later, as though the atmosphere of cruelty and violence had drawn them back."[8] Much of the violence, however, was the work of professionals pursuing what they saw as defense of the nation.

National security doctrines, which drew heavily on French and US counterinsurgency doctrines of the 1950s and 1960s, provided an all-encompassing ideological framework for the military regimes of the Southern Cone. The state was viewed as the central institution of society. The military in turn was seen as the central institution of the state, the only organization with the combined insight, commitment, and resources needed to protect the interests and values of the nation.

The nation and its values were seen as under assault from an international conspiracy that was centered on, but by no means limited to, international communism. For example, a diagram used at Argentina's Air Force Academy depicts a tree of subversion with three roots: Marxism, Zionism, and Freemasonry.[9] Progressive Catholicism appears at the top, and new growths at the bottom include human rights organizations, women's rights, pacifism, nonaggression, disarmament, the Rotary Club, the Lions Club, and junior Chambers of Commerce. The main branches off the trunk are communist parties, the extreme totalitarian Right (Nazism and fascism), socialist parties, liberal democracy, revolutionary front parties, Protestants, sectarians and anti-Christians, armed revolutionary organizations, and "indirect aggression." The branches off the limb of "indirect aggression" are particularly striking: drug addiction, alcoholism, prostitution, gambling, political liberalism, economic liberalism, lay education, trade union corruption, "hippieness," pornography, homosexuality, divorce, art, newspapers, television, cinema, theater, magazines, and books.

All-out war was the only "reasonable" response to such a pervasive threat. The process would not always be pretty, especially when applied to the agents of "indirect aggression." But even if many "subversives" were more misdirected or gullible than malicious, they were still guilty and had to be treated as such. As General Iberico Saint Jean, military governor of Buenos Aires, put it in May 1976, "First we will kill all the subversives; then we will kill their collaborators; then . . . their sympathizers; then . . . those who remain indifferent; and finally we will kill the timid."[10]

The metaphor of disease was also common. "Subversives" were an infection, the armed forces the nation's antibodies. An infected member of the body politic had to be isolated (detained) to stop the spread of the disease. If treatment was possible, so much the better—although even a cure might be painful (torture). If the member was beyond repair, though, permanent surgical removal (death) was demanded. What mattered was the long-run health of the body politic.

This paranoid vision helps to explain the wide range of victims. Violence against terrorists was not unexpected; in both Argentina and Uruguay, it had been official policy even before the coups. Most of the disappeared, though, had no connection at all to the guerrillas.[11] Yet they too were considered guilty because of their "dangerous" political views.

Uruguay carried this ideology to its totalitarian extreme, creating Certificates of Democratic Background. An "A" rating indicated political reliability. A "B," or suspect, rating subjected one to police scrutiny and harassment. Those rated "C"— sometimes for an "offense" as minor as having been involved in a protest march twenty years earlier—were absolutely banned from public employment, a serious penalty in a country where the state was the largest employer. Many had trouble finding even private-sector jobs because hiring a "C" (or even a "B") citizen often led to harassing government audits and ominous questions about the employer's own loyalty.

The military sought to penetrate and "purify" all aspects of Uruguayan life. Each school received a new, politically reliable director. Every class had a "teacher's aide" to take notes on the behavior of students and teachers. A permit was required to hold a birthday party. Elections for captains of amateur soccer teams were supervised by the military, which could veto the results. A public performance of Ravel's *Piano Concerto for the Left Hand* was banned because of its sinister title.

National purification also had a major economic dimension. In Chile, the Pinochet government tried to reverse not only Allende's reforms but also those of the 1960s. In 1975 the junta applied "Shock Treatment" *(Plan Shock)*. Government spending declined by more than one-fourth. Public investment was cut in half. Uruguay and Argentina pursued similar plans somewhat less vigorously. The aim was to privatize the economy and weaken or destroy organized labor, which was seen as a focal point for subversion. In Argentina, as many as half of the disappeared were labor activists.

This forced march toward "free" markets produced a rapid decline in living standards. For example, real wages in Chile were one-third lower in 1976 than in 1970. Infant mortality increased dramatically. But after the initial shock, there was limited economic recovery, especially in Chile. Although most of the benefits of growth were concentrated in the hands of a small elite, employment and wages increased while inflation declined. Economic success helped to calm at least some of the discontent with military rule. In fact, all three military governments relied on economic growth to deflect attention from, or compensate for, political repression.

The beneficiaries of the national security state were somewhat less clear than the victims. Some members of the upper and middle classes profited from the privatization of the economy and the lifting of government controls. Industrialists seem to have strongly supported military control over labor. But neither local industrialists nor multinational corporations (MNCs) seem to have had much influence on economic policies. Furthermore, many local industrialists were left extremely vulnerable to foreign competition. And although the military amply rewarded itself—for example, between 1968 and 1973, Uruguayan spending on education declined from 24.3 percent to 16.6 percent of the budget, while military spending rose from 13.9

percent to 26.2 percent—economic advantage seems to have been a secondary concern.[12] In their economic policies as much as in their political strategies, ideology was central to the policies of the military regimes of the Southern Cone.

4. HUMAN RIGHTS NGOs

If the Southern Cone provides a particularly striking example of human rights violations, it also provides one of the most moving examples of resistance. On April 30, 1977, fourteen middle-aged women, frustrated in their search for their disappeared children, met publicly in the Plaza de Mayo (the main square of Buenos Aires) in front of the Casa Rosada (the president's residence). The weekly Thursday-afternoon vigil of the Mothers of the Plaza de Mayo—white scarves on their heads, silently walking around the square—became a symbol of both the cruelty of the military regime and the refusal of at least some ordinary people to bow to repression. Although subject to harassment and even attack—nine people associated with the mothers, including two French nuns, permanently disappeared on December 10, 1977, after evening mass—the mothers persevered and grew in numbers and in strength. By 1980, they had almost five thousand members and were able to set up a small office.

The following summer, similar groups from several Latin American countries joined to form the Federation of Families of Disappeared Persons and Political Prisoners (FEDEFAM). Its first president was Lidia Galletti, one of the leaders of the mothers. Patrick Rice, the Irish priest mentioned earlier who survived his trip to ESMA, became its volunteer secretary, operating out of a small office with a borrowed typewriter in Caracas, Venezuela. FEDEFAM became an important source of information and a focus for concerted international action by relatives' groups throughout Central and South America.

The Grandmothers of the Plaza de Mayo were organized in October 1977 to deal with one of the most bizarre aspects of Argentina's "Dirty War," the traffic in children. Young children and infants were occasionally picked up with their parents. Others were born while their mothers were in captivity. The total numbered around eight hundred. They were usually given or sold to childless military couples. One torturer estimated that about sixty babies passed through ESMA and that all but two—whose heads were smashed against the wall in efforts to get their mothers to talk—were sold.[13] Even today, the grandmothers continue to try to trace and recover these victims.

Several other human rights NGOs operated in Argentina. For example, the Center for Legal and Social Studies (CELS) was established in the summer of 1979 to investigate individual cases involving the security forces. Within a year of its founding, CELS had become affiliated with both the Geneva-based International Commission of Jurists and the New York–based International League for Human Rights. The Argentine Human Rights Commission was formed in 1975 to protest right-wing death-squad killings. It was forced into exile in 1976 but opened branches in Geneva, Mexico, Rome, and Washington to spread information about the nature of the repression in Argentina. Adolfo Pérez Esquivel, a leader of the Service for Peace and Justice (SERPAJ), received the Nobel Peace Prize in 1980, three years after having been imprisoned and tortured by the military regime. Important work was also done by the Permanent Assembly for Human Rights (APDH) and the Families of Those Detained and Disappeared for Political Reasons.

The Argentine Catholic Church, however, despite the disappearance or assassination of two bishops and twenty priests, nuns, and seminarians, was never a vocal critic of the military. Although SERPAJ was a religious organization and the Ecumenical Movement for Human Rights was active, the church as an institution was not part of the opposition. In fact, some military chaplains actively participated in the system of torture.

In Chile, by contrast, the church was at the center of the human rights movement. The Committee of Cooperation for Peace (COPACHI) was formed in October 1973, the month after the coup, under the joint leadership of the bishops of Chile's Catholic and Lutheran Churches. A month later, a legal-aid organization was established in space provided by the Catholic Church. By August 1974, CO-PACHI had more than one hundred employees in the capital of Santiago alone.

When Pinochet ordered COPACHI dissolved in November 1975, the Catholic Church responded by organizing the Vicaría de la Solidaridad (Vicariate of Solidarity).[14] The Vicaría provided aid and support for relatives of the disappeared and legal assistance to victims of state terror. Its Health Department organized soup kitchens and child-nutrition programs, especially in poorer urban areas that had been severely affected by Pinochet's economic reforms. Peasant organizations and unions, which had been special targets of repression, also received special support. And as military rule dragged on, the Vicaría began an extensive program of documentation and analysis. Although some lay human rights groups were also active, particularly the Chilean Human Rights Commission, in Chile, as in much of the rest of Latin America, the Catholic Church could do things that were impossible for lay organizations and even other churches.

In addition to aiding victims and their families, human rights NGOs were an important source of information. In fact, the lists of disappeared people prepared by CELS and APDH provided much of the factual basis for initial action by the United Nations and the Organization of American States (OAS). Given the efforts of the juntas to hide the scope of their violence, this may have been a significant achievement.

Human rights NGOs also allowed Argentineans and Chileans a limited opportunity to struggle against, rather than simply acquiesce to, military rule and the Dirty War. (In Uruguay the system of repression was so totalitarian that no effective local human rights NGOs were able to function until the final two or three years of military rule.) Taken together, NGO activities probably played a significant role in the failure of the military governments to "normalize" their rule.

5. THE COLLAPSE OF MILITARY RULE

The Argentine military, ironically, finally fell from power after it lost a conventional war with Britain over control of the obscure Falkland Islands. Argentina had long protested British occupation and control of the Malvinas, as they are known in Latin America. In April 1982, the junta decided to reclaim them by force, a ploy to deflect public attention from the collapse of the economy during the global recession of the early 1980s.

When Britain decisively repulsed the invasion, though, the military's humiliation was complete. Having attacked its own people, brought the economy to the brink of ruin, and then embarrassed itself and the country before the entire world, the Argentine military had little choice but to permit a return to civilian government. On October 30, 1983, Raúl Alfonsín won the national presidential election. He took office on December 10, the thirty-fifth anniversary of the adoption of the Universal Declaration of Human Rights.

In Chile, the economy also collapsed in the early 1980s. In 1982, per capita gross domestic product (GDP) declined by one-sixth. By March 1983, one-third of the labor force was unemployed. The minimum wage lost between one-fifth and one-half of its purchasing power. Close to half of Chile's children were malnourished, an appalling situation in a country that had previously been relatively prosperous. A wave of bankruptcies brought hard times even to the middle and upper classes.

As the junta approached its tenth anniversary in power, opposition increased in all sectors of society. Working-class residential neighborhoods began to organize. The old political parties (especially the centrist Christian Democrats, which had never been forced entirely underground) began to act, cautiously, in public. Strikes by truck drivers and copper miners in June 1983 were labor's first major challenge since the coup, followed by a successful general strike in July. Between May and November, several Days of National Protest culminated in a demonstration by close to a million people in Santiago.

The military, however, also found new resolve. As opposition grew, so did repression. Several deaths and more than one thousand arrests accompanied the July general strike. Mass arrests increased dramatically, as did banishments, exiles, torture, and political deaths. By late 1984, the government was forced to reimpose a state of siege, and repression became more brutal. For example, two young Chileans were set on fire by the police during a protest demonstration, killing one and savagely maiming the other. Although the government claimed that the youths had accidentally set themselves aflame with a Molotov cocktail, a third victim was torched a week later, as if to remind opponents that it had been no accident.

Popular resistance, however, could not be crushed this time. In October 1988, the military tried a plebiscite to legitimate its rule. The majority of Chileans, however, rejected a new eight-year term for Pinochet. On December 14, 1989, an opposition alliance of seventeen parties, led by Patricio Aylwin, won the first free elections in Chile in nearly two decades.

The Uruguayan military was also hit hard by the economic crisis of the early 1980s. By 1984, real wages were less than half their 1968 levels, and more than 10 percent of the population had left the country, including one-seventh of the country's university graduates and close to one-fifth of the economically active population of the capital city of Montevideo.[15] But the military, after some initial indecision, was unwilling to adopt the Chilean strategy of increased repression in the face of growing opposition. Elections were held in 1984, and an elected civilian government returned to power in 1985, even without a Falklands-like blunder.

6. *NUNCA MÁS:* SETTLING ACCOUNTS WITH TORTURERS AND THE PAST

Elections, or at least the transfer of power from one elected civilian government to another (as occurred in both Argentina and Uruguay in 1989, and in Chile in 1993), are sometimes seen as the solution for human rights problems. But a nation that has suffered gross and systematic violations of human rights remains no less scarred than individual victims and their families, friends, and acquaintances. Furthermore, successor regimes face the problem of dealing with those responsible for human rights violations under the old order.

When the torture stops, it may not be clear how to deal with those responsible—especially when they retain political influence and control the weaponry that supported their dictatorial rule. Defining the terms of retributive and restorative justice is part of a process of national reconciliation necessary to keep the wounds inflicted under military rule from festering. The experience of the countries of the Southern Cone, however, provides some sobering lessons. The post–cold war world in Central and Eastern Europe has faced similar problems, as have South Africa, Cambodia, and a number of other countries.

Two weeks before the election that brought a return to civilian rule, the Argentine junta issued a Law of National Reconciliation that created a blanket amnesty for all offenses connected with the "war against subversion." In his first week as president, however, Raúl Alfonsín delivered on his campaign promise to prosecute all nine members of the three military juntas that had run Argentina from 1976 to 1982.

No less significant was Alfonsín's decision to create the CONADEP, which would conduct an official investigation of the Dirty War. CONADEP's September 1984 report contained more than fifty thousand pages of documentation and provided an extensive, official, public accounting of the Dirty War. The summary, published under the title *Nunca Más* (Never Again)—a phrase that first attained wide political currency in the aftermath of the Holocaust—became an instant best seller.

Where so much of the violence was clandestine, to know the nature of the crime was the essential first step to overcoming its legacies. *Nunca Más,* at minimum, finally recognized and publicly memorialized the victims, whose very existence had for so long been officially denied. Truth, however, is only a first step. Punishment or pardon usually follows, and preventing future abuses must be a high priority.

Argentina made several changes in domestic law and ratified several international human rights treaties. The military command structure was reorganized. Military spending declined from 4.3 percent of gross domestic product in 1983 to 2.3 percent in 1987. In April 1988, a new Law of Defense defined the role of the armed forces as protecting against external aggression, effectively renouncing the national security doctrine.

Punishment was pursued through the courts. A defense of obedience to orders, however, effectively pardoned ordinary soldiers and lower-ranking officers. In a gesture to the dignity of the military, the Supreme Council of the Armed Forces was given initial jurisdiction to deal with its own through the system of military justice. But when the supreme council could find nothing illegal in any actions of the military government, the civilian Federal Court of Appeals took over the cases.

Sentences were handed down on December 9, 1985, the day before the second anniversary of the return of civilian government. Five leaders of the juntas received prison sentences, including life sentences for General Videla, the leader of the first junta, and Admiral Massera, the commander most intimately associated with the Dirty War. In addition, the court left open the possibility of further trials against more than 650 additional members of the armed forces.

Under extreme pressure from the military and its supporters, Alfonsín in December 1986 pushed through the *Ley de Punto Final*—literally, the Law of Full Stop (period), or the "final deadline." No new prosecutions could be filed after sixty days. The hope was that the legendary slowness of the Argentine judicial bureaucracy would leave most officers untouched. *Punto Final,* however, actually spurred monumental efforts by human rights groups and the courts. Judges even canceled their summer vacations to meet the deadline. Four hundred new indictments were registered against more than 100 officers.

On April 15, 1987, rebellious soldiers occupied several garrisons throughout the country and forced Alfonsín to push through the Law of Due Obedience, which limited prosecutions to chiefs of military areas. Even this, though, was not enough for the hard-liners. In January and December 1988 and in December 1990, new (but much less effective) revolts broke out, suggesting a precarious balance of power between hard-liners and moderates in the military and between the armed forces and the government.

Argentina's second civilian government, under President Carlos Menem, pardoned thirty-nine senior military officials in October 1989, effectively halting ongoing investigations of high leaders such as General Galtieri, the leader of the last junta. Hundreds involved in the military uprisings were also pardoned. Another eight senior officers, including General Videla, were pardoned at the end of December 1990. Although neither side was satisfied—Julio Strassera, who had prosecuted Videla, resigned from his position as Argentina's representative to the UN Commission on Human Rights, while General Videla publicly indicated that even this gesture was not enough, asking instead for a full vindication of the military—Argentine politics has since increasingly left the past behind.

Uruguay's new civilian government, when it took power in 1985, faced the even more difficult task of dealing with a military that had not been humiliated on the battlefield. It is thus not surprising that President Sanguinetti chose to accept the military's self-amnesty. In December 1986, Uruguay adopted the Law of Limitations, which protected the military against prosecution for crimes committed while it ruled the country.

The reaction against *impunidad* (impunity) for the military—there had not been a single prosecution, or even an official investigation—was dramatic.[16] In February

1987, a campaign was launched to hold a national referendum. By Christmas Eve, petitions had been signed by 634,702 people, out of a total population of about 3 million. This was equivalent to obtaining nearly 50 million signatures in the United States.

In the April 16, 1989, plebiscite, however, a majority chose to let the amnesty stand. Despite heavy rain, voter turnout was more than 80 percent: 53 percent voted "yellow," to let the amnesty stand, and 41 percent voted "green," to overturn it. The example of military resistance in Argentina seems to have been the deciding factor—especially after public statements by highly placed members of the Uruguayan military suggested that they would not allow the amnesty to be overturned.

Although not an entirely free choice, Uruguayans had the opportunity to choose whether to try to punish the military. Many victimized nations have not had even that much. For example, in Guatemala the military declared an amnesty just before leaving office in 1986. And to remind everyone where real power still resided, five dozen mutilated bodies appeared in various places in the country in the first three weeks of "civilian" rule. There was no plebiscite, or even an investigation of the tens of thousands of disappearances and arbitrary executions.

Chile, following the lead of Uruguay and the lesson of Argentina, chose to forgo prosecutions, which the military made clear it would not permit. In April 1990, however, President Aylwin created the Commission for Truth and Reconciliation (also known as the Rettig Commission). Its March 1991 report documents close to one thousand disappearances that resulted in death. (The commission's mandate did not include other violations, including tens of thousands of cases of torture.)

Although these efforts suggest that even where punishment is impossible, the guilty may be denied complete impunity, "men are unable to forgive what they cannot punish."[17] These words of Hannah Arendt, which have often been cited by those in the Southern Cone struggling against impunity, capture the central problem with military-imposed amnesties. Pardon is an act of charity or compassion. Punishment is an act of justice (and a deterrent to injustice). New civilian regimes are often unable to punish because the guilty retain considerable political power. The pardons thus received by torturers and murderers may have legal effect. Morally, however, they are profoundly defective. This corruption of both punishment and pardon by power also makes preventing future abuses more difficult.

Nonetheless, the task of prevention is likely to be greatly aided by the truth, which can sometimes be a partial substitute for punishment or pardon. A public declaration of the crimes of the guilty may help to put the past behind and focus a country's energy and attention on preventing future abuses. At the very least, a nation unable to acknowledge its past publicly is less likely to be able to prevent new human rights violations.

The official name of Chile's Commission for Truth and Reconciliation was thus particularly well chosen. Especially where suffering has been denied, truth may permit mourning and provide a public solace that may help to make reconciliation possible. There may even be a punishment of sorts in being forced to face a public demonstration of one's crimes. South Africa's truth commission, under the leadership of Nobel Laureate Bishop Desmond Tutu, was particularly forceful and effective in its efforts to uncover, and thus help to overcome, the horrors of the past.

Truth alone is never enough. Sometimes, though, it may make inroads against power. In any case, the task of human rights advocacy is to speak truth to power, in the name of past and present victims and in the hope of preventing future victims.

> *accuracy is essential*
> *we must not be wrong*
> *even by a single one*
> *we are despite everything*
> *the guardians of our brothers*
> *ignorance about those who have disappeared*
> *undermines the reality of the world.*[18]

Nunca más. Never again. Never *this* horror again. Ultimately, this is the meaning of the struggle against systematic violations of human rights.

7. POSTSCRIPT: MAINTAINING CIVILIAN RULE

Perhaps the most remarkable aspect of the return of civilian rule in the Southern Cone has been its persistence. Although the military remains an important institution, soldiers have remained in their barracks. Even in times of severe economic and political crisis, they have not threatened to retake power.

Argentina provides perhaps the most striking example. The financial crisis that began in July 1997 in East Asia spread in 1998 to Russia, then Brazil, and at the end of the year Argentina. After a series of failed internal measures in 1999, Argentina was forced to negotiate a $7.2 billion agreement with the International Monetary Fund (IMF) in March 2000, followed by a massive $40 billion package of assistance in December. The country nonetheless plunged into deep depression, forcing Argentina into default on its international loans.

Real GDP declined every year from 1999 through 2002, with a staggering 10.9 percent decline in 2002 alone. In 2002, the inflation rate was more than 40 percent, and well over 100 percent when measured in world prices (reflecting the collapse of the Argentinean peso, which lost three-quarters of its value during the year). Unemployment was approaching 20 percent, and well over half of the population was in poverty (as compared to less than 40 percent before the crisis). Perhaps most ominously, in light of the history of the 1970s, in December 2001 Buenos Aires and other major cities experienced significant episodes of looting and rioting. Nonetheless, the military did not intervene, despite a series of questionable decisions by the civilian governments in their attempts to deal with the crisis.

The deepening of the consensus on civilian rule can also be seen in the fate of General Pinochet in Chile. Although Pinochet stepped down as head of state in 1990, he continued to head the military until 1998, when he was named senator for life—a position that granted him parliamentary immunity from prosecution.

However, in October 1998, a Spanish special judge issued an international arrest warrant, which was served on Pinochet while he was visiting London. After a period of detention, the British government decided that he was not fit to be extradited and allowed him to return to Chile in March 2000.

On returning to Chile, Pinochet was stripped of his parliamentary immunity and arrested. In July 2002, however, the case against him was dismissed by the Chilean Supreme Court, on the (highly debatable) technical grounds of mental incapacity. But his legal troubles continued. In May 2004, the Chilean Supreme Court reversed itself and found him mentally competent, and in August 2004, the Supreme Court confirmed the stripping of his immunity for many of his crimes connected with Operation Condor during the Dirty War. Legal wrangling continued until his death, on December 10, 2006. Although he was never brought to trial, on a very personal level General Pinochet was denied impunity.

Throughout all of these wranglings, the Chilean military remained in the background. Although still a significant political force, they seem to have accepted the idea that their influence is to be exercised only from their barracks. Even more encouraging, in January 2005 the Chilean army formally accepted institutional responsibility for past abuses.

It would be foolish to proclaim civilian rule absolutely safe. Nonetheless, democratic rule and respect for human rights seem to be deeply entrenched. For example, Freedom House, which issues annual rankings of "freedom" that are generally accepted as a good measure of civil and political rights, rated Argentina "not free" from 1976 to 1982, "partly free" in 1983 and in the crisis years of 2001 and 2002, and "free" for all other years through 2010. Chile was rated "not free" from 1973 to 1978, "partly free" from 1979 through 1989, and "free" from 1990 through 2010 (with the best possible score from 2003 to 2010). And Uruguay was rated "not free" from 1976 through 1979, "partly free" from 1980 to 1984, and "free" from 1985 to 2010 (with the highest possible score from 2000 to 2010).

The people of Argentina, Chile, and Uruguay deserve most of the credit for this achievement. Nonetheless, international action, especially the global and regional spread of human rights values, does seem to be a significant part of the story, both in supporting local human rights advocates and in delegitimating their opponents.

DISCUSSION QUESTIONS

1. When we talk about human rights violations, numbers of victims can take on a strangely abstract character. To make the suffering behind the numbers more concrete, try this simple exercise. Count all the people you know personally. For most people, the number will be several hundred. This is far fewer than the number disappeared in Argentina or Chile. It is about the number of people killed in a single day in June 1989 in Tiananmen Square in China. Now add all the people you know of (actors, writers, celebrities, people in the news). The total will probably be a few

thousand. In Argentina, more people disappeared than you can even name. In the early 1980s in Guatemala and El Salvador, this many people were being killed every few months.

2. Are there situations in which torture or disappearances could be justified? (Don't answer too quickly, whatever your initial inclination.)

3. How can people become torturers? Even if they are not applying the electric shocks to the victims, how can people work in institutions that regularly practice torture or arbitrary execution? Consider the following possibilities:
   - Sadism: they enjoy it.
   - Commitment: they believe it is necessary to achieve a higher good.
   - Self-interest: they see an opportunity to get ahead.
   - Coercion: they are forced to participate.
   - Cowardice: they find themselves in a system they are afraid to resist.
   - Denial: they try to convince themselves that things are other than they appear.
   - Inertia: they go with a flow that they don't try to resist.
   - Does it make a difference why people engage in torture and commit murder? Does it make a *moral* difference? At what point in your thinking about "justification" does the issue of motive become relevant?

4. Chile and Uruguay had long and relatively well-established democratic traditions. Nonetheless, they endured more than a decade of extraordinarily repressive military rule. How can this be explained? Although you may lack the factual information to make a truly informed judgment, speculating on possible reasons can be useful, particularly if we want to use these cases to think about prospects for democracy elsewhere.

5. Is it easier to build or to destroy a democracy? Once it is destroyed, how (and how easily) can it be fixed? Does the way it was destroyed—and the length of time it took—have a significant impact on the prospects for recovery or repair? Does the particular way that democracy was (re)instituted have an impact on its future prospects?

6. It obviously makes sense to distinguish between large and small numbers of human rights violations. But does it make sense to distinguish between different types of violations? If so, which ones are especially heinous? Why?

7. Is there a qualitative difference between a regime that tortures people but feeds everyone well and one that allows people to suffer from malnutrition but tortures no one? Or between a regime that allows free political participation but requires everyone to work sixty-hour weeks and one that provides thirty-five-hour workweeks but no political participation? There are differences, certainly, and they are likely to be of considerable political importance. But are the differences of any *moral* significance?

8. Are the only important (moral) distinctions between human rights violations ultimately quantitative? This would seem to be the implication of the claim that all human rights are interdependent and indivisible. But is

the moral difference really just the number of people and the number of rights violated?

9. However you have answered the preceding set of questions, you can construct a list of human rights violations and then rank them from more to less severe. Having done that, what foreign policy implications can you draw? Suppose we concentrate on the worst cases. The reasons to do so are fairly obvious, but are there drawbacks? Suppose someone were to suggest that we focus on *less* severe violators because the chances for improving practices there are greater. Or consider the claim that we should focus on the trend in a given country. If we accept this, should an improving or a worsening trend receive greater weight? What other relevant considerations can you think of? States clearly cannot concentrate on all human rights violators equally, but how should they prioritize cases?

10. How should new governments deal with former torturers and dictators and the members of the repressive apparatus of the old regime? Suppose that there are no political constraints imposed by the continuing power of these forces. Who should be punished—and who shouldn't—for what, and how severely? How should vengeance, justice, mercy, and reconciliation be balanced? Now suppose that the old forces of repression do still hold considerable power. How far should the demands of justice be pressed? At what point does bowing to power corrupt or undermine the new political order? Is there a practical alternative to accepting the lesser of two evils? Are practical alternatives the only ones that should be adopted?

11. Although economic, social, and cultural rights received some attention in this chapter, the central focus was on violations of civil and political rights. This reflects the focus of international discussions of human rights violations in the Southern Cone. Is that focus the best one? Was the distinctive character of human rights violations in the Southern Cone significantly connected with economic, social, and cultural rights? Even if the distinctive nature of the repression concerned civil and political rights, should there have been greater international attention to economic and social rights?

SUGGESTED READINGS

Readers interested in more information on human rights violations in the Southern Cone should begin with Ian Guest, *Behind the Disappearances: Argentina's Dirty War Against Human Rights and the United Nations* (Philadelphia: University of Pennsylvania Press, 1990). Guest, a journalist who covered the United Nations Commission on Human Rights for a number of years, and later became a human rights activist, makes particularly powerful use of personal accounts of some of the victims and thoroughly examines both UN action and US policy during both the Carter and the Reagan years. Somewhat narrower, but even more moving for being a first-person account by a journalist victim of the Dirty War, is Jacobo Timerman, *Prisoner Without a Name, Cell Without a Number* (New York: Alfred A. Knopf,

1981). Eric Stener Carlson, ed., *I Remember Julia: Voices of the Disappeared* (Philadelphia: Temple University Press, 1996), is also powerful and evocative.

John Simpson and Jana Bennett, *The Disappeared: Voices from a Secret War* (London: Robson Books, 1985), is another useful example of political journalism, providing detailed information on the internal politics of the Dirty War. A much more idiosyncratic, but penetrating, analysis by a cynical external observer can be found in V. S. Naipaul, *The Return of Eva Perón* (New York: Vintage Books, 1981). For a more general discussion of disappearances as a technique of human rights violations, see Amnesty International USA, *Disappearances: A Workbook* (New York: Amnesty International USA, 1981). Jeffrey A. Sluka, ed., *Death Squad: The Anthropology of State Terror* (Philadelphia: University of Pennsylvania Press, 2000), offers interesting comparative case studies.

The horror of the Dirty War is difficult to capture even in good journalism (let alone in dry academic prose). Literary representations can thus be particularly useful. Among fictional accounts, I particularly like Lawrence Thornton, *Imagining Argentina* (New York: Doubleday, 1987), a novel in the "magic realist" tradition of García Márquez.

For an excellent academic account of the human rights movement in Argentina, see Alison Brysk, *The Politics of Human Rights in Argentina* (Stanford, CA: Stanford University Press, 1994). On Chile, Pamela Lowden, *Moral Opposition to Authoritarian Rule in Chile, 1973–1990* (Houndmills, UK: Macmillan Press, 1996), is strong on domestic opposition. Darren G. Hawkins, *International Human Rights and Authoritarian Rule in Chile* (Lincoln: University of Nebraska Press, 2002), thoroughly reviews the record of international human rights diplomacy. Sonia Cardenas, *Conflict and Compliance: State Responses to International Human Rights Pressure* (Philadelphia: University of Pennsylvania Press, 2007), looks comparatively at this important topic.

Another journalistic account, Lawrence Weschler, *A Miracle, a Universe: Settling Accounts with Torturers* (New York: Pantheon Books, 1990), is perhaps the best place to begin further reading and reflection on the difficult process of overcoming the legacy of repression. Among the now immense academic literature on reconciliation and transitional justice, the following volumes are useful for their breadth of coverage and extensive comparative case studies: Neil J. Kritz, ed., *Transitional Justice: How Emerging Democracies Reckon with Former Regimes,* 3 vols. (Washington, DC: US Institute of Peace Press, 1995); A. James McAdams, ed., *Transitional Justice and the Rule of Law in New Democracies* (Notre Dame, IN: University of Notre Dame Press, 1997); Carol A. L. Praeger and Trudy Govier, eds., *Dilemmas of Reconciliation: Cases and Concepts* (Waterloo, Canada: Wilfred Laurier University Press, 2003); and Chandra Lekha Sriram, *Confronting Past Human Rights Violations: Justice vs. Peace in Times of Transition* (London: Frank Cass, 2004). Mark Ensalaco, *Chile Under Pinochet: Recovering the Truth* (Philadelphia: University of Pennsylvania Press, 2000), is excellent on Chile. Eric Wiebelhaus-Brahm, *Truth Commissions and Transitional Societies: The Impact on Human Rights and Democracy* (Hoboken, NJ: Taylor & Francis, 2010), combines statistical and case study analyses to try to measure the impact of truth commissions.

On broader issues of human rights in transitional societies, see Shale Horowitz and Albrecht Schnabel, eds., *Human Rights and Societies in Transition: Causes, Consequences, Responses* (Tokyo: United Nations University Press, 2004). The website of the International Center for Transitional Justice, http://www.ictj.org/, is useful for recent information on transitional justice issues around the world. The Truth Commission Digital Collection, http://www.usip.org/library/truth.html, provides basic information. For useful links, see the Truth Commissions page on the site of the Transitional Justice Forum, http://tj-forum.org/files/Truth-comms-from-JE.html#reps.

PART TWO
Multilateral, Bilateral, and Transnational Action

5

Global Multilateral Mechanisms

In this chapter we look at multilateral mechanisms with a global scope. I follow the conventional distinction between "Charter-based bodies" (considered in §§5.1 and 5.2) and "treaty-based bodies" (considered in §5.3), that is, those that draw their authority from the United Nations Charter and those that are rooted in other, more specialized, treaties. This chapter also briefly notes the work of other global multilateral actors (§5.4) and provides a case study of the global antiapartheid regime (§5.5). The following chapter considers regional human rights regimes, the other major multilateral actors.

1. THE HUMAN RIGHTS COUNCIL

The Human Rights Council[1] was created in 2006 to replace the Commission on Human Rights. As we have seen, the commission during its first two decades of work laid the foundations of the global human rights regime, doing the principal work on the drafting of the Universal Declaration of Human Rights and the International Human Rights Covenants. In the late 1960s and 1970s, it began very limited monitoring of state practices. In the 1980s and early 1990s, its monitoring activities expanded substantially, including many more countries and issues. But in its final decade, the commission became hopelessly politicized, as symbolized by the election in 2003 of Mu'ammar Gadhafi as its chair.

The council, though, remains severely constrained by its composition. Its members are states, elected by the UN General Assembly largely without regard to their human rights record. For example, Bahrain, China, Cuba, Gabon, Kyrgyzstan, Libya, Mauritania, Qatar, Russia, and Saudi Arabia—all countries with poor to dismal human rights records—were members of the council in 2010–2011.

Given this membership, perhaps the most notable fact about the Human Rights Council is that it regularly does work of real value. It remains a largely impartial forum for the consensual development of new international human rights norms. For example, the concluding work on the conventions on persons with disabilities and on disappearances was done by the council and its wide-ranging resolutions are part of the global process of promoting adoption of international human rights norms.

The council also tries to promote the implementation of internationally recognized human rights and engages in limited monitoring. These efforts are somewhat less impartial. Some countries, for political reasons, receive more attention than their human rights record would suggest, while others receive less. (Israel and China, respectively, are often presented as examples.) But those countries that are considered are generally examined on the basis of well-documented violations.

The council's new system of "universal period review"[2] subjects the human rights record of all states to public discussion every four years. Although the process generates a lot of predictable political posturing, in some instances a frank and open discussion of some value does occur. But there are no sanctions, other than publicity, associated with the review. And because it covers the full range of human rights practices, it tends to elicit scattered observations that are "all over the map."

Of much more value are the special procedures and mechanisms[3] originally developed by the commission in the 1980s. For example, in 1980 the commission created a Working Group on Enforced or Involuntary Disappearances to assist families and friends in determining the whereabouts of disappeared persons (see §4.2). After examining communications detailing a disappearance, the working group transmits the case to the government in question. If necessary, reminders are sent, at least once a year. More than nineteen thousand cases were handled in the group's first decade of work. And in its first thirty years of work, through 2010, the working group has inquired into the fate of more than fifty-three thousand individuals.

In close to one in five cases—more than ten thousand cases in total—the whereabouts or fate of the individual has been clarified. Special urgent-action procedures for disappearances within the three months preceding the communication, when most victims suffer torture or execution, but also when they are most likely to reappear, have resolved a somewhat higher percentage of cases. There is good reason to believe that a significant number of those identified by this procedure owe their lives to it.

Ironically, the first urgent inquiry concerned Mohamed al-Jabiri, Iraq's representative to the Commission on Human Rights. He had been active in establishing the working group and was slated to be its first chair. But al-Jabiri apparently ran afoul of Iraqi dictator Saddam Hussein, was recalled to Baghdad, and disappeared. Theo van Boven, director of the UN Division of Human Rights, began diplomatic inquiries and threatened to publicize the case. About a week later, van Boven received a handwritten note from al-Jabiri saying that he had decided to retire. It is uncertain what al-Jabiri's fate would have been without immediate UN intervention. His case does suggest, though, that aggressive international procedures can help at least a few victims. Furthermore, the working group's annual inquiries about unresolved cases, even when they are ignored, are a reminder that someone is watching and still cares.

The special procedures are manned by independent experts, not state representatives. Because of their greater impartiality and their narrower focus, their investigations typically are more penetrating and their efforts more aggressive than those of the council itself—which, after all, is a political organ of the United Nations.

In 2011 there were thirty-three active "thematic" special rapporteurs or working groups dealing with a range of issues, from arbitrary detention, torture, and freedom of religion to the rights to food, adequate housing, and education, as well as topics such as protecting human rights defenders, the use of mercenaries, and toxic and dangerous products and wastes. In addition, nine independent "country" experts or special rapporteurs addressed the human rights situations in Cambodia, Côte d'Ivoire, North Korea, Haiti, Iran, Myanmar (Burma), the Occupied Palestinian Territories, Somalia, and Sudan. (Côte d'Ivoire and Iran were added to the list in 2011, and the mandate on Burundi was allowed to expire.) These bodies often have well-established records of improving the conditions of individual victims. The offices of the rapporteurs on torture, arbitrary executions, and violence against women are especially well known and respected.

The stature of the "mandate holder" (i.e., rapporteur or expert) can also be used to increase the impact of these special procedures. For example, Juan Mendez (from Argentina), the current special rapporteur on torture, is the former head of Human Rights Watch and the International Center for Transnational Justice. John Ruggie (from the United States), the special representative of the secretary-general on human rights and transnational corporations and other business enterprises, is one of the world's leading scholars of international relations (teaching at Harvard and having previously been a dean at Columbia), a former assistant secretary-general of the United Nations, and the founder of the Global Compact (a leading international actor in the area of corporate responsibility in the areas of human rights, labor, environment, and corruption).

The immediate impact of these bodies is ultimately a matter of the willingness of governments to engage in conversations with them, allow them to visit their countries, and listen to their concerns and advice. But particularly when either the body or the mandate holder has a prominent international reputation, many states are willing to make improvements in the treatment of particular individuals. And some of the reports by these experts are important sources of information about abuses that is used by national and transnational advocates.

The council has also inherited and revised older commission procedures for considering complaints about violations in particular countries. They have been much less significant than the work of thematic and country experts. Complaint procedures in the context of the relatively political council are simply too adversarial to elicit cooperation from governments with the sorts of gross and persistent violations that are required to have a case raised under these mechanisms.

In addition, the council has regularly exercised its right to convene special sessions. Through 2011 there had been eighteen such sessions, addressing the Occupied Palestinian Territories, Lebanon, Sudan (Darfur), Myanmar (Burma), Democratic Republic of the Congo, Sri Lanka, Haiti, Côte d'Ivoire, Libya, and Syria, as well as international food prices and the global economic and financial crisis. These sessions have brought additional international attention to these situations and in some cases have provoked a slightly more cooperative response from rights-abusive states. Especially notable are the three special sessions held on Syria in 2011. These reflect the dramatic changes in the region and perhaps even suggest somewhat more aggressive monitoring by the council in the future.

2. THE HIGH COMMISSIONER FOR HUMAN RIGHTS

The council's (and earlier the commission's) activities reflect an information-advocacy model of human rights implementation. They seek to acquire and disseminate authoritative information on violations to encourage (embarrass) governments to improve their practices. They rely on the desire of states to be respected, both by their peers and by their citizens, and on the damage to state reputations that can be caused by well-publicized systematic human rights violations.

The UN Office of the High Commissioner for Human Rights (OHCHR), created after the 1993 Vienna World Conference, personifies this information-advocacy approach. The high commissioner has the global reach of the council, without its cumbersome procedures and politicization. Like the special rapporteurs, the high commissioner may deal directly with governments to seek improved respect for internationally recognized human rights—but with the added advantage of an explicit mandate to deal with all governments on all issues. And in practice the high commissioner has emerged as a prominent global advocate for human rights.

The first incumbent, José Ayala-Lasso of Ecuador, adopted a very low profile during his tenure (1994–1997). His successor, however, Mary Robinson, the former president of Ireland, turned the office into a major force. The quality of the secretarial support work was brought to a high level, the budget increased substantially, and Robinson became a well-known public figure across the globe, as a result of her difficult-to-resist combination of intellectual brilliance, moral commitment, and hard work, combined with an unusual mix of diplomatic skill and a constant willingness to push the bounds of what her targets were willing to tolerate from an international public servant.

Robinson left her successor, Sérgio Vieira de Mello of Brazil, a completely transformed organization when she moved on to other work in 2002. Sadly, he was among the victims of the bombing of the UN offices in Baghdad in August 2003. The acting high commissioner, Bertrand Ramcharan of Guyana, a career UN official and a noted scholar of international human rights law, was succeeded in 2004 by Louise Arbour of Canada, another high-profile high commissioner—she was previously the chief prosecutor for the International Criminal Tribunals for the former Yugoslavia and for Rwanda—who exercised her mandate aggressively on behalf of human rights and victims of violations. She was in turn succeeded in 2008 by Navanethem (Navi) Pillay of South Africa, a former judge of the International Criminal Court and former president of the International Criminal Tribunal for Rwanda.

Although the public activities of the high commissioner draw the most attention, the significance of the behind-the-scenes work of her office should not be underestimated. The OHCHR website (http://www2.ohchr.org) is a model of clarity and comprehensive coverage that is of great value to activists, scholars, ordinary citizens, and victims. The office also provides direct administrative support for the council and the treaty bodies (which are discussed in the next section), engages in original research (with special attention to the Vienna Programme of Action and the right to development), and provides capacity building and advisory services to governments seeking to improve their national practices.

At the end of 2010, the OHCHR had established twelve country offices (in Bolivia, Cambodia, Colombia, Guatemala, Guinea, Kosovo, Mauritania, Mexico, Nepal, the Occupied Palestinian Territories, Togo, and Uganda) and ten regional offices (for East Africa, Southern Africa, West Africa, Central America, Latin America, Europe, Central Asia, Southeast Asia, the Pacific, and the Middle East). It also had 635 international human rights officers and national staff placed in fourteen international peacekeeping operations, as well as resident human rights advisers in sixteen countries. And the budget of the Office of the High Commissioner more than tripled in the 2000s, from a little more than $100 million in 2000–2001 to more than $350 million in 2009–2010.

Compared to the resources devoted to development assistance, such efforts are very modest. (For example, the World Bank made loans totaling more than $44 billion in 2010, and its administrative expenses of $1.4 billion were close to four times the total budget of the Office of the High Commissioner.) Nonetheless, they represent a considerable expansion of activities. And they illustrate the possibilities for progressive cooperative action with governments that have some degree of openness to a combination of pressure and assistance from the outside world, especially when it comes through the politically less partisan mechanisms of multilateral organizations.

3. TREATY-REPORTING SYSTEMS

An important cluster of global human rights institutions derive their authority from multilateral human rights treaties. (See Table 5.1.) The principal activity of the committees created by these treaties ("**treaty bodies**") is to review reports on compliance submitted by the parties. Many also consider "individual communications" (complaints from alleged victims of violations) and issue "general comments" that attempt to advance international human rights jurisprudence.

A. Reporting

The principal and most important activity of the treaty bodies is to review periodic reports on compliance that parties are required to submit, usually every four or five years. Based on the report and additional information gathered by the committee, questions are prepared and submitted to the state in writing. A state representative participates in the committee's public discussion of the report. A follow-up written exchange often ensues.

TABLE 5.1 Treaty Bodies

Committee (Treaty Supervised)	Parties to Treaty	Established	Meetings (Per Year)	Individual Communications (First Year Received)
Human Rights Committee (ICCPR)	167	1976	9 weeks	Yes (1976)
Committee on Economic, Social and Cultural Rights (ICESCR)	160	1985	6 weeks	Not yet*
Committee on the Elimination of Racial Discrimination (ICERD)	175	1969	6 weeks	Yes (1982)
Committee on the Elimination of Discrimination Against Women (CEDAW)	187	1981	9 weeks	Yes (2003)
Committee Against Torture (CAT)	149	1987	6 weeks	Yes (1987)
Committee on the Rights of the Child (CRC)	193	1990	9 weeks	Not yet*
Committee on Migrant Workers (ICRMW)	45	2004	3 weeks	Not yet*
Committee on the Rights of Persons with Disabilities (ICRPD)	107	2009	2 weeks	Not yet*
Committee on Enforced Disappearances (ICED)	30	2011	2 weeks	Not yet*

* The required number of parties has not yet been reached to put the process into practice.
Data as of various dates in the second half of 2011.

The reporting process thus is an exchange of information that provides limited, noncoercive monitoring. The extent of state participation, beyond submitting its report, ranges from active cooperation to a largely nonresponsive presence. There are no sanctions of any sort associated with the reporting procedure, even if the country refuses to submit its report (as a few do).

Complaints about the "weakness" of reporting systems, however, assume that the goal is coercive enforcement. In fact, though, the aim is to encourage and facilitate compliance. Judged in these terms, reporting often has a significant positive effect. The most constructive part of the process is the preparation of the report. Periodic reviews of national practice, if undertaken with any degree of conscientiousness, require states, agencies, and officials to step back from their day-to-day work and reflect on their processes, procedures, and institutions.

Reporting is especially valuable in countries with an active civil society. NGOs are sometimes directly involved in preparing the national report. Often they lobby the officials that draft the report. And they can use preparation of the report and its public review by the treaty body as occasions for campaigning. NGOs may also participate indirectly in the committee review through contacts with individual members. And the public hearing and comments by the committee often provide an occasion for amplified publicity. Paradoxically, then, reporting is most likely to have an impact where it is not critically needed: that is, where human rights records are relatively good. Nevertheless, any victim who is helped is a victory for international action, wherever that person resides.

One might even argue that the greatest virtue of treaty-reporting systems is their ability to address violations that are not sufficiently severe to merit scrutiny by the council or a special procedure. Particularly for countries and violations that do not have a high international profile, reporting may actually provide greater scrutiny.

Furthermore, small-scale incremental progress, which is a realistic possibility in the case of any state that takes its reporting obligation seriously, is not to be sneered at—especially when we consider the typically modest impact of higher-profile investigatory or complaint procedures. And even if stronger mechanisms are available, the periodic self-study that reporting requires is a valuable contribution.

Two major limits of reporting systems, however, deserve note. First, the positive effects of reporting depend ultimately on the willingness of the state to change—either because of a positive desire to improve or because of an openness or vulnerability to criticism (which all but the most repressive of regimes possess to some degree). Second, the changes produced by such mechanisms are limited and incremental.

States typically engage in massive violations only when they feel something of great importance is at stake. The national and international political costs of negative publicity and advocacy campaigns are almost never sufficient to overcome the political incentives to continue gross and persistent systematic violations. But where the violations are relatively minor or narrowly circumscribed—for example, particular rules on the treatment of prisoners, activities of a single part of the government bureaucracy, particular nondiscrimination policies, or the treatment of a single individual—all but the worst governments may be willing to consider improvements.

For all their limits, then, such modest improvements are not insignificant. And over time, they may accumulate. This is especially true as the process is repeated in multiple treaty bodies—and as the reporting process interacts with other national, transnational, bilateral, and multilateral advocacy.

B. General Comments

Treaty bodies also issue "general comments." This practice, first developed and most effectively employed by the Human Rights Committee, attempts not only to improve the reporting process but also to influence the progressive development of international human rights law by offering quasi-authoritative interpretations of the obligations under the treaty.

Consider a more or less arbitrarily chosen example, General Comment 20 of the Human Rights Committee, adopted in 1992. It interprets Article 7 of the International

Covenant on Civil and Political Rights, which states (in its entirety), "No one shall be subjected to torture or to cruel, inhuman or degrading treatment or punishment. In particular, no one shall be subjected without his free consent to medical or scientific experimentation." This pithy statement certainly could benefit from some elaboration, which General Comment 20 seeks to provide.

Paragraph 2 states that the aim of the article "is to protect both the dignity and the physical and mental integrity of the individual"—offering a relatively expansive reading that links the provision to the foundational claim in the preamble of the Covenants that "these rights derive from the inherent dignity of the human person." Paragraph 2 also explicitly links this article to the provision in Article 10 that "all persons deprived of their liberty shall be treated with humanity and with respect for the inherent dignity of the human person." And it explicitly applies these obligations to agents of the state not just when acting in their official capacity but also when operating "outside their official capacity or in a private capacity."

Paragraph 3 draws attention to the fact that no exceptions are permitted in times of emergency. (Along similar lines, paragraph 15 expresses concern over amnesties for torturers that have been granted by some states.) And in holding that "no justification or extenuating circumstances may be invoked to excuse a violation of Article 7 for any reasons, including those based on an order from a superior officer or public authority," the committee in effect applies the provisions of the 1984 Convention Against Torture to the interpretation of the covenant. (The prohibition of the use of evidence obtained by torture, advanced in paragraph 12, does much the same thing.)

Paragraph 4 holds that it is neither necessary nor productive to draw up a list of prohibited acts. Nonetheless, paragraph 5 emphasizes that mental suffering falls within the acts prohibited by Article 7 and that its protections extend to certain forms of corporal punishment, including protection of "children, pupils and patients in teaching and medical institutions." Paragraph 6 explicitly places prolonged solitary confinement within the coverage of Article 7.

Paragraph 8 claims that the state obligation is not simply to legislatively prohibit such actions but also to take positive steps of protection. Paragraphs 10–13 specify some of those steps, including widely disseminating information on the ban on torture, systematically reviewing interrogation practices, and prohibiting incommunicado detention.

Such observations and interpretations are not formally binding. They do, however, have considerable informal authority. General comments thus have become a modest yet significant device for the progressive development of international human rights jurisprudence that has been of use to national and international human rights advocates.

C. Complaint Procedures

The six core treaties also allow individual "communications." (Complaints were approved for economic, social, and cultural rights in 2006, and in 2011 a mechanism

TABLE 5.2 Statistical Overview of Individual Communications

Committee	Parties Allowing Complaints (Percent of Parties)	Registered Communications (Number of Parties Against; Percent of Parties Allowing)	Pending Cases	Inadmissible or Discontinued (Percent Concluded)	Views (Percent Violation)
HRC	113 (68%)	1996 (82; 73%)	409	838 (55%)	749 (81%)
CAT	64 (44%)	439 (29; 45%)	102	168 (50%)	169 (31%)
CERD	54 (31%)	45 (10; 19%)	4	17 (41%)	24 (42%)

Data as of various dates in the second half of 2010.

finally was established under the Convention on the Rights of the Child, although neither has yet entered into force.) Complaint procedure are also envisioned under the treaties on migrant workers, persons with disabilities, and disappearances. Table 5.2 provides basic statistical data on the three most used individual complaint mechanisms.

Participation in these procedures, however, is voluntary; states that are party to the treaty must affirmatively "opt in" (or, in the case of torture, may "opt out"). Depending on the treaty, between one-third and two-thirds of the parties do not allow individual complaints. Not surprisingly, some of the worst violators choose not to participate. In addition, the number of cases considered is tiny. And, in the end, complaint procedures are not even binding in international law.

Although the details differ from body to body, there is a clear general pattern. Communications from individuals are screened by the United Nations Secretariat. Those that show potential merit are registered. Registered complaints are then screened carefully for admissibility. (The principal requirements are that the alleged violations fall under the scope of the treaty and that local remedies have been exhausted.)

Once the procedural hurdles have been scaled, the committee corresponds with the government in question, and sometimes with the petitioner (or her representative). It also often carries out inquiries into public records and independent sources of information. It then states its views as to whether there has been a violation of the treaty and makes suggestions and recommendations as to remedies. These findings are, explicitly, merely the view of the committee. They are not binding even in international law (let alone national law). In fact, the state has no obligation even to respond to the committee's views. Nonetheless, many states, especially those with an active civil society, do take the findings seriously. Individuals often receive remedy as a result of their complaints. In some cases—prominent examples include complaints of discrimination on the basis of sexual orientation in Australia and against indigenous women in Canada—national legislation has been changed in response to the recommendations of the committee.

4. ADDITIONAL GLOBAL ACTORS

At least four other global multilateral actors merit note: the International Labor Organization (ILO); the United Nations Educational, Scientific, and Cultural Organization (UNESCO); the International Criminal Court (ICC); and the UN Security Council. Each has a functional mandate that centrally includes, but is not limited to, human rights.

The International Labor Organization is the "granddaddy" of multilateral human rights organizations, founded in 1919.[4] Major ILO conventions (treaties) have dealt with freedom of association, the right to organize and bargain collectively, forced labor, migrant workers, and indigenous peoples, as well as a variety of issues of working conditions and workplace safety. Even nonbinding ILO recommendations provide an important international reference point for national standards.

ILO monitoring procedures, which date back to 1926, have been the model for other international human rights reporting systems. The Committee of Experts meets annually to review periodic reports submitted by states on their implementation of ratified conventions. If apparent problems are uncovered, the committee may issue a "direct request" for information or for changes in policy. Over the past two decades, more than a thousand such requests have brought changes in national policies. If the problem remains unresolved, the committee may make "observations," that is, authoritative determinations of violations of the convention in question.

The Conference Committee, which is made up of ILO delegates rather than independent experts, provides an additional level of scrutiny with greater political backing. Each year it selects cases from the report of the Committee of Experts for further review. Government representatives are called upon to provide additional information and explanation. Special complaint procedures also exist for violations of the right to freedom of association and for discrimination in employment.

No less important than these inquisitorial or adversarial procedures is the institution of "direct contacts," a program of consultations and advice, often initiated by a government concerned about improving its performance with respect to a particular convention. The ILO is a leader in cooperative resolution of problems before they reach international monitoring bodies.

Part of the ILO's success can be attributed to its unique "tripartite" structure. Intergovernmental organizations typically are made up solely of state representatives. NGOs often participate in deliberations but have no decision-making powers. In the ILO, however, workers' and employers' representatives from each member state are voting members of the organization, making it much more difficult for states to hide behind the curtain of sovereignty. The transideological appeal of workers' rights has also been important to the ILO's success. In addition, the Committee of Experts, the ILO's central monitoring body, deals principally with technical issues such as hours of work, minimum working age, workplace safety, and identity documents for seamen. In monitoring such technical conventions, the committee develops and confirms expectations of neutrality that can help to moderate controversy when more contentious "political" issues do arise.

UNESCO has addressed a variety of human rights issues explicitly.[5] Its 1960 Convention on Discrimination in Education was an important normative instrument during the doldrums while the covenant languished in the commission. Its 2005 Declaration on Bioethics and Human Rights has helped to globalize the discussion of this important topic. And UNESCO has done important normative and programmatic work on cultural rights, especially connected with preserving cultural heritages and languages.

The International Criminal Court, which was created in 2002, is a permanent tribunal that provides individual criminal liability for genocide, crimes against humanity, and war crimes.[6] The symbolic significance of individual accountability for particularly egregious, systematic violations of human rights is undoubtedly great. But virtually all violations of internationally recognized human rights lie outside of the jurisdiction of the ICC (which addresses human rights violations only indirectly as they arise in genocide, war crimes, or crimes against humanity). And it can deal with only a very small number of situations and cases. (It handed down its first judgment in March 2012, against Thomas Lubanga Dyilo in a case involving the use of child soldiers in the Democratic Republic of the Congo.)

Nonetheless, in 2011 the ICC was pursuing prosecutions concerning situations in the Democratic Republic of the Congo (involving four cases against five individuals), the Central African Republic (involving one case against one individual), Uganda (one case against four individuals), the Darfur region of Sudan (four cases against six individuals, including the sitting president of the country), Kenya (one case against three individuals), Libya (one case against two individuals), and Côte d'Ivoire (one case against the former president). This is a not unreasonable sampling of major cases in recent years. And the fact that national leaders have been charged is of considerable significance.

Finally, the Security Council regularly addresses human rights issues, which over the past quarter century have become a part of most peacekeeping and peace-building operations. It also has the authority to authorize the threat or use of force, which it has occasionally exercised in response to genocide (for example, in Bosnia)—although its tragically limited response to the emerging genocide in Rwanda is notorious and its limited response to genocide in the Darfur region of Sudan has provoked considerable international criticism.

In a more comprehensive survey, we might also consider the human rights work of organizations within the UN systems that do not have an explicit human rights mandate. For example, the secretary-general often speaks out on severe violations. Human rights are also an increasing part of many other functional organizations within the broad UN system. For example, the World Health Organization and the Food and Agriculture Organization engage in work that is obviously related to human rights and have in recent years begun to employ human rights language in their documents and human rights concepts in their programs. The World Bank and other development assistance organizations have also increasingly addressed their activities in terms of human rights and even directly monitored the human rights implications of their activities. This is perhaps most notable in programs focusing on women in development, which have been a prominent focus of multilateral development programs for three decades. This process of "mainstreaming," in which human rights penetrate arenas of action that previously did not explicitly consider human rights questions, illustrates the continued spread of human rights norms even as the explicit norm-creation process in the Human Rights Council and other bodies has slowed and become less important in recent decades.

In a still more comprehensive account, we might also look at the human rights impact of multilateral agencies that even today typically do not employ the language of human rights in their work. The structural adjustment programs of the International Monetary Fund are the most prominent example. The resistance of the IMF to the language and concepts of human rights is itself an interesting topic, although one clearly beyond our scope here.

5. CASE STUDY: THE ANTIAPARTHEID REGIME

One of the most extensive and vigorous of all international human rights regimes was also its narrowest, the regime against apartheid. For nearly a half century, South Africa was synonymous with **apartheid,** a distinctive style of unusually deep and wide-ranging systematic racial domination. Officially abolished in 1992, apartheid was a major international human rights issue for thirty years and provides a good illustration of the strengths and weaknesses of multilateral mechanisms.

A. A System of Racial Domination

Racial discrimination in South Africa goes back to the initial Dutch colonization in 1652. Indigenous hunter-gatherers (San, or "Bushmen") were largely killed off or pushed out, and local herding peoples (Khoikhoi, or "Hottentots") were forced off their lands. Slaves began to be imported in 1658. Blacks, discriminated against in voting from the very beginning, lost the formal right to vote in 1936. They were legally excluded from many jobs after 1911.

With the electoral victory of the conservative Nationalist Party in 1948, race became the basis for regulating all aspects of life in South Africa. The Nationalist government created a totalitarian bureaucracy to enforce racism throughout South African society. The official rationale was racial and cultural preservation—separation and separate development. In practice, though, apartheid meant white privilege and domination.

The Population Registration Act of 1950, the cornerstone of apartheid, required racial registration of each person at birth. The Group Areas Act of 1950 (amended in 1957) consolidated and extended earlier laws designating land by race. The 1954 Natives Resettlement Act provided for forced removals of blacks from white-designated land.

These racial designations, however, did not necessarily have any connection to previously existing facts. For example, in 1956 and 1957, Sophiatown, a black freehold section of Johannesburg, was rezoned white and the residents forcibly removed. In 1966, District Six of Cape Town was declared white, although the population was 90 percent Coloured (a socioracial category intended to designate "mixed race" people that were not classified as white, black, or Asian). More than 3.5 million blacks were removed from "white" areas, and more than 1 million were forced to relocate within designated black areas, often great distances away from their actual homes.

Controls on the movement of nonwhites resulted in a series of "pass laws" and regulations that made it illegal for most blacks to be in urban areas for more than seventy-two hours without special permission. The result was the creation of black "townships," with inferior housing, education, and social services, on the outskirts of (white) cities, often two hours away from where residents worked. Because of the absurdities of the system of restrictions on movement, the ordinary nonwhite was subject to the constant threat of prosecution. More than one-fifth of the nonwhite population could expect to be prosecuted for pass-law violations within a ten-year period, a staggering level of legal intrusion on the basis of just one set of rules. And because prosecutions often led to expulsion from the area and the loss of a person's only source of income, the pass laws were an extraordinarily powerful instrument of social control.

According to the 1980 official census, 48 percent of all blacks were living in white areas. And it was a good thing, for the land defined as black "homelands" was largely barren and completely unable to support the population. (This was no coincidence. In fact, one could largely plot economically worthless land by looking at a map of the homelands. For example, Bophuthatswana was made up of nineteen separate pieces. KwaZulu contained twenty-nine major and forty-one minor pieces of unconnected territory. And mineral rights were not even formally placed under the control of the homeland governments.) Getting everyone where they "belonged" would have produced mass starvation for blacks and the collapse of white standards of living and the white economy, which were built around cheap (black) labor.

Interracial marriage and sexual relations between whites and nonwhites were prohibited. The 1953 Reservation of Separate Amenities Act removed the formal legal requirement that racially segregated facilities be equal. The Native Laws Amendment Act of 1957 prohibited holding classes, church services, or any meeting by blacks in designated white areas. The euphemistically named Extension of University Education Act of 1959 effectively removed nonwhites from most existing universities and established new, and decidedly inferior, ethnic universities.

Increasingly repressive internal-security laws were passed to prevent political opposition. By 1967, few legal safeguards remained for those suspected of political offenses. At least one hundred people died while being detained by the police or security forces, usually after having been tortured. The best-known victim was black-consciousness activist Steve Biko.

Many who were not formally detained were brought in by the authorities for questioning, often as a not-so-subtle warning. Any organization could be banned (that is, outlawed) and the printing or dissemination of any publication prohibited. South Africa also "banned" individuals, restricting their movements, limiting whom they might see (sometimes to their immediate family), and prohibiting them from speaking publicly or being quoted in the media. Most nonparliamentary opposition was thus forced underground.

This does not mean that there was no resistance. The African National Congress (ANC), the leading political group in contemporary South Africa, was founded in 1912. The 1952–1953 pass-law demonstrations marked the beginning of organized resistance to apartheid. Resistance took new forms, however, after the police fired on a group of peaceful demonstrators on March 21, 1960, killing sixty-nine people and wounding about two hundred others in what quickly came to be known as the Sharpeville Massacre.

When the ANC and several other groups were banned, a number of leading activists of the 1950s, including Nelson Mandela, concluded that peaceful protest alone could not be successful and launched a (quite ineffective) sabotage campaign. When Mandela and several other leaders were convicted in 1964 and sentenced to life imprisonment, the ANC was forced into exile. The government weathered mass protests and riots in 1976 and 1977 through a combination of force, new restrictions, and minor concessions.

Peaceful opposition also continued, despite government efforts to make it illegal. South African churches became particularly important, since almost all overtly political opposition organizations were banned. The award of the Nobel Peace Prize in 1984 to Bishop Desmond Tutu symbolized this struggle. Black trade-union activity also increased and became politically important in the mid-1980s.

New and unusually violent uprisings in the townships broke out in the fall of 1984 and lasted for nearly two years. Torture and abuse of those detained increased dramatically. Official violence against those not detained also increased. Symbolic of all this was the widely seen footage of armed security-force personnel popping up from their hiding place inside a passing vehicle and opening fire on unarmed children. Even more ominous was the dramatic increase in violence by police-sponsored vigilante groups.

Direct repression was accompanied by no less severe social and economic exploitation and degradation. For example, the average white under apartheid had an income more than twelve times that of the average black. A black child was almost ten times more likely to die before the age of one than a white child. Other standard statistical measures revealed a similar picture.

B. The International Campaign Against Apartheid

Although the United Nations addressed racial discrimination in South Africa as early as 1946, it became a priority only after the 1960 Sharpeville Massacre. In the subsequent thirty years, a flood of resolutions sought to mobilize international support for the national and international struggle against apartheid.

In 1962, the UN General Assembly called on states to break diplomatic relations and boycott all trade with South Africa. The decisions of the General Assembly, however, are only recommendations, and until the 1980s they were largely ignored by most powerful states. The Security Council, which does have the authority to impose mandatory sanctions, established only a voluntary arms embargo in December 1963.

A mandatory arms embargo finally was approved in November 1977, after the murder of Steve Biko and the ensuing riots and repression in Soweto (Johannesburg's largest black township). Both nationally and internationally, the death of the charismatic Biko was a crucial turning point in South African history. Although a comprehensive, mandatory trade embargo was never established, several states did reduce or end diplomatic, cultural, and commercial relations with South Africa.

The UN developed a complex web of procedures and forums to pressure South Africa. The Special Committee on Apartheid, created in 1962, promoted a broad international campaign against apartheid. National support committees were formed, and opinion leaders in several countries were targeted. In 1975, the Trust Fund for Publicity Against Apartheid was established. The United Nations Educational and Training Program for Southern Africa, established in 1964, made more than twenty thousand grants to South Africans studying abroad. The United Nations Trust Fund for South Africa, established in 1965, provided more than $30 million in legal, educational, and humanitarian assistance to the victims of apartheid, including refugees. The 1973 International Convention on the Suppression and Punishment of the Crime of Apartheid came into force in 1976 and had eighty-eight parties by the end of 1990, when apartheid was on its last legs.

Reiteration of antiapartheid norms and associated condemnations of South Africa became a regular feature of most international organizations. For example, the ILO paid considerable attention to questions of workers' rights in South Africa. Other specialized agencies, such as the World Health Organization, also closely scrutinized South African policies in their areas of competence. Others instead excluded South Africa, beginning with the International Telecommunication Union in 1965. The South African government was even prevented from taking its seat in the United Nations General Assembly in 1970.

The norm of isolation was applied with particular force in sports, culminating in the 1985 International Convention Against Apartheid in Sports. South Africa was unable to participate in the Olympics from 1964 until 1992. The Special Committee on Apartheid also kept and publicized a list of sporting contacts with South Africa, in an attempt to pressure national sporting federations to join the boycott. Less systematic efforts were made to monitor, deter, and give adverse publicity to entertainment and cultural contacts.

The principal positive influence of the apartheid regime was probably the support, encouragement, and justification it provided for individuals and national and international NGOs trying to alter the foreign policies of individual states. We will see some evidence of this in the discussion of US policy toward South Africa in §8.4. International pressure undoubtedly played a role in the process of reform that led the Botha government to agree to the abolition of apartheid. But the fact that fundamental change in South Africa came only after thirty years of unusually strong and sustained international action underscores the limits of international human rights action in the face of truly recalcitrant violators.

DISCUSSION QUESTIONS

1. You have read in this chapter about a large number of global multilateral mechanisms. What kind of overall evaluation would you draw? Clearly, there is a reasonably large amount of international activity. What sort of impact has it had? Is that impact worth all the effort?

2. There is a diverse array of global multilateral bodies and procedures: comprehensive and single issue, individual and situation oriented, political and legal. What are the strengths and weaknesses of each type? Is there, in your view, one type that is preferable to the others? What is the relationship between the best type and the other possible types in this area?

3. How would you assess international reporting schemes? Be sure to consider not only what they have (and have not) accomplished, but also what the costs have been and what the alternatives are.

4. Make an inventory of alternative multilateral approaches that either have not yet been tried or in your view have not been adequately exploited. Then consider why they haven't been used and whether these impediments are likely to persist.

5. I have suggested that international human rights procedures are likely to have their greatest impact where the human rights abuses are less egregious. What does this suggest about the most effective forms of international action? Are you comfortable with the idea of writing off the worst cases (which some may conclude is the central policy implication of this argument)? Is there a practical alternative?

6. Multilateral human rights institutions concentrate heavily on civil and political rights. What are the reasons for this? Is this a defensible allocation of resources and attention? What would have to change to bring about a more comprehensive system of international human rights monitoring?

7. Even when we consider only civil and political rights, we find that monitoring focuses on a relatively small number of rights, especially egregious violations of personal liberty and bodily integrity and cases of discrimination. There has been relatively little attention to the *political* aspects of civil and political rights. How can this be explained? How should it be evaluated? What are the alternatives, both theoretical and practical?

8. Return now to the issue of national implementation of international human rights norms. Do we have the right mix of national and international mechanisms of implementation and enforcement? How does your answer to this question change when you shift between moral and political perspectives? Is national implementation anything more than an unfortunate compromise with the realities of a world of sovereign states?

SUGGESTED READINGS

Primary source information on most of the bodies considered in this chapter is available on the comprehensive and easy-to-use website "United Nations Human Rights" (http://www.ohchr.org) run by the Office of the High Commissioner for Human Rights.

Among the extensive published scholarly literature, special note should be made of the recent second edition of Philip Alston, ed., *The United Nations and Human Rights: A Critical Appraisal* (Oxford: Oxford University Press, 2011). Two other wide-ranging readers are Gundmundur Alfredsson, Jonas Grimheden, Bertrand D. Ramcharan, and Alfred Zayas, *International Human Rights Monitoring Mechanisms: Essays in Honour of Jakob Th. Möeller*, 2nd ed. (Leiden: Martinus Nijhof, 2009), and Geoff Gilbert, ed., *The Delivery of Human Rights: Essays in Honour of Professor Sir Nigel Rodley* (Hoboken, NJ: Taylor & Francis, 2010).

The standard work on treaty monitoring is Philip Alston and James Crawford, eds., *The Future of UN Human Rights Treaty Monitoring* (Cambridge: Cambridge University Press, 2000). It covers the full range of venues and issues. Christof Heyns and Frans Viljoen, *The Impact of United Nations Human Rights Treaties on the Domestic Level* (The Hague: Kluwer International, 2002), provides considerable illustrative material on the domestic impact of international human rights treaties. The literature on individual bodies is immense.

The following recent books provide a good start for those interested in more details: Yogesh Tyagi, *The UN Human Rights Committee: Practice and Procedure* (New York: Cambridge University Press, 2011); Alex Conte, *Defining Civil and Political Rights: The Jurisprudence of the United Nations Human Rights Committee* (Farnham: Ashgate, 2009); Hanna Beate Schöpp-Schilling and Cees Flinterman, eds., *The Circle of Empowerment: Twenty-Five Years of the UN Committee on the Elimination of Discrimination Against Women* (New York: Feminist Press at the City University of New York, 2007); Andrew Byrnes and Jane Connors, *The International Bill of Rights for Women: The Impact of the CEDAW Convention* (Oxford: Oxford University Press, 2008); Meena Shivdas and Sarah Coleman, eds., *Without Prejudice: CEDAW and the Determination of Women's Rights in a Legal and Cultural Context* (London: Commonwealth Secretariat, 2010); Fleur van Leeuwen, *Women's Rights Are Human Rights: The Practice of the United Nations Human Rights Committee and the Committee on Economic, Social, and Cultural Rights* (Antwerp: Intersentia, 2010); Catherine Rutgers, ed., *Creating a World Fit for Children: Understanding the UN Convention on the Rights of the Child* (New York: International Debate Education Association, 2011); Trevor Buck, *International Child Law*, 2nd ed. (Hoboken, NJ: Taylor & Francis, 2010); and Manfred Nowak and Elizabeth McArthur et al., *The United Nations Convention Against Torture: A Commentary* (Oxford: Oxford University Press, 2008). The websites for all the individual treaty bodies can be accessed through http://www.ohchr.org/EN/HRBodies/Pages/HumanRightsBodies.aspx. Finally, Joel E. Oestreich, *Power and Principle: Human Rights Programming in International Organizations* (Washington, DC: Georgetown University Press, 2007), examines human rights in the work of UNICEF, the World Bank, and the World Health Organization.

6

◄○►

Regional Human Rights Regimes

Regional human rights regimes run the gamut from a system of authoritative judicial enforcement in Europe to the absence of any formal regional mechanism in Asia and most of its subregions.

1. THE EUROPEAN REGIONAL REGIME

The forty-seven-member Council of Europe operates a strong system of regional human rights enforcement.[1] Its normative core is the (European) Convention for the Protection of Human Rights and Fundamental Freedoms, which covers mostly civil and political rights, and the European Social Charter, which addresses a wide range of economic and social rights in considerable detail. The most notable element of the system, though, is the European Court of Human Rights, which exercises binding jurisdiction with respect to the European convention and whose decisions create binding legal obligations for states.[2] (The European Social Charter is not subject to judicial enforcement.)

Since the reorganization of the court in 1998, individuals in any member country have direct access, subject to minimal procedural restrictions (most notably the requirement that local remedies have been exhausted). The court is organized into five sections, each with nine or ten judges. A Grand Chamber hears cases of special interest or importance.

The European Court of Human Rights has issued more than ten thousand judgments.[3] Some of its more prominent decisions have led to significant changes in national law. Most of its decisions, when in favor of the petitioner (as is the case about two-thirds of the time), have brought relief, including monetary damages. The system, however, has become a victim of its own success, with a huge backlog of unprocessed petitions and lengthy delays in the conclusion of cases.

One of the most important and innovative features of the court has been its adoption of a principle of "evolutive interpretation." Treaty provisions are interpreted not according to the understandings at the time of drafting (which is the norm in international law and many national legal systems) but in light of current

95

understandings and practices. The court thus serves as an important mechanism for the progressive evolution of regional human rights obligations.

The Council of Europe system also includes other important human rights mechanisms. The Council of Europe Commissioner for Human Rights (currently Thomas Hammarberg, a Swedish diplomat and human rights activist) has extensive powers to investigate and publicize human rights issues on either a thematic or a country basis.[4] Special procedures exist in the case of torture, including the right of the European Committee for the Prevention of Torture to visit all places of detention in any member state.

Important European regional mechanisms also exist under the Organization for Security and Co-operation in Europe (OSCE),[5] a group of fifty-six states from Europe, central Asia, and North America. Its work on minority rights has been especially important, with its high commissioner on national minorities being a leading regional actor on this topic of immense historical and contemporary importance. It also has notable programs to support elections and rule of law (through the Office for Democratic Institutions and Human Rights) and media freedom (through the OSCE Representative on Freedom of the Media) and to combat human trafficking (through the Office of the Special Representative and Coordinator for Combating Trafficking in Human Beings).

The activities of the twenty-seven-member European Union (EU), especially those dealing with social policy, also have an important human rights dimension.[6] The Court of Justice of the European Communities, the supreme judicial organ of the EU, has been particularly forceful in its insistence that fundamental human rights, especially principles of nondiscrimination, are an essential part of EU law.[7]

Citizens of Europe thus have a considerable array of regional multilateral mechanisms available to them not just to encourage their governments to implement their obligations but in many instances to make legally binding findings of violations. And given the context of extensive and intensive regional cooperation, most states usually comply with most decisions.

2. THE INTER-AMERICAN SYSTEM

The American Declaration of the Rights and Duties of Man was adopted by the General Assembly of the Organization of American States (OAS) in April 1948. Like the Universal Declaration, it is not technically binding. The 1969 American Convention on Human Rights, which is a legally binding instrument, came into force in 1978. As of late 2011, it had been ratified by twenty-four of the thirty-five OAS members, including all Latin American states (but not the United States, Canada, and a number of Caribbean states). The other major normative instrument of the system is the 2001 Inter-American Democratic Charter, which today is arguably as important as the declaration and the convention.

The Inter-American Commission on Human Rights (IACHR) was established in 1959.[8] Much like the UN's Human Rights Council, it operates independently of the convention, in this case as an autonomous organization within the OAS (whose thirty-five members include all the independent states of the Western Hemisphere). Its seven members are elected by secret ballot by the OAS General Assembly and serve in their personal capacity.

The Inter-American Commission conducts country studies and examines thematic issues of regional concern. During the 1970s and 1980s, the commission was particularly aggressive in using its independent authority to pressure repressive governments. Its reporting on Chile under military rule was particularly important to both internal and international human rights advocates.

As the overall regional human rights situation has improved in the post–cold war world, the reports of the commission have become less prominent. Nonetheless, they remain significant. For example, commission reports on Honduras in 2009 and 2010 drew attention to serious problems. And at the end of 2009, it issued an important report on citizen security and human rights. It also works to publicize prominent individual cases.

The commission also plays a central role in processing individual petitions, of which more than a thousand are received every year. After an initial procedural screening, the commission conducts its own fact-finding and typically attempts to facilitate a friendly settlement between the petitioner and her government. If this is not successful, it issues a report, indicating its findings and recommendations. And if the state does not accept those recommendations, the commission may refer the case to the Inter-American Court of Human Rights, if the state has accepted the court's jurisdiction. (Currently, twenty-one states have recognized the jurisdiction of the court.) In practice, the commission usually forwards the case to the court when that is the wish of the petitioner.

The Inter-American Court sits in San José, Costa Rica.[9] Its seven members are elected by state parties to the convention (although nationals of any OAS member state may serve, even if their state is not a party to the convention). Individuals do not, however, have direct access to the court. Only the commission and parties to the convention can submit cases. Through December 2011, the court had issued more than 230 judgments.[10] One of the more interesting and innovative procedures of the court is the use of interim measures to attempt to protect persons in danger of irreparable harm or death.

This disappointingly small number of cases heard by the court indicates the relative weakness of the Inter-American regime compared to its European counterpart. But we should be careful not to confuse cause and effect. As we will discuss further below, strong multilateral measures are largely a consequence, not a cause, of a high level of national practice throughout the region. Even the European system did not allow individuals direct access to the court until 1998. (Until then it relied on a two-stage commission-court process, on which the Inter-American system was modeled.) States agree to, utilize, and comply with strong measures out of a strong sense of national commitment.

As noted above, the democracy norm has become especially important in the Inter-American system. In July 2009, the OAS General Assembly suspended Honduras after its elected government was deposed by a military coup. And the regional democracy norm seems to have played an important role in the United

States deciding in 2002 not to support the coup against Hugo Chávez in Venezuela, despite its strong opposition to Chávez's national and international policies.

As in Europe, a number of other mechanisms operate within the Inter-American regime broadly understood. The Protocol of San Salvador addresses economic and social rights. (The American Convention on Human Rights deals almost exclusively with civil and political rights.) There are regional conventions on torture, violence against women, disappearances, and discrimination against persons with disabilities. And the OAS has adopted resolutions and declarations on a variety of topics, including freedom of expression, indigenous peoples, and racism and discrimination.

3. THE AFRICAN REGIONAL REGIME

A regional human rights regime also operates in Africa, based on the 1981 African Charter on Human and Peoples' Rights. It is substantively much weaker than its European and American counterparts. Nonetheless, it is of great regional symbolic significance and has provided considerable encouragement and support to national activists.

The norms in the African Charter are riddled with "clawback clauses" that weaken the protections. For example, Article 6 states, "No one may be deprived of his freedom except for reasons and conditions previously laid down by law." In other words, so long as a government bothers to pass a law first, it can deprive people of their freedom for pretty much any reason it chooses. In addition—and quite oddly for a human rights instrument—the charter gives considerable emphasis to individual duties. More positively, the charter also attempts to advance the idea of collective people's rights, although in practice this seems to have had no discernible impact.

The institutions for monitoring and enforcement are extremely weak. The African Commission is elected by the Assembly of Heads of States and Government of the African Union, from nominees proposed by states.[11] The members thus are much less independent than their European and American counterparts. The reporting system is plagued by poor reports—a reflection of both lack of resources in most states and lack of interest by many—and by underfunding of the commission. As for the investigation of complaints, few states cooperate, and the decisions of the commission have been criticized for their vagueness with respect to suggested remedies.

The African Court resembles its Inter-American counterpart in that its jurisdiction is optional—twenty-five states had accepted its jurisdiction through 2010—and only states and the commission (not individuals) may submit cases.[12] It first met in July 2006 and issued its first judgment in December 2009.

In a sad irony, though, the court rejected the case (against Senegal) for lack of jurisdiction. The case involved an effort by a Chadian national residing in Switzerland to stop proceedings in Senegal against Hissein Habré, the former head of state of Chad. That the commission allowed the court's first case to be one that was highly politicized, had an obscure relationship to the charter, and came from an applicant who did not even reply to Senegal's response to his initial application suggests questionable judgment that does not bode well for the near-term future of the court. Much the same is true of its March 2011 order for provisional measures against Libya, which were completely ignored and, given the evolving situation in the country, largely beside the point. And by the end of 2011, it had only four pending cases (including the now largely moot case against Libya).

Despite all these limitations, the African Commission is a leading regional voice for human rights. Its meetings provide the occasion for valuable networking by NGOs from across the continent. Its activities have helped to socialize African states to the idea that their human rights practices are legitimately subject to regional scrutiny—a not insignificant achievement given the radical notions of sovereignty and nonintervention that dominated the continent in the 1970s and 1980s. And there is an infrastructure in place that African states can build on in the future.

4. THE ARAB WORLD AND ASIA

Regional human rights machinery in Asia and the Middle East is almost nonexistent, although this may be beginning to change.

The League of Arab States created the Permanent Arab Commission on Human Rights in 1968, largely in response to the 1967 occupation of Palestinian territory in the West Bank and Gaza. That has remained its principal focus ever since. Although recent meetings have addressed developing and spreading an Arab human rights culture, the practices of member states are not subjected to even the most delicate scrutiny by the commission. As I delivered this manuscript to the publisher, though, an Arab League observer delegation was in Syria. Its activities, although not without problems, may represent a historical turning point.

The 2005 Arab Charter of Human Rights, which entered into force in 2008, created the Arab Human Rights Committee.[13] It is still too early to judge its activities. They are, however, formally restricted to the review of state reports. And there is nothing to suggest that such reviews are likely to be in any way penetrating, given that most current members hold government positions.

Nonetheless, even the most toothless of instruments represents rather substantial progress in a region where the mean and median levels of performance are probably most charitably labeled poor. Once again, we see that the character of regional mechanisms is a consequence, rather than a cause, of the regional pattern of human rights performance—although the Arab Spring of 2011 suggests that we might expect some improvements in the next few years.

In Asia there is no regional mechanism of any sort. Part of the reason is that Asia is largely a geographical entity, not a true cultural, economic, or political region. But even at the subregional level, "regional organizations" that might have a human rights dimension are rare. Southeast Asia is the only region comparable to Europe, the Americas, Africa, and the Arab world as understood above, in that only the

Association of Southeast Asian Nations (ASEAN) includes as members all the countries of the geographical region and has a long tradition of collective multilateral consultation.[14]

ASEAN is (in)famous for its extreme deference to state sovereignty understood in almost absolutist terms. But in 2008—building on more than a decade of work by the Working Group for an ASEAN Human Rights Mechanism—the ASEAN foreign ministers created the High Level Panel to draft terms of reference for an ASEAN human rights organ. In 2009 the ASEAN Intergovernmental Commission on Human Rights was created.

As an intergovernmental body, not much can be hoped for in terms of independent action. Its website (http://www.aseansec.org/22769.htm) is difficult to find and includes little real information other than formal press releases on the meetings of the commission. Neither its original five-year work plan nor the new plan for 2013–2015 that was adopted in December 2011 is readily available anywhere on the Internet. And its decisions in 2011 to study corporate social responsibility and the right to peace suggest a serious lack of interest in the human rights practices of member states.

Nonetheless, as in the Arab case, any formal entity within the organization represents a genuine step forward. And if democratic states in the region, especially Indonesia, become more assertive in their interest in addressing human rights issues regionally, some further modest progress in the medium term is likely.

5. CASE STUDY: CHILE AND THE INTER-AMERICAN COMMISSION

In Chapter 4 we considered human rights violations in the Southern Cone of South America. Here we will look at the Inter-American Commission's response to military rule in Chile. (US policy will be examined in §8.3.)

Within a week of the coup on September 11, 1973, the commission cabled Chile expressing its concern and asking for information. In October, its executive secretary, Luis Reque, visited Chile. His report advised a formal on-site visit by the Inter-American Commission, which took place July 22–August 2, 1974.

During its visit, the Inter-American Commission interviewed government authorities, received 575 new communications, and took statements from witnesses to support previously submitted communications. Commission members also observed military tribunals, studied trial records of military and civil courts, and gathered information on the junta's legislation. Their visits to detention centers led to some minor changes and helped to identify facilities where torture was being practiced.

The commission's report concluded that the government of Chile was guilty of a wide range of human rights abuses, including systematic violations of the rights to life, liberty, personal security, due process, and civil liberties. In October 1974, this was hardly news. Nonetheless, the report was thorough and tough. It also provided authoritative confirmation of the charges that had been made against the Chilean junta. This made it much more difficult for sympathetic foreign governments to dismiss the complaints of exiles and human rights activists as partisan or unsubstantiated. For example, the report was a standard source of information in US congressional hearings.

Over the next two years, the commission focused on individual communications. In 1975 it considered more than 600 cases of torture and 160 disappearances. The government, however, was uncooperative. Furthermore, as noted earlier, individual communications are not well suited to handling systematic, gross violations. Not much came of these investigations—beyond added publicity and greater detail on individual violations.

The commission's second report on Chile, in 1976, applied new pressure on the Pinochet regime. Although noting a decline in some violations, it documented continuing systematic abuses and concluded that government actions and policies continued to be an impediment to the restoration of respect for human rights in Chile. This helped to undercut arguments made by and on behalf of Chile that the situation was returning to normal.

The political organs of the OAS, however, refused to follow the commission's lead. The first report on Chile provoked an innocuous resolution that did little more than ask for additional information. The OAS was so little moved that in 1975 the members overwhelmingly accepted Chile's offer to host the next session of the OAS General Assembly. Following the commission's second report, Chile was asked "to continue adopting and implementing the necessary procedures and measures for effectively preserving and ensuring full respect for human rights in Chile." By implying more progress than had in fact occurred, this resolution was in some ways worse than nothing. And after the third report, in March 1977, the OAS General Assembly did not even extend the formal courtesy of asking for a further study.

This icy reception underscores the limits of even aggressive and independent monitors in an organization with little concern for human rights. Nonetheless, the commission persisted. Its annual reports for 1977, 1978, and 1979–1980 included sections on Chile. The reports for 1980–1981 through 1982–1983, in a concession to the generally hostile organizational environment, contained no references to particular countries. But the 1983–1984 report returned to a tougher stand, with a chapter on violations in several states (including Chile).

In May 1984, in response to the worsening situation in Chile, the commission began work on a new country report, issued in 1985. A resolution criticizing Chile by name failed by a single vote in the OAS General Assembly in December 1985. And the IACHR continued to pressure the Pinochet government until it was finally removed from office.

What can we conclude from all this? A cynic can point to "the bottom line," namely, the persistence of military rule in Chile. If a state is willing to accept the costs to its reputation, which rarely exceed strained relations and reduced foreign aid, it can flout international human rights regimes.

But to expect recalcitrant states to be forced to mend their ways is wildly unrealistic. The Inter-American Commission, like most other multilateral human rights agencies, works primarily with the power of publicity. It can promote the regional implementation of human rights norms. It can monitor and publicize violations and try to persuade states to improve their practices. But it cannot, and is not intended to be able to, force a state to do anything. Sovereignty remains the overriding norm in the Inter-American human rights regime—as in all other international human rights regimes (except Europe).

Nonetheless, in summarizing the commission's work on Chile, Cecilia Medina, who herself was forced into exile by the military government, has argued that "in a situation of gross, systematic violations, the constant attention of the international community is of the highest importance; it serves as a support and encouragement for those suffering and opposing repression within the country, and at the same time prompts, and serves as a basis for, further international action by other governmental and nongovernmental international organizations."[15] This is particularly true when a state is subject to scrutiny in multiple intergovernmental organizations and by several national and international NGOs.

Perhaps the strongest evidence for the importance of international publicity is the diplomatic effort states exert to avoid it. In the late 1970s and early 1980s, both Argentina and Chile devoted much of their diplomacy—in the United Nations, the OAS, and the United States—to avoiding public criticism.[16] If rights-abusive regimes take international condemnation seriously enough to struggle to avoid it, the work of international human rights agencies is unlikely to be entirely pointless.

We must also remember that "the bottom line" includes individuals who are helped. States often respond to international pressure by releasing or improving the treatment of prominent victims. These small victories for international action are victories nonetheless—and of immense significance to individual victims.

In rare cases, there may even be a systematic impact. For example, the 1978 IACHR report on Nicaragua increased the pressure on the dictatorial Somoza government. Furthermore, the OAS call for Somoza to resign in June 1979 shook his political confidence and seems to have hastened his departure.

Reports, though, are only reports. Decisions on individual cases are only nonbinding resolutions. Real change requires additional action by states. This is an inherent shortcoming of almost all international human rights regimes.

Nonetheless, the Inter-American Commission has aggressively exploited its powers, to at least some effect. Its activities have improved the treatment of many thousands of victims of human rights violations. If we compare it not to Europe but to global mechanisms discussed in the preceding chapter, the record of the Inter-American regime, even in the difficult environment of the cold war, appears in a relatively good light.

DISCUSSION QUESTIONS

1. The following chapter compares global and regional mechanisms. Before turning to my assessment, what do *you* see as the principal strengths and weaknesses of each?

2. Which are more striking, similarities or differences between regional and global mechanisms?
3. Is the example of Europe more encouraging or discouraging for the prospects of stronger action in other regions in the near future?
4. Bilateral action will be considered in Chapters 8 and 9 and compared with multilateral action in Chapter 11. Based on what you know so far, though, in what areas does multilateral action have an advantage over bilateral action? Where does the advantage lie with bilateral action? Are their respective strengths and weaknesses sufficiently complementary that the two together may add up to more than the sum of their parts?
5. Now ask the same questions about transnational action by international human rights NGOs. (I pose these questions now so that you do not take multilateral action as in any way the norm, just because it is considered first in this book.)

SUGGESTED READINGS

Dinah Shelton, *Regional Protection of Human Rights* (Oxford: Oxford University Press, 2008), provides an exhaustive survey of regional regimes. Recent works on particular regional mechanisms include the following: Council of Europe, *The European Court of Human Rights in Facts and Figures* (Strasbourg: Council of Europe, 2010); Jonas Christoffersen and Mikael Rask Madsen, eds., *The European Court of Human Rights Between Law and Politics* (Oxford: Oxford University Press, 2011); Thomas Hammarberg, *Human Rights in Europe: No Grounds for Complacency; Viewpoints by the Council of Europe Commissioner for Human Rights* (Strasbourg: Council of Europe, 2011); Malcolm Evans and Rachel Murray, eds., *The African Charter on Human and Peoples' Rights: The System in Practice, 1986–2006* (Cambridge: Cambridge University Press, 2009); and Monica Serrano and Vesselin Popovski, eds., *Human Rights Regimes in the Americas* (New York: United Nations University Press, 2010).

7

Assessing Multilateral
Mechanisms

We have now looked at several global and regional multilateral mechanisms. This very brief chapter steps back to look historically at the evolution of international human rights regimes and assess the strengths and weaknesses of the mechanisms we have examined.

1. THE EVOLUTION OF INTERNATIONAL HUMAN RIGHTS REGIMES

Table 7.1 summarizes the character of the regimes considered above (plus the genocide regimes which is addressed in Chapter 13). I identify four types of human rights regimes: (1) declaratory regimes (which include norms but no significant decision-making procedures, except for developing norms); (2) promotional regimes (which encourage states to implement norms and disseminate information concerning state practices); (3) implementation regimes (which involve formal or informal powers to determine whether violations have occurred); and (4) enforcement regimes (where multilateral bodies have at least some binding enforcement authority, usually of a judicial or quasi-judicial character, but ranging all the way up to the use of force). This section examines the pattern of growth in these regimes from 1945 to 2010. The following section provides a more evaluative assessment of the character of these regimes.

The most striking pattern is the near-complete absence of international human rights regimes in 1945, in contrast to the presence of several in all the later periods. We can also note both the fairly steady growth of single-issue regimes and the gradual strengthening of most international human rights regimes over the past thirty years. Even today, though, promotional regimes remain the rule.

Once states accept norms stronger than nonbinding guidelines, declaratory regimes readily evolve into promotional regimes. It is difficult to argue against promoting the

TABLE 7.1 Change in International Human Rights Regimes, 1945–2010

	1945	1960	1975	1990	2000	2010
Global Regime	—	**Declaratory**	**Promotional**	**Strong Promotional**	**Strong Promotional**	**Strong Promotional**
Norms	—	Guidelines	Standards with exemptions	Standards with exemptions	Standards with exemptions	Standards with exemptions
Procedures	—	Weak promotion	Strong promotion	Strong promotion/ weak monitoring	Promotion/ monitoring	Promotion/ monitoring
Regional Regimes						
European Regime	—	**Implementation**	**Enforcement**	**Enforcement**	**Enforcement**	**Enforcement**
Norms	—	Guidelines/ regional norms	Authoritative regional norms	Authoritative regional norms	Authoritative regional norms	Authoritative regional norms
Procedures	—	Promotion/ monitoring	Regional decisions	Regional judicial enforcement	Regional judicial enforcement	Regional judicial enforcement
Inter-American Regime	—	**Declaratory**	**Promotional**	**Promotional/ Enforcement**	**Promotional/ Enforcement**	**Promotional/ Enforcement**
Norms	—	Guidelines	Standards with exemptions	Regional norms	Regional norms	Regional norms
Procedures	—	Weak promotion	Monitoring	Monitoring/ regional decisions	Monitoring/ regional decisions	Monitoring/ regional decisions
African Regime	—	—	—	**Declaratory**	**Declaratory/ Promotional**	**Declaratory/ Promotional**
Norms	—	—	—	Standards with exemptions	Standards with exemptions	Standards with exemptions
Procedures	—	—	—	Weak promotion	Weak promotion	Promotion/ weak monitoring
Arab Middle East	—	—	—	—	—	**Weak Declaratory**
Norms	—	—	—	—	—	Guidelines
Procedures	—	—	—	—	—	Weak promotion
Asia	—	—	—	—	—	—*

Single-Issue Regimes

Worker's Rights	Promotional	Promotion/Implementation	Promotion/Implementation	Promotion/Implementation	Promotion/Implementation	Promotion/Implementation
Norms	Weak standards	Standards with exemptions	Strong standards with exemptions	Strong standards with exemptions	Strong standards with exemptions	Strong standards with exemptions
Procedures	Promotion/monitoring	Promotion/monitoring	Promotion/monitoring	Promotion/monitoring	Promotion/monitoring	Promotion/monitoring
Racial Discrimination	—	—	Strong Promotional	Strong Promotional	Strong Promotional	Strong Promotional
Norms	—	—	Strong standards with exemptions	Strong standards	Authoritative global norms	Authoritative global norms
Procedures	—	—	Promotion/monitoring	Promotion/monitoring	Promotion/monitoring	Promotion/monitoring
Women's Rights	—	Declaratory/Promotional	Declaratory/Promotional	Strong Promotional	Strong Promotional	Strong Promotional
Norms	—	Guidelines	Guidelines	Standards with exemptions	Global norms	Global norms
Procedures	—	Promotion	Promotion	Promotion/weak monitoring	Promotion/weak monitoring	Promotion/weak monitoring
Torture	—	—	Weak Declaratory	Promotional/Implementation	Implementation	Implementation
Norms	—	—	Guidelines	Standards with exemptions	Authoritative global norms	Authoritative global norms
Procedures	—	—	None	None/promotion	Monitoring	Monitoring
Genocide	—	Declaratory	Declaratory	Declaratory	Implementation/Enforcement	Implementation/Enforcement
Norms	—	Guidelines	Guidelines	Guidelines	Authoritative global norms	Authoritative global norms
Procedures	—	None	None	None	Military enforcement	Military enforcement
Disabled	—	—	—	Weak Declaratory	Weak Declaratory	Promotional
Norms	—	—	—	Guidelines	Guidelines	Standards with exemptions
Procedures	—	—	—	None	None	Promotion

* Weak Declaratory regime in Southeast Asian (ASEAN) sub-region.

Regimes are classified, in order of increasing strength, as declaratory, promotional, implementation, and enforcement.

Norms are classified, in order of increasing strength, as guidelines, standards, and authoritative norms.

Procedures are classified, in order of increasing strength, as promotion, monitoring, decisions, and enforcement.

further spread and implementation of norms that one has accepted. However, the move to implementation or enforcement involves a major qualitative jump that most states resist, often with vigor and usually with success.

National commitment is the single most important contributor to a strong regime; it is the source of the often-mentioned "political will" that underlies most strong regimes. If a state has a good human rights record, then not only will a strong regime appear relatively unthreatening, but the additional support it provides for national efforts is likely to be welcomed. The European regime's unprecedented strength provides the most striking example of the power of national commitment.

Cultural community, however, is no less important. In the absence of sociocultural and ideological consensus, strong procedures are likely to appear too subject to partisan use or abuse to be accepted even by states with good records and strong national commitments. For example, opponents of stronger procedures in the global human rights regime and in single-issue regimes include major countries from all regions with national human rights records that range from good to poor. The very scope of all but the regional regimes undercuts the relative homogeneity that seems almost necessary for movement beyond a promotional regime.

Finally, we must stress the importance of dominant power and ideological hegemony, which should be kept analytically distinct. The effective exercise of even preponderant material power usually requires an ideological justification sufficiently powerful to win at least acquiescence from nonhegemonic powers. The seemingly inescapable ideological appeal of human rights over the past half century, even during the ideological rivalry of the cold war, thus has been an important element in the rise of international human rights regimes.

A hegemonic idea such as human rights may actually draw power to itself; power may coalesce around, rather than create, hegemonic ideas, such as human rights and the regimes that emerge from them. Hegemonic ideas thus can be expected to draw acquiescence to relatively weak regimes. But to move beyond promotional activities—which requires significant sacrifices—something more, typically external material power or internal substantive commitment, is needed. Hegemony thus also points toward the pattern of limited growth, with strong barriers at the threshold between promotional and implementation regimes.

2. ASSESSING MULTILATERAL HUMAN RIGHTS MECHANISMS

How do we assess the welter of multilateral institutions we have examined in the two preceding chapters? I will focus on differences in regimes that arise from the source of their authority (based on a treaty or rooted in a wider international organization), their range or focus, and the character of their powers. Each type of mechanism has its own strengths and weaknesses. Table 7.2 summarizes the discussion that follows.

Human rights institutions based in international and regional organizations can draw on the prestige and influence of the broader organization. This is one of the

TABLE 7.2 Comparing Multilateral Implementation Mechanisms

	Strengths	*Weaknesses*
Basis of Authority		
Organization	Political support/prestige issue linkage within organization	Political bias
Treaty	Impartiality voluntary acceptance	No political linkages/ limited coverage
Means		
Reporting	Least adversarial/can address less severe violations	States set terms of discussion
Investigation	Proactive advocacy	States not required to cooperate
Petition	Quasi-judicial resolution/ specificity of individual case	Small number of cases

greatest resources of the High Commissioner for Human Rights and the Human Rights Council. Organization-based institutions may also benefit from internal political linkages. The other objectives states pursue within the organization may constrain them from resisting the organization's human rights initiatives.

In addition, the decisions of international organizations represent the collective activities of states, with their associated power resources. This may allow mobilizing a different kind of influence than that available to committees of independent experts. For example, the impact of the Inter-American Commission's activities on Chile and Argentina was increased by the support of the regional hegemon, the United States, especially during the Carter presidency.

Politicization, however, is the price often paid for the political power of multilateral organizations. For example, in the UN during the cold war, countries were singled out for scrutiny largely on the basis of their (lack of) international political support. Even though serious violations were addressed, the procedures were corrupted by the taint of political partisanship. The position of the Inter-American Commission in the 1970s and 1980s also illustrates the problems that can arise if the broader organization is substantially less interested in human rights.

Committees of independent experts have been relatively nonpartisan. Even during the cold war, the Human Rights Committee, for example, was far less politicized than even the UN Commission, let alone the General Assembly. Given the heavy reliance on publicity and persuasion, a reputation for integrity and fairness can be a powerful tool.

Combining these two lines of argument suggests that an international human rights institution can maximize its impact if it is backed by a broader organization while avoiding the taint of politicization. This assessment is confirmed by the record of the UN Human Rights Council/Commission, the Inter-American Commission, and the European Court. The Inter-American Commission was far more aggressive, and effective, than the highly politicized OAS General Assembly. The UN Commission, especially in the 1980s and early 1990s, was able to draw on the combination of a reputation for relative impartiality and the prestige of the broader organization. This enabled, for example, improved access for special rapporteurs in closed countries such as Iran and Burma. Likewise, the widespread voluntary compliance with the decisions of the European regime rests on a combination of the Council of Europe's prestige and influence and the unparalleled reputation for neutrality of its human rights machinery. This line of argument also helps to explain the emergence of the high commissioner as a major international actor.

Single-issue and country-specific initiatives have largely complementary strengths and weaknesses. Because thematic or single-issue mechanisms avoid singling out individual countries, even when they do address particular state practices, the inquiry is likely to be somewhat less threatening. Thematic and single-issue initiatives may also appear less threatening because they do not address the full range of human rights issues. Although initiatives on single issues may appear timid and almost beside the point in countries guilty of gross violations, significant incremental improvements in particular areas may result from single-issue mechanisms even where systematic violations persist. Whether the initiatives are countrywide or issue specific, the concrete achievements usually are, at best, incremental improvements in limited areas, such as the release of prominent political prisoners or the modification of particular laws, decrees, or administrative practices.

In examining particular implementation mechanisms, we again see a picture of complementary strengths and weaknesses. The principal tools available within these various regimes are (1) state reports, characteristic of the treaty-based regimes; (2) information-advocacy procedures, such as those undertaken by the IACHR or the UN Commission's thematic and country rapporteurs; and (3) individual communications (complaints), as in the European regime and the activities of the Human Rights Committee. The strengths and weaknesses of reporting systems were considered in §5.3. Here I focus on investigations and communications.

The individual petition system in Europe often appears to be the ideal mechanism. From an individual victim's point of view, the near-universal compliance with the decisions of the European Court is undoubtedly preferable to the uncertainties of reporting and investigatory-diplomatic methods. The Inter-American system, however, suggests that it is not so much the formal availability of individual petitions that is crucial but the commitment of states not simply to abide by the resulting quasi-judicial proceedings but to do the tough domestic legal and political work of implementing regional decisions.

Regional or global petition systems thus are best seen as modest supplementary elements in an effective system of enforcing human rights. This is particularly true where, as with the Human Rights Committee and the Inter-American Court, the procedure is optional—presenting a striking example of the typical trade-off between the scope and the strength of international procedures. Even the European regime is an example of the strongest procedures applying only to a relatively small group of states with relatively good human rights records.

The other obvious drawback of individual complaint mechanisms is the small number of cases they can address. Even the thousands of cases handled by the European Court, the Inter-American Commission, and the Human Rights Committee are the tiniest drop in the bucket—or, rather, the sea—of human rights violations. Nonetheless, the focus on individual cases gives these procedures a valuable specificity and concreteness. Because violations are personalized and detailed evidence of individual violations is provided, it is more difficult for states to deny responsibility.

Individual petitions, like the other kinds of procedures, occupy a special niche. They are particularly desirable when violations are either narrow or sporadic. Investigation and reporting mechanisms will continue to be needed for a very long time. I am even tempted to argue that they are the heart of multilateral human rights activity. In a world still organized around sovereign states, the international contribution to implementing human rights rests on persuasive diplomacy, which itself rests considerably on the power of shame that lies at the heart of investigatory and reporting mechanisms.

If this is true, the key to change in state practices probably lies not in any one type of forum or activity but in the mobilization of multiple, complementary channels of influence—which leads us to the remaining chapters in Part 2, which consider bilateral and transnational action.

8

Human Rights in American Foreign Policy: Cold War–Era Cases and Comparisons

We now turn to two chapters on bilateral international human rights policies, the first historical and case oriented, the second more conceptual and focused on issues of means and mechanisms. Our primary focus in this chapter will be on the international human rights policies of the United States. Chapter 1 provided a brief overview of major events in postwar international human rights. For the United States, we can distinguish six phases.

1945–1948: initial enthusiasm, culminating in the adoption of the Universal Declaration of Human Rights

1949–1973: human rights concerns subordinated to anticommunism and cold war rivalry with the Soviet Union

1974–1980: emergence of human rights as a prominent element in the public diplomacy of the United States, first in Congress and then during the Carter presidency

1981–1988: the (ultimately unsuccessful) Reagan attempt to subordinate human rights to the (new) cold war

1989–2001: post–cold war spread and deepening of human rights concerns

2001–present: partial subordination of human rights to antiterrorism

Here we will focus on the cold war, and especially the third and fourth of these periods. Human rights became a regular part of foreign policy in these years. And the United States not only led this process, but its policies had the greatest global impact. In addition to the historical significance of this material, it provides a point of comparison for the chapters in Part 3, which focus on the post–cold war era.

The heart of the chapter (§§5.2–5.4) is three case studies, on US policy toward Central America, the Southern Cone, and South Africa. Each is self-contained;

read or skip them as you see fit. Together, though, they provide a broad overview of US international human rights policy during its formative decades. The final two sections compare US policy with that of smaller "like-minded" Western countries, represented here by the Netherlands and Norway.

1. ANTICOMMUNISM AND AMERICAN EXCEPTIONALISM

During the cold war, even during the "liberal" Democratic presidencies of Truman, Kennedy, Johnson, and Carter, fear of communism was an overriding concern. The Korean War began under Truman. Kennedy and Johnson began and prosecuted the war in Vietnam. Carter's Central American policy was strongly shaped by the desire to avoid "another Cuba."

Although individual presidents certainly disagreed on strategy and tactics, anti-communism had the highest foreign policy priority in every administration from Truman through Reagan. As a result, the United States usually supported avowedly anticommunist governments. Whether this was good foreign policy or bad, its human rights consequences were disastrous.

Totalitarian, Soviet-style communism, which has largely been eliminated from the contemporary world, systematically violated most internationally recognized civil and political rights. But the fact that anticommunist regimes were often guilty of serious, and sometimes no less severe, violations did not stop the United States from regularly equating anticommunism with the pursuit of "freedom" and human rights. In country after country—Bolivia, Chile, Guatemala, Haiti, Iran, Liberia, Pakistan, Paraguay, Somalia, South Africa, South Korea, South Vietnam, Sudan, and Zaire, to name just a few—the United States supported repressive military dictatorships and narrow civilian oligarchies (along with US interests) in the name of democracy and human rights.

This confusion of anticommunism with human rights has been strengthened by what students of domestic politics in the United States call **American exceptionalism**, the belief that the United States is different from (and generally superior to) most other countries, in large part because of its domestic commitment to individual rights. The isolationist variant of American exceptionalism, expressed with particular clarity in George Washington's Farewell Address, has seen the country as a beacon of hope for an oppressed world—but only an example, not an active participant in the struggle for freedom overseas. No less powerful, however, has been interventionist exceptionalism, which stresses an active American mission to spread its values through direct foreign policy action and even military force.

This interventionist strand has often led to identifying the international interests of the United States with democracy and human rights. During the cold war, the "logic" was roughly the following: Communism is opposed to human rights. The United States favors human rights. Therefore, American action against communism is action on behalf of human rights.

The interaction of exceptionalism (the American tendency to denigrate economic and social rights, other than the right to property) and anticommunism (the emphasis of Soviet-bloc regimes on economic and social rights) contributed to an American tendency to react suspiciously to regimes and opposition that emphasized economic and social rights, especially when it involved redistributing wealth. By labeling economic and social reformers "communists" and "subversives," right-wing rulers could generally retain US support for systematic repression to protect their own wealth, power, and privilege, often under an American banner of "democracy." Beyond the devastating human rights consequences, such policies frequently prevented the achievement of professed US goals. For example, repressive dictatorships of the Right often eliminated not only the Far Left but also the political moderates that the United States claimed to support.

Anticommunism was also at the heart of a striking American inconsistency toward elections. The United States regularly, and rightly, criticized one-party elections in communist countries. But the mere existence of elections in anticommunist countries, even in the face of clear evidence of restrictions on political participation, corruption, intimidation of voters, or outright fraud, was usually accepted as evidence of the ruling regime's democratic character. And when the United States disapproved of governments brought to power through free and fair elections, it was not above using force to remove them. Striking examples include sponsorship of the 1954 military coup in Guatemala, subversion in Chile in the early 1970s, and continued support for the Nicaraguan "contras" (violent anticommunist revolutionaries) after the 1984 election.

Elections that brought (alleged) communists to power were bad and had to be overturned. When force or fraud brought anticommunists to power, that was an acceptable price to pay to keep communists out of power and on the run. And the United States, the leader of the "Free World," was the self-appointed judge of "democratic" credentials.

2. CASE STUDY: US POLICY IN CENTRAL AMERICA

Central America, the geographical area that lies between North America (Canada, the United States, and Mexico) and South America, became a major international human rights concern in the 1980s largely because of US support for the right-wing government of El Salvador and parallel US efforts to overthrow the leftist government of Nicaragua. These countries, and to a lesser extent Guatemala, will be our focus here.

A. Human Rights in El Salvador

Salvadoran independence from Spain in the 1820s was in many ways less significant than the economic reforms in the second half of the nineteenth century that transferred one-third of the country's land to a small coffee oligarchy. For the following half century, protests by dispossessed peasants were ruthlessly suppressed, culminating in the systematic killing of at least ten thousand people and as many as thirty thousand in the *matanza* (massacre) of 1932.

After World War II, the Salvadoran economy grew, but the benefits of growth were distributed extremely unequally. In the mid-1970s, more than two-thirds of the children under age five suffered from malnutrition. Three-fourths of rural families (who made up about two-thirds of the total population) were landless. Less than 40 percent had access to piped water. Half lacked the income necessary for a minimum healthy diet. Urban poverty was only somewhat less extreme.[1] And the ruling oligarchy regularly used force against those seeking a more egalitarian society.

Elections were held regularly, but the official military-backed party used patronage, threats, and, when necessary, blatant fraud to ensure victory for its candidates. As disillusionment grew, "popular organizations" emerged that engaged in direct nonviolent action—sit-ins, strikes, demonstrations, civil disobedience. A few opponents also turned to armed insurrection, but in the mid-1970s they were of negligible political significance.

The security forces and their paramilitary supporters, however, made few distinctions between peaceful opponents and violent revolutionaries. The government of General Carlos Humberto Romero, installed after the fraudulent elections of 1977, imposed total press censorship, outlawed not only strikes but also public meetings of all sorts, and suspended judicial due process. Death squads, which worked closely with both the party and the Salvadoran security forces, became a regular part of the Romero regime's repressive apparatus.

In an attempt to head off civil war, reformist junior officers staged a coup in October 1979. In January 1980, however, all the civilian members of the cabinet resigned because of the government's inability to control the security forces. For example, military sharpshooters opened fire from the top of the National Palace on a peaceful demonstration commemorating the *matanza* of 1932, killing between twenty and fifty people. A second junta collapsed in March, again because the military refused to allow civilian political control. This was vividly illustrated by the assassination on March 24, 1980, of Archbishop Óscar Arnulfo Romero. As opposition continued to grow, the government declared a state of siege.

Although the intensification of repression led all other civilian political parties to refuse to participate, the conservative wing of the Christian Democrats, led by José Napoleón Duarte, joined the third junta. Political deaths jumped from fewer than two thousand in 1979 to twelve thousand in 1980. In November 1980, six leaders of the Democratic Revolutionary Front, a party made up principally of Social Democrats and the left wing of the (centrist) Christian Democrats, were dragged from a meeting and brutally murdered. After this, most of the remaining leaders of the nonviolent opposition went underground or into exile. Duarte, however, remained in the fourth junta, which instituted a reign of terror. Americas Watch estimated that out of a total population of fewer than 5 million, there were more than thirty thousand government-sponsored murders in 1980–1983 alone (roughly equivalent to killing about one and a quarter million Americans).

Duarte's election as president in 1984 (largely as a result of US pressure) helped to reduce the level of violence. The human rights situation, however, remained dismal. The government estimated that death squads were killing "only" about thirty people a month in 1985, and most independent observers put the number substantially higher. Torture continued. The number of political prisoners even increased, apparently because of the decline in political murders.

El Salvador thus settled into a sad routine of widespread and systematic human rights abuses. At the end of the decade, most civil and political rights were still being regularly violated. The country's poor economic situation remained, at best, unchanged (and that only because of massive US aid). The guerrillas, whose strength grew along with the repression in the early and mid-1980s, continued to operate, but with no real success. Peaceful political opposition, and economic organization by workers and peasants, remained dangerous.

The electoral transfer of power between civilian governments in March 1989 was a notable event in Salvadoran political history. But under Alfredo Cristiani's right-wing National Republican Alliance government, political space in El Salvador actually contracted in 1989. At least seventy human rights activists were arrested, labor activists came under increased attack, the offices of the Committee of Mothers of Political Prisoners, Disappeared, and Assassinated in El Salvador were bombed, and six Jesuit priests and two laywomen were murdered by the military. A UN-mediated end to the civil war was finally agreed to at the end of 1991. The arrival of UN monitors in 1992 stopped the fighting and initiated efforts at structural political reform (especially greater civilian control over the armed forces). And by 1997, in the annual Freedom House ratings of political rights and civil liberties, El Salvador had returned to the level of the early 1970s (just barely "free" in the Freedom House categorization) and has maintained this ranking consistently since then.

B. Human Rights in Nicaragua

Nicaragua's early political history was not much different from that of El Salvador. In 1936, however, Anastasio Somoza García seized power and initiated what would be more than forty years of authoritarian family rule. When Somoza was assassinated in 1956, power passed first to his son Luis Somoza Debayle and then to his younger son, Anastasio Somoza Debayle, who ruled until overthrown in 1979.

Although the Somozas retained the forms of democracy, elections were rigged and civil and political rights regularly violated. (Large-scale systematic killings, though, were not part of their repertoire.) Economic and social rights were also systematically infringed, both through the predatory accumulation of immense personal wealth by the Somozas and their cronies and through disregard of social services. For example, in the early 1970s, the Nicaraguan government spent three times as much on defense as on health care. Its neighbors typically spent about equal amounts on each.

Massive corruption in the cleanup and recovery effort following the 1972 earthquake in the capital city of Managua, which left perhaps ten thousand dead and hundreds of thousands homeless, exacerbated and highlighted the endemic problems of inequality. Two years later, Somoza was reelected in a contest that even by Nicaraguan standards was farcical. In January 1978, the pace of disaffection accelerated after the assassination of Pedro Joaquín Chamorro, the leader of the moderate opposition. Even the business community turned against Somoza, under whom it had profited, organizing a general strike to protest Chamorro's death. Eighteen months later, Somoza was forced into exile.

Somoza was swept from power by a mass popular revolt incorporating many different social and political groups. Although its military forces were led by the Sandinista National Liberation Front (FSLN), established in 1961 as a radical breakaway from the Soviet-oriented Nicaraguan Socialist Party, during his final two years in power Somoza was opposed even by Nicaragua's conservative Catholic Church and by the United States, the Somozas' traditional patron.

The revolution, although widely supported, had immense human and economic costs. About one-fifth of Nicaragua's population of roughly 2.5 million became refugees. Casualties included 40,000–50,000 people killed, 150,000 wounded, and perhaps 40,000 orphaned. The war also disrupted agricultural production and most other sectors of the economy. The nation's gross domestic product fell by one-fourth in 1979 and by another one-fifth in 1980. Direct economic losses from the revolution were about $2 billion, or roughly Nicaragua's entire annual GDP.

Human rights conditions generally improved in revolutionary Nicaragua. The Sandinista government increased spending on social programs, especially health care, and redirected spending for education toward mass literacy. Personal and legal rights were fairly widely respected. Internationally recognized civil liberties were extensively implemented for the first time in Nicaraguan history. Mass political participation was actively fostered, and the 1984 election was generally considered by outside observers to have been relatively open and fairly run.

The government itself admitted serious human rights violations during the forced relocation of Indian populations on the Atlantic Coast. Restrictions on freedom of the press, freedom of association, and due process were imposed. Sandinista mass popular organizations and the government-controlled media received preferential treatment. Nonetheless, political opponents operated under fewer constraints, and with far less fear of retaliation, than Somoza's opponents had. Human rights NGOs such as Americas Watch consistently judged the human rights situation to be significantly better than in neighboring El Salvador and Guatemala.

This record, although acceptable only in relative terms, was noteworthy because the Sandinista government was under intense attack from US-financed "contras" (a shortened form of the Spanish word for counterrevolutionaries). The contras originated in the Nicaraguan Democratic Forces, a group of former Somoza national guardsmen led by Colonel Enrique Bermúdez. In 1981, the US Central Intelligence Agency (CIA) began financial and logistical support, which by 1983 involved $100 million provided to a force that had grown to more than ten thousand guerrillas.

Contra strategy emphasized terrorism, including kidnappings, assassinations, and attacks on farms, schools, health clinics, and civilian economic targets. Nonetheless, the rights to life and security of the person were generally respected by the Nicaraguan government. In sharp contrast, US-supported governments in neighboring Guatemala and El Salvador typically justified state terrorism by the need to combat guerrilla violence.

With the winding down of the contra war in 1988 and 1989, respect for civil and political rights again improved. Peaceful political opposition was generally tolerated during the 1989–1990 election campaign. And in national elections in February 1990, the Sandinistas were voted out of power. This was particularly noteworthy because it involved not merely a change in government, as in neighboring El Salvador and Guatemala, but a change in social and political philosophy as well.

Over the past two decades, there has been a lively contestation between Left and Right. Daniel Ortega lost the next two presidential elections, in 1996 and 2001. In 2006, however, he won—although in part because of electoral reforms that critics have argued were intended to give the FSLN and its principal rival, the Constitutional Liberal Party, an effective lock on power. The second Ortega administration has worked aggressively, and with at least some success, on economic and social rights. A mediocre record on civil and political rights, however, has become more problematic. And in November 2011, in elections that the head of the OAS observer mission described as "worrying," Ortega was reelected (after the Sandinista-dominated Supreme Court overturned term limits).

In other words, the human rights situation, especially with respect to civil and political rights, is not good, and has recently deteriorated. Nonetheless, it is still far better than in the Somoza years before the revolution. And the fears that dominated American foreign policy in the 1980s have proved largely baseless.

C. US Policy in Central America

In the early twentieth century, US policy in Central America was directed toward establishing military, economic, and political hegemony. Central America was strategically significant for its proximity to the United States, the Panama Canal, and Caribbean sea-lanes. US pressure and intervention were also regularly used to further the interests of US banks and corporations. By the 1920s, Central America had become a special US sphere of influence, "our backyard," as it was still often put in the 1980s.

After World War II, however, the role of economic concerns in US policy declined dramatically. Although the 1954 US-backed overthrow of the freely elected government of Jacobo Árbenz Guzmán in Guatemala reflected the interests of the United Fruit Company, which had special influence in both the State Department and the CIA, anticommunism was probably a stronger motivating force. By the 1980s, when Central America reemerged as a central issue in US foreign policy, economic interests were largely irrelevant. For example, US exports to Nicaragua averaged just under $200 million per year from 1976 to 1978, and total US direct foreign investment was a meager $60 million.

Human rights concerns, however, did not replace economic interests. US policy was driven instead by the fear that domestic instability might increase support for local communists and their Soviet (and Cuban) backers. US policy in Central

America thus oscillated between neglect (during periods of domestic calm) and intervention (at times of domestic instability). In both modes, though, US policy usually supported the military and traditional civilian elites, to the detriment of the rights of most Central Americans.

Consider Nicaragua. In 1912, US troops prevented a liberal political revolution and then remained until 1933, except for eighteen months between 1925 and 1927. Furthermore, the United States was the leading force behind the creation of the National Guard, the principal base of Somoza power. Economic interests and strategic concerns over a potential second canal through Nicaragua explain the initial US involvement. But after World War II, the Somozas' support of US cold war policies became their major asset. The (probably apocryphal) assessment of the senior Somoza attributed to Franklin D. Roosevelt aptly summarized the relationship: "He's a son of a bitch, but he's *our* son of a bitch."

US policy in Guatemala and El Salvador was similar. Following the overthrow of Árbenz in 1954, the United States supported a series of vicious Guatemalan military governments. In El Salvador, although dictatorship was established with little American involvement, the United States supported a series of military-dominated governments.

The postwar US record on economic and social rights in Central America was more mixed. The Alliance for Progress, a major foreign aid initiative for Latin America launched in 1961, brought substantial increases in US aid to Central America. This seems to have contributed to rapid economic growth in the 1960s and early 1970s. US aid also helped to improve life expectancy and literacy. The benefits of growth, however, were distributed so unequally that the gap between rich and poor widened in the 1960s and 1970s. And in El Salvador, Guatemala, and Nicaragua alike, US-backed governments regularly used their power against political parties, trade unions, peasant organizations, and most other groups that tried to foster more rapid reforms or structural changes in society or the economy.

There were signs of US uneasiness. For example, after martial law was imposed in Nicaragua in 1974, the Ford administration moved to distance itself from Somoza (although not so far as to support any alternative). Nonetheless, the logic of anticommunism dominated US policy in Central America in the first three decades after World War II.

The Carter administration entered office in 1977 intent on giving human rights at least equal place in its policy. In Central America, the administration took both concrete and symbolic action. For example, early in 1977 Guatemala's military government announced that it would not accept US aid if it was contingent on public US reporting of Guatemalan human rights practices. Neither Congress nor Carter, however, was willing to leave it at that. Military assistance credits to Guatemala were banned in 1978, and the United States refused to support multilateral loans to Guatemala in 1979 and 1980. The United States also carried out an active program of public diplomacy, including a well-publicized visit by Assistant Secretary of State William Bowdler. But although new military aid to Guatemala was cut off, already committed ("pipeline") aid was continued. And Carter never seriously pressed for major structural reforms.

When Nicaragua emerged as a major concern of US foreign policy, in the fall of 1978, internal turmoil rather than human rights was the major American concern. Carter's goal was to remove Somoza without yielding power to the Sandinistas, who were seen as too closely tied to Cuba and the Soviet Union. The desire to avoid "another Cuba" dominated policy.

The United States tried to strengthen the political center, but it was suffering under political and financial retaliation by Somoza, and the assassination of Pedro Joaquín Chamorro had deprived it of its most respected and effective leader. After four frustrating months of US mediation, Somoza simply refused to leave. Carter responded by terminating military and economic aid, withdrawing the Peace Corps, and halving the size of the US Embassy in Managua. But when these sanctions failed to convince Somoza to step down, there was little that could be done short of the use of force—which Carter refused to consider, for reasons of principle and policy alike.

In June 1979, when the Sandinistas (FSLN) launched their "final offensive," the United States again tried to promote a centrist "third force." The pace of events, however, combined with the moderate opposition's lack of organization and foresight, proved fatal. When Somoza left in July, power passed to a provisional coalition government dominated by its most astute and best-organized faction, the FSLN.

The Carter administration attempted to set aside its suspicions. Food and medical supplies were sent almost immediately. When Carter left office in January 1981, eighteen months after Somoza's fall, the United States had provided $118 million in aid to Nicaragua. This was more than the United States gave to any other Central American country in the same period and was the largest amount provided to Nicaragua by any Western government.

In El Salvador, because of human rights concerns, the United States backed the October 1979 coup led by reformist military officers. But even after most of the civilians in the junta resigned (in January 1980) and Colonel Majano, the leader of the reformist faction in the military, was forced out of the junta (in December 1980), the United States continued to characterize the Salvadoran government as reformist—despite massive and mounting violations of civil and political rights and lack of progress on land reform and economic and social rights.

It is also important to note that even Carter's limited efforts on behalf of human rights met with substantial domestic opposition. For example, in June 1979 more than one hundred members of Congress signed a full-page ad in support of Somoza that ran in the *New York Times* under the headline "Congress Asks: Please, Mr. President, Not Another Cuba!" The Carter administration itself also included skeptics among its high officials, most prominently the national security adviser, Zbigniew Brzezinski. As these elements increasingly came to dominate policy making, the Carter administration began moving the United States toward what would become President Ronald Reagan's new approach.

Central America (along with Afghanistan) became a test case for the Reagan administration's new global political strategy. By summer 1981, the CIA was working with the military opposition in Nicaragua. On March 14, 1982, the war began when two bridges were destroyed by former members of the National Guard who had been trained by the CIA.

The "Kirkpatrick Doctrine" provided a rationale for this new approach. In an influential article that helped to earn her the position of US ambassador to the UN, Jeane Kirkpatrick argued that Carter had failed to understand that the most serious threats to human rights were posed not by authoritarian dictatorships but by totalitarian communists. Furthermore, because many authoritarian dictatorships were US allies, Carter's policy hurt US friends while giving insufficient attention to communism, the most serious threat to human rights.[2] As one conservative group summed up the Carter approach, "Faced with the choice of an occasionally deplorable ally and a consistently deplorable enemy, since 1977 the United States has aided its adversary and alienated its ally."[3] For the Reagan administration, global strategic rivalry with the Soviet Union *was* a struggle for human rights, regardless of the actual human rights practices of the governments in question.

Many in Congress, however, had a more complex vision of Central America. They were supported by a wide range of liberal interest groups. The Reagan administration thus faced constant, but only sporadically successful, resistance to its requests for aid to the contras. Although aid was suspended by Congress in July 1983, "humanitarian" assistance resumed in June 1985, and military aid was approved the following summer. Not until February 1988, during Reagan's last year of office, was military aid again stopped.

The Reagan administration blocked multilateral loans to Nicaragua, cut the import of Nicaraguan sugar by 90 percent in 1983, imposed a complete trade embargo in May 1985, and orchestrated a massive assault on Nicaragua, using the full range of resources short of the direct use of US troops—but including illegally mining Nicaraguan harbors in 1984. Funds were even illegally diverted to the contras, and those responsible lied under oath to Congress.

This campaign of military and economic aggression had devastating consequences. As many as forty thousand people were killed and at least a quarter-million displaced. Food production declined by at least one-fourth. Advances in health care and social services were reversed by terrorist attacks on clinics, schools, and social service offices. By 1988, Nicaragua's economy had been destroyed, with hyperinflation raging at 31,000 percent per year.

The intense US opposition to the government of Nicaragua contrasted sharply with the strong US support for the government of El Salvador. The human rights situation in El Salvador in the late 1970s and early 1980s was far worse than in Nicaragua under either Somoza or the Sandinistas. Salvadoran security forces regularly used indiscriminate violence against civilians. Clandestine paramilitary death squads, with links to the security forces and right-wing political parties, operated with impunity, kidnapping and killing politicians, labor leaders, peasant activists, intellectuals, church activists, and other civilians believed to sympathize with the guerrillas.[4] And in addition to the tens of thousands of Salvadorans killed, Americans were also victims. In December 1980, four American churchwomen were abducted, raped, and murdered. In March 1981, two officials of the American Institute for Free Labor Development were assassinated in the San Salvador Sheraton Hotel. Yet massive aid continued—about $500 million a year in 1984 and 1985 (compared to less than $100 million in 1979 and 1980 combined), totaling almost $4 billion for the decade.

To release American aid, Congress required the president to certify that the government of El Salvador was respecting internationally recognized human rights and had gained control over the armed forces. The first such certification came in January 1982, after a year in which the Salvadoran government and its paramilitary allies murdered well over ten thousand civilians. After four such cynical certifications, President Reagan vetoed new legislation requiring further certifications.

The human rights situation in neighboring Nicaragua was hardly ideal. For example, the 1984–1985 Americas Watch annual report noted "prior censorship of the press, political jailings, the denial of due process of law by special tribunals, the mistreatment of prisoners by incommunicado detention, and forced relocation."[5] But torture and extrajudicial executions, which were commonplace in El Salvador, were rare in Nicaragua. Nonetheless, the United States helped to launch and aggressively supported a guerrilla war of terrorism against Nicaragua. As Americas Watch put it, "So consistent is this double standard that it can be fairly said [that] the Reagan administration has no true human rights policy."[6] Criticisms of the human rights practices of leftist regimes and the defense of the human rights practices of "friendly" governments were simply a continuation of the struggle with the Soviet Union by other means.

Rhetoric, however, exaggerates the differences in the policies of the Carter and Reagan administrations. Carter spoke of human rights as the "heart" of US foreign policy, but in practice they were only a secondary goal. And Reagan's attempts to relegate human rights to the bottom of the list of US foreign policy objectives were at least partially defeated by Congress. Carter did significantly elevate the place of human rights in US policy toward Central America, but they never reached the top. Reagan did force human rights back down the list, but they never reached the bottom.

The first Bush administration's Central America policy, both in word and in deed, lay between its predecessors. Bush generally supported the Salvadoran and Guatemalan governments, despite their lack of control over the military. He did, however, act to prevent further deterioration. For example, he suspended military aid to Guatemala in late 1990 after an upsurge in political violence. Vice President Dan Quayle was sent to El Salvador twice in 1989 to express the administration's concerns. Bush supported the implementation of the UN-mediated end to El Salvador's civil war. And in Nicaragua he pursued a somewhat less belligerent strategy of opposition to the Sandinistas.

The end of the cold war led to a decline in Central America's geopolitical significance—and thus US attention. But human rights concerns have over the past twenty years been an important—and nonpartisan—part of US foreign policy in the region. And improvements in national human rights practices across the region have meant that US initiatives have often been met with less resistance—although with continued concern for national sovereignty and fear of US regional hegemony.

3. CASE STUDY: US POLICY
IN THE SOUTHERN CONE

As we saw in Chapter 4, Argentina, Chile, and Uruguay suffered under brutal military regimes in the 1970s and 1980s. What Argentineans call the Dirty War was a concerted campaign of violence directed against the political Left, trade unions, intellectuals, mainstream autonomous social organizations, and dissidents of all sorts, as well as ordinary apolitical citizens who were forced into or became accidentally enmeshed in the politics of torture and disappearances.

The United States played a significant supporting role in the rise to power of the Chilean military. The Nixon administration saw the 1970 election of Salvador Allende, an avowed Marxist, as an intolerable intrusion of communism in Latin America, despite Allende's fair and free election, strong democratic socialist background, and independence from Soviet and Cuban influence. Henry Kissinger, US national security adviser and later secretary of state, crafted a campaign of economic sabotage. In addition, US support encouraged dissident military officers (although the 1973 coup was largely a local Chilean initiative). Moreover, US diplomacy supported the military regimes in all three countries.

Congress tried to distance the United States from the junta in Chile, limiting economic aid and banning new military assistance. Kissinger, however, did his best to circumvent Congress. For example, in 1976 he publicly reprimanded the US ambassador to Chile for even raising the issue of human rights in private discussions. Even when human rights initiatives were undertaken, as in Argentina in 1976, they were low-key, private, and accompanied by public support for the military.

The Carter administration sharply reversed US policy. President Carter, Secretary of State Cyrus Vance, and Assistant Secretary of State for Human Rights Patricia Derian all drew public attention to human rights violations in the Southern Cone. No head of a Southern Cone military regime was invited for a state visit to Washington. Human rights activists and major figures in the political opposition, by contrast, were received at the State Department and in local US embassies.

During Carter's term, military aid to Southern Cone countries was halted (although Congress deserves much of the credit for this). The United States also supported UN and OAS activities directed against Argentina, Uruguay, and especially Chile. And unlike Central America, this new approach was sustained throughout the full four years of the Carter presidency.

These policies led to the release of many political prisoners, including prominent opposition journalist Jacobo Timerman and human rights activist (and future Nobel Peace Prize recipient) Adolfo Pérez Esquivel. Conditions of detention were eased for many others. The Carter administration also claimed credit for reductions in disappearances and political prisoners, although a more important factor was probably the success of earlier efforts at terror and repression, which reduced the number of potential new victims.

In 1981, the Reagan administration abruptly returned to the policies of Nixon, Kissinger, and Ford. In fact, Argentina and Chile were principal examples in Jeane

Kirkpatrick's criticism of the Carter administration for foolishly sacrificing more important US interests to the quixotic pursuit of human rights. For example, in August 1981, Ambassador Kirkpatrick paid a formal visit to Chile and called for the full normalization of US-Chilean relations. At the UN Commission on Human Rights, the United States voted against continuing the special rapporteur on Chile. Joint military exercises were reinstituted. For Argentina, the Reagan administration obtained the repeal of the 1978 Humphrey-Kennedy amendment that had banned US military sales and security assistance. General Viola, the leader of Argentina's second junta, was one of the first foreign leaders invited by Reagan for a state visit, in March 1981. And Ambassador Kirkpatrick did not even reply to a letter from the Mothers of the Plaza de Mayo asking for a meeting during her 1981 visit to Buenos Aires.

These signals of renewed US support led directly to new human rights violations. For example, immediately after Kirkpatrick's visit, Chile expelled several political leaders, including centrist Christian Democrats, and arrested and tortured a number of human rights activists. The United States issued no public response.

Although the Reagan administration did engage in **quiet diplomacy** on behalf of individual victims, human rights violations were treated as a matter for private discussions between friends. The overriding priority was to maintain close relations. Other interests were considered far more important than pervasive human rights abuses.

Even after Argentina's Falklands disaster, which proved to be the prelude to the return of civilian rule, the Reagan administration did not publicly raise human rights concerns. Although the new civilian government was embraced in Washington, the United States had nothing to do with its creation. In Uruguay as well, civilian rule returned despite, rather than because of, US policy.

In Chile, the Reagan administration did speak out against the intensified repression that led to the reimposition of martial law in 1984. Assistant Secretary of State Elliott Abrams, previously a vocal supporter of the Chilean junta, publicly criticized the Pinochet government. But in December 1985, the United States cast the decisive vote in the OAS General Assembly that removed reference to Chile from a resolution on human rights violations. Even after Pinochet lost the 1988 plebiscite for another eight-year term as president, US criticism of military rule remained low-key. Democracy returned to Chile too in spite, not because, of US policy.

4. CASE STUDY: US POLICY TOWARD SOUTH AFRICA

The human rights situation in South Africa was discussed in §5.4. Here we are concerned with the response of the United States. Before the Sharpeville Massacre in 1960, the United States treated apartheid as an internal South African matter. The turmoil following Sharpeville, however, raised the specter of revolution and mobilized American fear of communism. The United States thus began to treat apartheid as a matter of international concern. The Eisenhower administration even agreed to put apartheid permanently on the agenda of the UN Security Council.

The new Kennedy administration initiated a policy review in 1961 (which dragged on until 1964). Kennedy also imposed a selective arms embargo even before the Security Council called for a voluntary embargo at the end of 1963. As the crisis receded, however, so too did US attention. Sanctions remained in effect, but they were modest and had no discernible impact.

When Henry Kissinger took over as national security adviser to President Nixon in 1969, he instituted a series of policy reviews for all areas of the world. The resulting document on South Africa, National Security Memorandum 39 (NSM 39), proposed closer association with South Africa in order to put the United States in a better position to press for reform. The goal was to combine negative sanctions with more positive inducements to change and to use areas of mutual interest, such as regional security, as a wedge to open South Africa to US pressure on apartheid.

This approach, however, had no more impact than the Kennedy-Johnson strategy of dissociation. Part of the problem was weak and inconsistent implementation. For example, false certifications of the nonmilitary nature of certain arms were accepted. A 1978 US Department of Justice study found that 178 of South Africa's 578 military aircraft had been purchased from the United States during the embargo.[7] Furthermore, US concessions were tied to no particular demands on South Africa. In other words, there was no real policy on South Africa. NSM 39 was never seriously implemented.

There were also major conceptual flaws in both the Kennedy-Johnson and the Nixon-Kissinger approaches. The United States asked for changes that the South African government refused even to consider. Although willing to ease some elements of "petty apartheid" (for example, by desegregating some public facilities in large cities), the government was unwilling to end racial separation. Democratic majority rule was not even open for discussion. The negative sanctions and positive inducements the United States was willing to use fell far short of what would have been necessary to make the white government change its mind.

The other conceptual error in US policy was an excessive reliance on economic change and private enterprise. Liberals and conservatives alike believed that South Africa's atavistic racial policies would inevitably be eroded by the "modernization" that accompanied economic development. Trade and investment thus appeared as instruments for change rather than as support for apartheid. In practice, however, reforms required by economic necessity were prevented from spilling over into social and political changes. South Africa's immense bureaucracy, which intervened with totalitarian thoroughness in all aspects of life, largely prevented unplanned changes in the fundamental character of apartheid from going unnoticed or unchecked.

After the Portuguese coup in April 1974, which led to the rapid decolonization of Angola and Mozambique, even these modest US efforts were largely abandoned in favor of a focus on "regional security"—that is, containing expanding Soviet influence. South Africa now appeared as a pro-Western regional power. Kissinger even met Prime Minister Vorster twice in 1976, the first official meeting at this level in thirty years.

The Soweto riots of 1976 returned apartheid to the center of international attention. Soon afterward, the election of Jimmy Carter changed the US approach. But actions such as US support in the Security Council for a mandatory arms embargo were largely symbolic. Furthermore, there were tensions within the Carter administration. Zbigniew Brzezinski, Carter's national security adviser, favored a policy that, like Kissinger's, emphasized regional security. As Brzezinski's influence grew in the second half of Carter's term, US policy took on an increasingly cold war tone, stressing the Cuban presence in Angola and the Soviet naval threat in the South Atlantic and Indian Oceans. Even more than in Central America, the end of the Carter administration is best seen as preparing the way for Reagan's policies.

Reagan's policy of "constructive engagement" returned to the Nixon-era strategy of pursuing closer relations in order to increase US leverage. Assistant Secretary of State Chester Crocker, the principal architect of the policy, had been a staff member on Kissinger's National Security Council. In the 1980s, he tried to turn the idea behind NSM 39 into an effective policy.

Despite international calls for new sanctions, the United States eased many that were already in place. Restrictions on the sale of aircraft, computers, and nuclear-related equipment with dual military and civilian uses were eased. In fact, the United States became South Africa's largest trading partner. Total private investment and loans rose to $10 billion.

The stated aim of constructive engagement was to foster change through enlightened private enterprise and support for moderate forces of social change, such as trade unions and education. In practice, though, the United States devoted almost no resources to education or trade unions. The reforms introduced by US corporations helped a small number of employees but had no systematic impact on apartheid. And, as in the early 1970s, the United States did not insist on any concrete human rights improvements in return for closer relations. Furthermore, South African intentions continued to be misjudged. The government of P. W. Botha was willing to modernize apartheid but not to eliminate it.

Events in South Africa, however, again forced a reevaluation of US policy. Violence erupted in August 1984 in protest over elections held under the new constitution of 1983, which completely excluded blacks from direct political participation. When repression once more tightened rather than eased, constructive engagement lost any remaining credibility. But as late as July 1986, Reagan still argued that "we and our allies cannot dictate to the government of a sovereign nation—nor should we try"—despite supporting a terrorist war against the freely elected government of Nicaragua and the decades-old policy of comprehensive sanctions against Cuba.

Change in US policy came from a bipartisan congressional coalition that in 1986 overrode a presidential veto of a new sanctions bill. This reflected the culmination of the mobilization of antiapartheid by NGOs over many decades.

Activity on South Africa by US NGOs goes back to at least 1912, when the National Association for the Advancement of Colored People was involved in the initial formation of South Africa's African National Congress. The American Committee on Africa was formed in 1953 in response to the pass-law demonstrations. In the late 1970s and 1980s, groups like TransAfrica focused their efforts on apartheid. Other NGOs, such as the American Friends Service Committee, the Interfaith Council on Corporate Responsibility, and the Lawyers' Committee for Civil

Rights Under Law, made South Africa a major priority. In addition, churches, state and local governments, colleges and universities, student organizations, unions, and black organizations divested assets in corporations that did business in South Africa. Many of these actions were coordinated with divestment campaigns in other countries, with international antiapartheid groups such as the International Defense and Aid Fund and with other international NGOs such as the World Council of Churches and the Lutheran World Fund. They were also facilitated by Bishop Desmond Tutu's Nobel Peace Prize and his well-publicized visit to the United States at the end of 1984.

It is important not to overestimate US efforts. American sanctions were limited and quite incomplete. Nonetheless, South Africa was losing access to international capital (although in the short run more from lender fear caused by the 1984–1986 township riots than from sanctions). And the loss of US support, even if the Reagan administration never actively opposed the white government, created concern among many of South Africa's less conservative leaders and citizens, particularly in light of the growing internal crisis.

Apartheid ultimately collapsed because of the inability of the white government to keep opposition repressed. Nonetheless, changes in US policy, particularly in the context of the global antiapartheid campaign, made a small contribution to the final demise of apartheid. And even though American sanctions were largely symbolic, it was a very different sort of symbolism than had been typical of US policy in the preceding years.

5. OTHER WESTERN APPROACHES
TO INTERNATIONAL HUMAN RIGHTS

Although the United States led the way in the 1970s in introducing human rights into bilateral diplomacy, other countries also incorporated human rights into their foreign policies. Particularly notable were the efforts of the **like-minded countries,** a dozen smaller Western countries that since the mid-1970s have attempted to act together in international diplomacy as intermediaries between the larger Western countries, with which they are formally or informally aligned, and the countries of the Third World, for whose aspirations they have considerable sympathy. Norway and the Netherlands, in particular, have emphasized human rights in their foreign policies, signaled by white papers on the subject in 1977 and 1979.

Even more than in US policy, foreign aid has been a central instrument in the international human rights policies of the like-minded countries. Development assistance tends to be not only an important element of their foreign policies but a matter of consensus among the major political parties. In the Netherlands, there is even a separate minister for development cooperation within the foreign ministry. By contrast, in the United States, foreign aid is a relatively peripheral part of foreign policy yet, during the 1970s and 1980s, a subject of considerable partisan political controversy.

Furthermore, the United States tends to base initial foreign aid decisions on political and humanitarian factors, modifying allocations at a later stage in light of human rights concerns. The like-minded countries, which lack the resources to engage in a massive, global foreign aid program, target their development assistance at a small set of countries—variously called "core," "program," or "priority" countries—with which they seek to develop relatively intensive, long-term aid relations. The Dutch and Norwegians, in particular, have emphasized both civil and political rights and economic, social, and cultural rights in selecting program countries. In Norway, selection criteria since 1972 have included a strong preference for countries in which "the authorities of the country concerned [are] following a development-oriented and socially just policy in the best interests of all sections of the community," reflecting the fact that social justice is given roughly equal priority with civil and political rights largely across the Norwegian political spectrum. And as early as 1973, the Dutch officially emphasized a "close relationship between peace, a just distribution of wealth, international legal order and respect for human rights."[8]

Even more striking than the selection of priority countries has been the relatively rapid response of the like-minded countries to changes in human rights conditions. For example, Norway broke its aid relationship with Uganda in 1972, the year that Idi Amin overthrew the government of Milton Obote and embarked on a dictatorial career that made him one of the most notorious human rights violators of the decade. The Netherlands dropped Uganda from its list of program countries in 1974. The United States, by contrast, was Uganda's largest trading partner until October 1978, less than a year before Amin was overthrown.

Sweden stopped all assistance to Chile shortly after Pinochet's coup and was a significant international supporter of the work of the Vicaría. Canada was also a vocal critic of military rule in the Southern Cone. In the 1980s, as ethnic violence escalated in Sri Lanka, a country with which Norway had developed close ties in the 1970s, the Norwegians dramatically downgraded their relationship. Canada, the Netherlands, and the Nordic countries all increased their aid to Nicaragua in the 1980s, reflecting a radically different understanding of human rights than the Reagan administration.

The Dutch response to the deteriorating human rights situation in their former colony of Suriname is especially revealing. They strongly condemned the 1980 military coup. Following the execution of fifteen opposition figures in 1982, the Netherlands not only suspended all aid but refused to provide new aid for the remainder of the decade. The Dutch also led the effort to apply international pressure on Suriname. The contrast to US behavior toward its Caribbean Basin clients in Guatemala and El Salvador, who were guilty of much more severe human rights violations, is striking. The Dutch even carried human rights into relations with Indonesia, a country of far greater importance, and accepted some real economic and political costs as a result.

The like-minded countries also adopted an approach to South Africa very different from that of the United States in the 1970s and 1980s. Starting in 1969, Sweden and Norway provided both political support and development assistance funds to the ANC during its exile from South Africa. The Dutch adopted a similar policy in 1973. And in the 1980s, these efforts were expanded into broad, high-priority programs for the whole region of southern Africa and a leading role in the international movement for sanctions against South Africa.

We should be careful not to romanticize the policies of the like-minded countries. Considerations other than human rights are central, sometimes even overriding, in their foreign policies. For example, Dutch aid sanctions against Indonesia did not extend to trade or other economic relations. Canada also pursued close relations with Indonesia for commercial reasons. Economic interests in South Africa seriously delayed Canada's decision to adopt sanctions and led Norway to exclude shipping from its initial sanctions. Nonetheless, the overall international human rights record of the like-minded countries is clearly superior to that of the United States, both in avoiding associations with severe violators and in responding to abuses in countries with which they have special relations. The like-minded countries have also given human rights a much higher priority in their multilateral foreign policies.

6. EXPLAINING DIFFERENCES IN HUMAN RIGHTS POLICIES

Jan Egeland, in comparing Norwegian and US international human rights policies, argued that "small and big nations are differently disposed to undertaking coherent rights-oriented foreign policies." In fact, Egeland asserted that the relatively meager international human rights accomplishments of the United States are "because of, rather than in spite of, her superpower status."[9] Small countries are not so much "better," in this analysis, as less constrained than large states. "The frequency and intensity of the conflict between self-interest and [international human rights] norms seems, in short, proportional to a nation's economic and military power, as well as to its foreign policy ambitions."[10] Large states have multiple interests and responsibilities that preclude the consistent pursuit of human rights objectives. Small states rarely have to choose between human rights and other foreign policy goals.

This explanation focuses on the structure of the international system. Large states are also more likely to pursue bilateral policies because they are more likely to have the power to achieve their aims without multilateral support. Small states, by contrast, tend to prefer international organizations because multilateral processes increase their opportunities for influence. Such structural explanations would also seem to be supported by the fact that larger powers, such as Britain, France, Japan, and to a lesser extent Germany, have international human rights policies closer to those of the United States than to Norway or the Netherlands.

Size alone, however, cannot explain even the differences that are influenced by relative power. For example, despite declining American power, the United States remains reluctant to operate through multilateral channels (unless it can control the organization). As Germany's power grows, it continues to rely heavily on multilateral organizations. Britain has tended to pursue a much more unilateral foreign policy than France, Germany, or Japan. Among small states, Sweden, Austria, and especially Switzerland have emphasized a neutral foreign policy. Canada, Belgium, and the Netherlands have had a strong Western orientation in their foreign policies. Size or power at most inclines states in certain directions.

Furthermore, numerous factors unconnected with size are also important. Why did the United States emphasize international human rights in the 1970s while other large powers did not, and Japan still does not? Why did Britain intervene in its sphere of influence so much less frequently than the United States? Why are human rights as a foreign policy issue so much more controversial in the United States than in most other Western countries? Why does Belgium have a much less active international human rights policy than the Netherlands? Such questions can be answered only if we take history, political culture, and institutions into account.

Throughout the cold war era, the United States viewed the world in East-West terms, reducing all foreign policy issues to US-Soviet rivalry. But the cold war was not simply a bipolar political rivalry between hegemonic states; it involved a heavy emphasis on ideology. As a result, Americans generally assumed that radical reformers and their programs were Soviet backed, inspired, or influenced. And without the ideological element, many actual or attempted political changes in the Third World would not have been deemed such a threat to the United States. Ideology, however, has nothing to do with size. Many small states, especially in Latin America, were at least as anticommunist as the United States. Conversely, it is historically rare for a large state to define its interests in ideological terms.

Consider also the tendency of the like-minded states to view international conflicts more in North-South than East-West terms. During the cold war, these countries saw the principal lines of international cleavage as dividing rich and poor, not capitalist (or liberal-democratic) and communist. For example, in 1982, Mark MacGuigan, the Canadian secretary of state for external affairs, argued, "Instability in Central America . . . is not a product of East-West rivalry. It is a product of poverty, the unfair distribution of wealth, and social injustice. Instability feeds poverty and injustice. East-West rivalries flow in its wake."[11] The Dutch and the Nordic countries shared this view.

Some part of this might be related to size. For example, it is not surprising that a country like Canada, which fears being overwhelmed by the United States, or the Netherlands, which borders on powerful Germany and is not far from France and Britain, is more sympathetic to a perspective that sees differences in power as no less important than differences in ideology. But size alone cannot explain the difference in ideological perspective.

We can see this even in Egeland's own analysis. In explaining the "strong moral impact" on Norwegian policy, he stressed four factors: (1) no legacy of imperialism and intervention, (2) a good domestic human rights record, (3) a high level of foreign aid and support for changes in the world economy to favor Third World countries, and (4) consistent support for decolonization and national liberation movements.[12] The first of these factors is perhaps related to size—although Belgium, Portugal, and the Netherlands had significant colonial holdings; German, Austrian, Russian, and American colonial holdings were small; and the Netherlands rapidly overcame its imperial legacy. The other three factors, however, have little or nothing to do with size.

Size explains almost nothing about internal human rights records, as a comparison of pairs of similarly sized countries such as the United States and the Soviet Union, China and India, Japan and Indonesia, and Costa Rica and Guatemala vividly illustrates. Nor does size have much to do with levels of foreign aid. The United States chooses to be niggardly, whereas Norway and the Netherlands (and Japan) choose to be generous.[13] And the United States has had a better record on supporting decolonization than small states such as Portugal and Spain or second-tier powers such as Britain and France.

Much the same can be said of the role of consensus in Norwegian international human rights and foreign policy, another factor Egeland emphasized. Foreign policy consensus is hardly characteristic of small states, as the varying policies of dozens of Third World countries indicate. In the Nordic countries, foreign policy consensus is a function of a parliamentary system, in which there is no sharp division between executive and legislative branches, a strong reliance on a professional foreign and civil service (in contrast to the extensive use of political appointees in the US bureaucracy), and a political tradition that ensures direct representation and special consideration for all major social groups.

Size does not explain why Norway and the Netherlands in the 1970s embarked on unusually active international human rights policies but Austria, Belgium, and Greece did not. Likewise, size cannot explain either the active (if inconsistent) international human rights policy of the United States or the lack of an active international human rights policy in Japan, let alone China.

How a country defines its interests certainly is constrained, and often shaped, by its power and its position in the international system. But power and position do not come even close to determining interests. Most impediments to strong international human rights policies lie in the relatively free decisions of states to give higher weight to other foreign policy objectives. Most of the factors that contribute to aggressive efforts to pursue international human rights in a country's foreign policy have much more to do with its national political culture and contingent political facts (for example, the election of Jimmy Carter) than with its international political position. For example, Dutch membership in Amnesty International, on a per capita basis, exceeds American membership in the National Rifle Association, one of the largest and most powerful interest groups in the United States.

National political culture is especially important in explaining the striking differences between the attitudes of the United States and the like-minded countries toward economic and social rights. American foreign aid has been used almost exclusively in the pursuit of civil and political rights objectives. Humanitarian objectives such as nutrition, literacy, and health care have been pursued, but in the United States these objectives simply are not perceived in terms of human rights. US foreign aid and human rights policy are seen as two fundamentally separate issues that are tactically linked. The like-minded countries, by contrast, see development assistance as central to their international human rights policies. They also emphasize the intrinsic importance of economic, social, and cultural rights and their interdependence with civil and political rights.

Differences between the United States and the like-minded countries are largely matters of choice. Norway and the Netherlands place a relatively high value on international human rights not because they are small and weak but because of how their citizens understand themselves, their place in the world, and the obligations associated with their identity.

PROBLEM 4: US RATIFICATION OF HUMAN RIGHTS TREATIES

The Problem

The United States is a leading global advocate of human rights. It regularly makes use of the body of international human rights law to criticize other states. But the United States is a party to only three of the six core treaties: the civil and political covenant (but not the economic, social, and cultural covenant) and the treaties on racial discrimination and torture (but not those on discrimination against women and the rights of the child). It does not permit individual communications under the treaties to which it is a party. And the United States is not a party to the regional American Convention.

This is widely seen by other countries as hypocrisy. (We see a similar, and even more striking, hypocrisy is the United States' support of the ICC, and the tribunals for the former Yugoslavia and Rwanda, but its refusal to include itself under the jurisdiction of the ICC.) This hypocrisy hinders American international action. And it undermines what I have argued is the most important contribution of the global human rights regime, namely, an agreed-upon set of comprehensive global standards.

A Solution

The obvious solution is for the United States to ratify these treaties. But this is almost certain not to happen in the foreseeable future. In other words, there is no practical solution. The best we can do is understand why this problem arose and persists.

Section 8.1 highlighted the importance of "American exceptionalism." For much of its history, the United States was indeed exceptional in its commitment to the practice of human rights. But other Western countries have at least caught up, as have a growing number of non-Western countries. American exceptionalism thus increasingly expresses itself in the perverse form of what John Ruggie (see the Suggested Readings below) nicely calls "exemptionalism," the insistence that the United States is exempt from international standards.

This, at best, reflects a deep-seated American arrogance. It is almost as if Americans believe that "we invented human rights" and have nothing to learn from the rest of the world: that *human rights* means how things are done in the United States. Others need international standards, because they are not Americans. But

Americans don't—because our political and legal history is inseparable from human rights.

We need not go back to genocide against Native peoples and slavery to see the folly—or shocking denial—of this view. Legalized racial discrimination has been taken off the books only in the past half century. Violence against women has been effectively criminalized in most jurisdictions for much less than that. Political dissidents were actively persecuted during much of the cold war. In most American jurisdictions today, felons who have served their time are denied "inalienable" rights such as the right to vote. And the shortcomings of the United States in the area of economic and social rights, especially with respect to health care and housing, are shocking to most citizens in all other Western countries.

Many Americans dismiss ratification as a mere formality. And for many rights it would be. But for others it would not—at least if the United States took legislative action to implement the treaties in American law. This, however, is even less likely than ratification. For example, the US ratified the International Covenant on Civil and Political Rights, only with the "reservation" that ratification would have no effect in American law. But even with such a reservation, there is little likelihood that the US will even ratify the other core treaties.

Here partisan politics plays a central role. Abstract arguments of sovereignty have become a staple of the political Right. Little in the substance of, say, the Convention on the Rights of the Child is objectionable. Nonetheless, the United States is the only country with a functioning government that is not a party to it. (Somalia is the only other country not to have ratified it.) This is a case of pure symbolism— of the most peculiar sort. (It is part of what led the United States to take forty years to ratify the genocide convention—not because the United States wanted to reserve for itself an international legal right to commit genocide but because during the 1970s and most of the 1980s, powerful political forces insisted, as a matter of principle, on exemptionalism.)

Only a small segment of the American population attaches positive significance to US ratification of international human rights treaties. And almost no one would vote on that basis. But an important part of the Republican electorate can be mobilized against ratification—and the charge of sacrificing American sovereignty has considerable resonance in the political center. The electoral calculus is thus clear: nothing is to be gained from supporting ratification, but something may be lost. Thus, those treaties sit on the shelf—even though the conventions on discrimination against women and the rights of the child actually have considerable substantive attraction to the majority of the American population.

Further Problems

International scrutiny is a mechanism to help states hold themselves to the highest standards. And they provide citizens of participating states with supplemental mechanisms that in some cases can help them to achieve effective enjoyment of their rights. This is particularly true in countries with relatively good human rights records and active civil societies—that is, countries such as the United States. The

United States is thus depriving its citizens of a limited but not insignificant mechanism to guarantee their rights.

Americans are also becoming increasingly isolated from the rest of the Western world, where the language of human rights is being incorporated into national law and politics. This too is likely to lead to slower improvements, both absolutely and relatively, in the United States.

If this continues, America's leadership role may be challenged. People across the globe have for two centuries looked to the United States as a human rights inspiration. The refusal of the United States to participate fully in the body of international human rights law and practice may ultimately lead to that leadership passing to Europe.

DISCUSSION QUESTIONS

1. Should we accept the description of post–World War II US foreign policy as dominated by anticommunism? Suppose that we do. Was it a poor policy decision? Should anticommunism have been assigned a less overriding priority? Or was the problem that anticommunism was pursued with unreasonable zeal? Is there an important lesson here about an ideological (or moralistic) foreign policy that leads to such excess? If so, should we reconsider the arguments of the realists?

2. Should the United States be able to define for itself which internationally recognized human rights it wishes to recognize or pursue? If so, why? How can we sustain and enforce an international human rights policy if states can pick and choose the parts they want to comply with? Why should the United States (or any other sovereign state) have to comply with international human rights norms, no matter how widely accepted they are?

3. The United States has a relatively active and aggressive bilateral international human rights policy but has been reluctant to participate in most multilateral international human rights regimes. (The United States did not ratify the International Covenant on Civil and Political Rights until April 1992, and even then it did not ratify the optional protocol.) Isn't this a double standard? Can it be justified? Why should other countries take US international human rights policy seriously when the United States is so reluctant to open itself to international human rights scrutiny?

4. In reviewing the evidence of US policy toward South Africa, Central America, and the Southern Cone, what strikes you more, the continuities or the changes between different US administrations? When all is said and done, just how different was Carter's policy from that of either Ford or Reagan? Were the differences largely symbolic? If they were, how serious a criticism is that? How large a role does symbolic rhetoric play in foreign policy? In international human rights policy?

5. The same question might be asked about the differences between the international human rights policies of the United States and the policies of

the like-minded countries. When it comes to making difficult choices, when it comes to sacrificing their own interests, just how different are Canada, Norway, and the Netherlands from the United States? Compare, for example, the Netherlands' policy toward Indonesia and its policy toward Suriname. Is the difference one of quality or merely a matter of degree?

6. Consider the emphasis of the like-minded countries on economic, social, and cultural rights. Is their approach better than or just different from that of the United States? Why? Does your answer change if you look at the issue from the perspectives of foreign policy, foreign aid policy, and international human rights policy?

7. Why do you think that international human rights policies were a matter of intense partisan controversy in the United States in the 1970s and 1980s but not in Norway and the Netherlands? What explains the fact that since the early 1990s there has been a nonpartisan consensus on the importance of international human rights policies in the United States as well?

SUGGESTED READINGS

Debra Liang-Fenton, ed., *Implementing U.S. Human Rights Policy* (Washington, DC: US Institute of Peace Press, 2004), provides more than a dozen superb case studies of US human rights policy toward a wide range of prominent countries, focusing on the post–cold war era. It is the single best source to get some sense of the texture and range of American international human rights policy in recent years. Kathryn Sikkink, *Mixed Signals: U.S. Human Rights Policy and Latin America* (Ithaca, NY: Cornell University Press, 2005), provides a comprehensive overview of US human rights policy toward Latin America, covering the entire post–World War II era. Michael Ignatieff, ed., *American Exceptionalism and Human Rights* (Princeton, NJ: Princeton University Press, 2005), is an excellent collection of essays covering a wide range of both domestic and international human rights issues. Harold Koh, "America's Jeckyll-and-Hyde Exceptionalism," and John Ruggie, "American, Exceptionalism, Exemptionalism, and Global Governance," are particularly good and especially relevant to the issues covered in this chapter. Taken together, these three books provide an excellent overview of the topic of human rights in American foreign policy. For a more critical assessment, see Julie Mertus, *Bait and Switch? Human Rights and U.S. Foreign Policy,* 2nd ed. (New York: Routledge, 2008). Harold Hongju Koh, "A United States Human Rights Policy for the 21st Century," *Saint Louis University Law Journal* 46 (Spring 2002): 293–344, is a powerful programmatic statement by Clinton's former assistant secretary of state. In my view, there is no single piece that does a better job of provoking serious thought about the appropriate contours of American international human rights policy.

For good illustrations of competing views on human rights and American foreign policy in the late 1970s and early 1980s, see (on the "liberal" side) Arthur Schlesinger Jr., "Human Rights and the American Tradition," *Foreign Affairs* 57, no. 3 (1979): 503–526, and Stanley Hoffmann, "Reaching for the Most Difficult: Human Rights as a Foreign Policy Goal," *Daedalus* 112 (Fall 1983): 19–49; and (on the "conservative" side) Jeane J. Kirkpatrick, "Dictatorships and Double Standards," *Commentary* 68 (November 1979): 34–45, and Henry A. Kissinger, "Continuity and Change in American Foreign Policy," in *Human Rights and World Order,* edited by Abdul Aziz Said (New York: Praeger, 1978).

On human rights in the foreign policies of other countries, Alison Brysk, *Global Good Samaritans: Human Rights as Foreign Policy* (Oxford: Oxford University Press, 2009), is the place to begin. (Brysk looks at Sweden, Canada, Costa Rica, Japan, and South Africa.) Older but still useful is David P. Forsythe, ed., *Human Rights and Comparative Foreign Policy* (Tokyo: United Nations University Press, 2000).

9

◄○►

Human Rights and
Foreign Policy

The preceding chapter considered cold war–era cases, with a focus on US policy. This (briefer) chapter takes a conceptual approach to bilateral policy. After a preliminary discussion of the relation between human rights and the national interest, it looks at the means used in bilateral human rights policies, their aims and effects, and the relationship between human rights policy and foreign policy (with special attention to issues of trade-offs and consistency).

1. HUMAN RIGHTS AND
THE NATIONAL INTEREST

Discussion of human rights and foreign policy in the 1970s and 1980s often centered on *whether* states ought to have an international human rights policy. And the answer given to that question was as often no as yes. Today, it is completely normal and largely uncontroversial for states to pursue human rights objectives in their bilateral and multilateral foreign policies. Especially in liberal democratic countries, the questions have become what should be included in a country's human rights foreign policy, where should it be pursued, and how aggressively. Such a change reflects a fundamental redefinition of the national interest.

In an earlier era, a distinction was often drawn between the "high politics" of security and other ("low politics") international concerns of states. The theoretical and policy perspective of realpolitik—political realism, power politics—went even further, advocating the idea of the national interest defined in terms of power. In such a world, human rights is a (merely) moral concern. Although states may choose to pursue international human rights objectives, out of a sense of compassion or justice, they must be rigorously subordinated to vital material national interests.

In fact, though, the national interest is whatever states and their citizens are interested in. If states feel that it is in their interest to expend some of their foreign

139

policy resources and attention on the rights of foreigners, there is no reason they should not. And the reasons for doing so need not be instrumental (e.g., the idea that rights-protective regimes are more peaceful or better trading partners). An intrinsic interest in living in a more just world fully justifies including international human rights in a country's definition of its national interest. And in fact, many countries have done precisely that.

Today, most democratic countries in all regions of the world have more or less ambitious international human rights objectives in their bilateral foreign policies. Most nondemocratic regimes support (or at least tolerate) the multilateral mechanisms discussed in Chapter 5. They do not, however, extend their international human rights policies to bilateral relations—for rather obvious reasons.

The rise of human rights on the foreign policy agendas of democratic states has both internal and international dimensions. Democracies tend to identify themselves internally with the pursuit of human rights. Carrying this pursuit over into their foreign policies thus seems "natural." It also gives expression to a sort of universal solidarity based on a common humanity (without challenging the system of national implementation of international human rights).

Democratic regimes, though, long predate international human rights norms. Bilateral human rights policies emerged along with the maturing of the global human rights regime. The expression of a "natural" internal inclination to pursue human rights in foreign policy was in fact greatly facilitated, and in some senses even created, by changes in international norms. States define their national interests as the result of the intersection of national and international influences. The deepening of the commitment to human rights in the national foreign policies of democratic states is in some ways as much the result of an active international human rights policy as a cause of such policies. It was no coincidence that Carter was elected in the same year that the International Human Rights Covenants came into force and took office in the same year that Amnesty International won the Nobel Peace Prize.

Foreign policy is about how a state sees itself, the world around it, and its place in that world. The global human rights regime has created a world in which a government's commitment to human rights is seen as essential to full national and international legitimacy. That has not only enabled the expression of existing tendencies to address human rights in national foreign policies but also created additional support for such policies. The transformation of the national interest represented by the rise of bilateral human rights policies is thus both a cause and a consequence of the domestic preferences of states and the global human rights regime's mutual interactions with one another to push policy in a particular direction.

2. MEANS AND MECHANISMS OF BILATERAL ACTION

Human rights, as an objective of foreign policy, can be legitimately pursued using all the means of foreign policy—short of the threat or use of force, which contemporary international law reserves for self-defense. These means fall into two broad groups: diplomacy, understood as the use of discursive means of action, and sanctions, understood as the use of material means. We can also divide the mechanisms of foreign policy into persuasive and coercive means, understood as a continuum. (These two distinctions overlap only partially. Although diplomatic measures tend to be persuasive, they sometimes have a coercive dimension. Sanctions tend to be relatively coercive. When they involve carrots rather than sticks, though, they are fundamentally persuasive.)

A. Diplomacy

Human rights diplomacy tends to have three principal targets: the treatment of particular individuals (usually dissidents and political prisoners), particular policies, and the character of the regime (with a focus on patterns of gross and systematic violations of internationally recognized human rights). These objectives are pursued through both public and private means.

Although most attention is rightly focused on public human rights diplomacy, private diplomatic initiatives—**"quiet diplomacy"**—can be important. This is particularly true when dealing with individual victims or attempting to change particular laws, policies, or practices. Nonetheless, private action alone, without at least the plausible threat of public action, rarely helps even in the most limited cases. And when gross and systematic violations are at issue, quiet diplomacy rarely is an adequate response to such severe provocations.

Public human rights diplomacy has at least three important dimensions: gathering and disseminating information, communicating opposing views, and mobilizing pressure. Although mobilizing pressure certainly is of central importance, we should not underestimate the importance of information gathering and the diplomatic exchange of views.

The international politics of human rights is largely a matter of mobilizing shame. Reliable information about national human rights practices thus is essential to human rights advocacy of any sort. Professional diplomats are well positioned to develop and disseminate such information, both through their own direct inquiries and through contacts with human rights advocates in their host country.

The United States in particular has made a major contribution through its annual Country Reports on Human Rights Practices.[1] These have, especially since the end of the cold war, become a major source of reliable information about national human rights practices that is used not only by foreign policy decision makers in numerous countries but also by national and transnational human rights advocates across the globe.

The private and public exchange of views, especially among friendly countries, is an often-overlooked means of exerting influence. This is often particularly effective in countries that have fair to good human rights records and where foreign policy initiatives support the work of local activists. Knowing that one's international allies—especially powerful friends—are watching and will raise an issue sometimes influences a government's actions. This is rarely the case when addressing gross and systematic violations. But when dealing with particular individuals or particular practices, it can be of considerable help. Especially when undertaken in concert with other national, international, and transnational action, persuasive diplomacy can make a difference. Sometimes it may even provide the decisive element that tips the balance.

But just as quiet diplomacy depends on the possibility of "escalation" to public pressure, the efficacy of exchanging partially diverging and partially converging views often depends on the public mobilization of shame. Escalation to direct public criticism may be used as a threat. No less important, though, the retreat to less publicly contentious means may allow a country to save some face. It may also facilitate the often-difficult internal and international negotiations associated with changes in policy.

Discursive policy, however, can be, and often needs to be, coercive, not merely persuasive. Rarely will the privately expressed views of other countries, or even polite public disagreements among friends, be sufficient to improve even very specific human rights practices. States in their relations with other states often may reasonably choose to allow other actors, both national and transnational, to bear the burden of vocal public criticism. But such criticism is almost always necessary to win even incremental improvements in human rights practices. And when confronting severe and systematic violations, anything less than public criticism will appear to be, if not complicity, then at least acquiescence to practices that simply should not be borne in silence.

B. Sanctions

Words are the principal tool of bilateral human rights policy. The same is true of multilateral action, as we saw above, and of transnational action, as we will see in the next chapter. States, however, typically have more material means at their disposal that can be utilized on behalf of internationally recognized human rights than most multilateral human rights actors and transnational human rights NGOs.

One strategy that has often been employed is to link foreign aid to the human rights practices of recipients. Two different kinds of strategies have been pursued. Many countries have reduced aid in response to human rights violations (and, to a somewhat lesser extent, increased aid to reward improved human rights performance). As we saw in the preceding chapter, though, "like-minded" "middle powers" such as Canada, the Netherlands, and the Nordic countries have gone further, choosing aid recipients in significant measure on the basis of good or improving human rights records.

States also have a variety of other relations that they can manipulate in order to support their bilateral human rights policies. At the lowest level, which shades into diplomacy, states may engage in symbolic gestures, such as recalling an ambassador for consultations or delaying the nomination of a new appointee to a vacant ambassadorial post. Cultural contacts can be expanded or curtailed, as can joint military or political actions. Trade relations have occasionally been curtailed. Very rarely, diplomatic relations may be broken. The use of material means of persuasion and coercion, however, is often problematic. As a result, there has been a general move away from most (but not all) sanctions over the past two decades.

Cutting development assistance, assuming that it had previously been effectively employed, perversely punishes people for being oppressed by their government. Major economic sanctions, although relatively rare, have also typically had such perverse results, particularly in the case of Iraq in the 1990s. (South Africa under apartheid is the one clear exception, in part because there was considerable support from the majority of the South African population for the sanctions but also because sanctions proved, in the end, not particularly punishing.)

There has thus been a move toward "targeted sanctions." For example, rather than seek to block investment in a country, the overseas bank accounts of right-abusive foreign leaders and officials are targeted. In rare cases, though, such as Burma (Myanmar) and North Korea, where a brutal government has insinuated itself in all areas of the economy and society, suspending all but the most narrowly defined humanitarian aid may prove the right course, all things considered.

But even—or, rather, especially—in these cases, the coercive power of sanctions is limited. Where human rights violations are so severe and systematic that comprehensive material sanctions seem appropriate, perhaps even demanded, they are unlikely to have much effect. Governments like Burma and North Korea need little from the outside world—because they are willing to make their people suffer the consequences of being denied access to external resources. Comprehensive sanctions thus are likely to have little direct or immediate impact.

Nonetheless, to most human rights advocates, sanctions often still seem the appropriate course of action, even though they have little prospect of altering the behavior of the target government. This raises the important question of what we expect international human rights policies to achieve.

3. THE AIMS AND EFFECTS
OF HUMAN RIGHTS POLICIES

The most obvious aim of international human rights policies and initiatives is to improve the human rights practices of the targeted government. This is indeed an important objective. But it is not the only aim. In fact, as the discussion of comprehensive sanctions has suggested, sometimes it is not even the principal purpose.

International human rights policies that do not eliminate or even reduce the violations directly addressed may nonetheless be important in preventing further deterioration or deterring similar future violations. States may be reluctant to appear to be bowing to external pressure. That pressure, though, may be factored into calculations in the future, especially if there is a reasonable prospect that it will be repeated. This seems to have occurred in the 1980s in El Salvador. It did not eliminate violations, but it seems to have moderated them.

Human rights initiatives that bring no direct change in a government's practices may nonetheless have positive effects by supporting local human rights advocates or delegitimating repressive regimes. By subtly altering the local human rights environment that a rights-abusive regime faces, human rights initiatives may have significant long-term effects. South Africa is a good example.

Altering the broader normative environment is another possible impact for international human rights policies. For example, sanctions imposed in the late 1970s and 1980s on governments in Central America and South America usually had little impact on the behavior of the target governments. Nonetheless, they were crucial elements in altering international expectations and giving new force to the norms of the Universal Declaration and other international instruments. Some of the most striking differences between cold war and post–cold war international human rights politics owe as much to these normative change as to changes in the global balance of power.

In addition, actions directed against country A may have an impact on country B. Knowing that one is likely to be subject to international pressure, because pressure has been applied elsewhere in a comparable case, may have a deterrent effect. This is especially true when the violations are not seen as crucial to the survival or prosperity of the regime—that is, when they are more of a "convenience"—against which the inconvenience of international pressure needs to be weighed—or a practice that is preferred, "all other things being equal," and international pressure makes other things no longer equal.

Actions with no direct effect on the "target" county may also alter the direction of foreign policy in the "sending" state. For example, the initial Carter decision to suspend aid to Guatemala in 1977 established a precedent that influenced policy in a number of later cases in the Americas and elsewhere.

International human rights policies may also be undertaken primarily to satisfy domestic constituencies. There certainly is something troubling in the notion of a "successful" policy that satisfies national political constituencies while having no international effect. If that is what it is designed to do, though, that reality must be acknowledged. For example, periodic changes in American support to the United Nations Fund for Population Activities seem driven mostly by the abortion debate in the United States.

We can also note that international human rights policies may have punitive effects even when they have no remedial effect. Making the lives of human rights violators less pleasant is a good thing, even if it does not improve the lives of their present or future victims.

Even where there is no discernible direct impact—immediately or in the future, remedial or punitive, in the direct target or in other countries engaging in similar violations—there may be a diffuse impact. International human rights policies reinforce and help to further disseminate international human rights norms. Over time, the cumulative effect of policies that reiterate both the substance and the binding nature of international human rights norms may subtly but significantly change the context of national or international action. In the most optimistic scenario, new generations of leaders and citizens may, as a result of regular and aggressive international human rights policies, internalize human rights norms to a much greater extent than their predecessors.

Finally, even if we have reason to believe that our policies will have no discernible impact on the world, they may nonetheless be appropriately undertaken simply because they are right. Our values demand that we act on them simply because they are our values. Taking a stand is something that we owe ourselves, and those who share our values.

4. FOREIGN POLICY AND HUMAN RIGHTS POLICY

Issues of trade-offs and (in)consistency are regularly raised in discussions of international human rights policies. Some human rights advocates are uncomfortable with—even critical of—the idea that human rights are often balanced against competing foreign policy. Human rights advocates are also often critical of "inconsistent" policies that treat comparable human rights violations in different countries differently.

Such criticisms fail to take seriously the idea that human rights are but one of many interests pursued in foreign policy. Human rights interests *should* be balanced against other national interests—which sometimes appropriately take priority. And states in their foreign policy should aim for *foreign policy* consistency, even if that means treating similar human rights violations differently.

Moralists may see the demands of human rights as categorical. Foreign policy decision makers, though, are not independent moral actors. Their job is not to realize personal, national, or global moral values but to pursue the national interest of their country. They are officeholders, with professional and ethical responsibilities to discharge the particular duties of their office.

There certainly are moral and legal constraints on the pursuit of the national interest. But the principal aim of national foreign policy is the national interest. The national interest includes many objectives. And those varied interests regularly conflict and thus must be balanced against one another.

Many countries today include fostering the international realization of human rights in their definition of the national interest. But the national interest—and thus the goals of foreign policy—are not reducible to human rights. The issue then is not whether human rights are appropriately balanced against other objectives of foreign policy—there is no viable alternative to such balancing—but the weights assigned to the values being balanced.

The foreign policies of most states can, in a highly stylized fashion, be said to include security, economic, and "other" goals. Most states tend to rank these classes of goals in roughly this order. But there are also gradations within each category. High-order security interests usually take priority over all other objectives of foreign policy, including human rights. And there is nothing wrong with that *as a matter of national foreign policy*. Low-level security interests, however, often are, appropriately, sacrificed to major economic or other, including human rights, concerns. And this too is entirely appropriate.

Setting priorities among various national interests is an essential part of the process of defining the national interest. International human rights law leaves states considerable latitude with respect to the weight they attach to human rights objectives in their foreign policy. There is no requirement that they include international human rights goals. But states are free to use the full range of foreign policy instruments, short of force, on behalf of international human rights objectives.

For those states that have included international human rights in their foreign policies, however, we can reasonably demand that human rights actually enter into calculations balancing competing interests, with a weight that roughly matches their stated place in the hierarchy of national interests. Two tests are particularly appropriate and revealing. If human rights objectives are pursued with "friends" and well as "enemies" and particular human rights policies cause problems in other areas of ongoing relations, there is at least prima facie evidence that human rights really are being taken seriously in a country's foreign policy.

People may reasonably disagree over whether a state has appropriately ranked its international human rights objectives or is doing enough on their behalf. At minimum, though, we should insist that pursuing human rights objectives should sometimes be inconvenient, even costly—as the pursuit of security and economic objectives regularly is. Otherwise, human rights are not really a part of foreign policy, but a moral add-on after the "real" foreign policy decisions have been made—which was the typical situation before the transformation of foreign policies, noted above, that took place in the 1970s, 1980s, and 1990s.

There certainly is something morally disquieting about subordinating international human rights objectives to even national security objectives, let alone economic objectives of foreign policy. But often this is the right thing to do, all things considered, *as a matter of national foreign policy.* Critics may reasonably argue for moving international human rights objects up on the list of national foreign policy priorities. In the foreseeable future, though, there is no prospect that they will reach the pinnacle, let alone occupy that pinnacle alone. The national interest and the "human interest" represented by universal human rights cannot be expected to coincide—although we can reasonably work to bring them closer together.

Issues of consistency do have a special force in moral reasoning. In fact, as the "golden rule" suggests, morality in significant measure means not making an exception for oneself (or those one is allied with). But even from a purely moral point of view, only comparable human rights violations require comparable responses. Human rights may be "interdependent and indivisible." That does not, however, require an identical response to every comparable violation of each right.

Even from a purely moral point of view, considerations of cost may be relevant. Few would consider the United States to be morally bound, all things considered, to risk nuclear war in order to remedy human rights violations in China simply because we acted strongly to remedy similar violations in, say, Guatemala. Conversely, the fact that no state is willing to threaten the use of force to free Tibet from Chinese domination, and thus risk nuclear war, does not mean that considerations of moral consistency should have precluded the use of force in, say, East Timor. Balancing competing values *requires* taking account of all the values involved. And consistency requires treating like cases alike, *all things considered,* not just looking at human rights violations.

We should thus not bemoan trade-offs of human rights to other foreign policy interests—any more than we bemoan the sacrifice of economic interests to human rights interests—so long as these trade-offs properly reflect reasonable assessments of the value of the interests at stake. And we should not criticize as inconsistent treating comparable human rights violations differently—any more than we bemoan pursuing comparable international economic interests more aggressively in some countries than in others—so long as the differences reflect a reasonable balancing of the full range of national interests at stake in the particular cases.

Hypocrisy, however, is a completely different matter. When subordinating international human rights objectives cannot reasonably be justified in terms of previously established foreign policy priorities, we have not a defensible foreign policy trade-off but an unjustifiable sacrifice of human rights interests. And if human rights almost always lose out in a contest with almost any other foreign policy objective, we have concrete evidence of a very low effective evaluation of the significance of a country's international human rights objectives. (The problem here, though, is not inconsistency. Rather, the complaint is that the state in question consistently gives inadequate weight or attention to international human rights objectives.)

I have drawn the distinction between morality and foreign policy overly sharply. In countries with international human rights policies, human rights are matters of both moral and national interest. Moral inconsistency thus does pose problems for foreign policy—although again, hypocrisy seems more the problem than inconsistency. And such cases should not be confused with a policy that carefully balances human rights against other national interests. Such a policy is not likely to undermine seriously the moral value of human rights. In fact, by identifying clearly just what place human rights have in a nation's foreign policy, such reasoned trade-offs may provoke discussions that lead to increasing the relative place of human rights in a nation's foreign policy.

It is too easy to simply say, "We value human rights in our foreign policy." The important question is what place they have in foreign policy. *How much* are human rights valued, both intrinsically and relative to other national interests? And how seriously are those values in fact taken in the practice of foreign policy?

Many states have made substantial progress toward a more serious incorporation of human rights into their foreign policy. Most if not all, though, could readily do more. We cannot be satisfied with the fact that compared to thirty years ago, most democratic states today have more aggressive and more effective international human rights policies. The moral demands of human rights continue to push for a deeper penetration of human rights into national foreign policy and a greater willingness to take full advantage of the space available for the pursuit of international human rights objectives.

DISCUSSION QUESTIONS

1. What do you think of the distinction drawn in the chapter between human rights policy consistency and foreign policy consistency? Is it really appropriate to treat similar human rights situations differently because of other foreign policy interests? How does your answer to this question change if you adopt the perspectives of, say, a foreign policy decision maker, a human rights advocate, a concerned citizen of your own country, or someone who sees herself as a citizen of the world?

2. How can one justify trading off human rights? Are human rights really the kind of thing that is appropriately balanced against, say, the economic interests of corporations? How do your answers vary when the human rights in question are those of your fellow citizens versus those of foreign citizens?

3. Can a viable international human rights policy be constructed by responding to violations according to the principles of severity, trends, responsibility, and efficacy? Are all of these criteria of equal weight? Are there other principles that are no less important?

SUGGESTED READINGS

Very little has been written separately on the general question of human rights and foreign policy—although many of the suggested readings in the preceding chapter address the issue. Perhaps the best general discussion is Peter R. Baehr and Monique Castermans-Holleman, *The Role of Human Rights in Foreign Policy,* 3rd ed. (New York: Palgrave Macmillan, 2004). And two pamphlets from the late 1970s remain well worth reading, even if here examples are dated. Evan Luard, *Human Rights and Foreign Policy* (Oxford: Pergamon Press, 1981), provides a good short introductory discussion, with an especially thorough presentation of the means available for use on behalf of human rights. An abbreviated version of this essay is available in Richard Pierre Claude and Burns H. Weston, eds., *Human Rights in the World Community* (Philadelphia: University of Pennsylvania Press, 1992). And Hans Morgenthau's *Human Rights and Foreign Policy* (New York: Council on Religion and International Affairs, 1979) offers a classic statement of the realist perspective.

10

Transnational Human Rights Advocacy

We now turn to the final major type of international human rights actor, transnational actors, understood as "private" actors (that is, not states or multilateral organizations) that operate across state borders. Among the diverse array of private actors, we will be concerned with nongovernmental organizations, that is, private, noncommercial groups with an issue-specific mandate. More precisely, we will be concerned with transnational or international nongovernmental organizations (INGOs), that is, NGOs that operate internationally. The Problem for this chapter, however, addresses the human rights responsibilities of businesses.

About three hundred transnational NGOs define themselves as human rights organizations. These will be our principal focus here. There are also, however, thousands of INGOs that define themselves in other terms but engage centrally in human rights programming and advocacy. For example, most of the large development-assistance and disaster-relief organizations today explicitly use the language of human rights to describe parts of their missions. In addition, tens of thousands of national NGOs deal centrally with human rights.

There are two principal types of self-identified human rights INGOs. Some, like Amnesty International, Human Rights Watch, and the International Federation for Human Rights, address human rights generally (although as a practical matter, they tend to have particular areas of special concern). Others focus explicitly on a subset of internationally recognized human rights, or even a single right. Prominent examples include Minority Rights Group, Anti-Slavery International, and Article 19 (which addresses freedom of expression, taking its name from the provision in the Universal Declaration).

Rather than discuss transnational human rights advocacy generally, though, the first half of the chapter presents two brief case studies, Amnesty International and Human Rights Watch. This focus on two cases arises in part from the great diversity of transnational human rights NGOs, which makes it difficult to talk about transnational action in general and almost impossible to provide anything even close to a comprehensive survey. This also partly explains the relative brevity of this chapter. But it also reflects a substantive judgment that states remain the decisive actors in both the national and the international politics of human rights. This is not meant to denigrate the activities or accomplishments of NGOs. Quite the contrary. Their role is often crucial, as I have argued in the cases of the Southern Cone and South Africa.

1. AMNESTY INTERNATIONAL

Amnesty International is in many ways *the* emblematic transnational human rights NGO.[1] To many people, especially in the West, human rights advocacy means, roughly, the kinds of things that Amnesty does. This is an unfortunately narrow understanding. There are many internationally recognized human rights that AI does not address systematically. Furthermore, there are many forms of action, including direct advocacy in foreign countries, that are not part of AI's repertoire. Nonetheless, Amnesty International is indeed one of the most important actors in the global human rights regime.

AI was founded in 1961 by British lawyer Peter Berenson, to draw attention to the plight of "prisoners of conscience"—individuals detained because of their political, religious, or other beliefs—across the globe. Individual prisoners were identified and verified by the organization, which both sought to publicize their plight centrally and organized local chapters to "adopt" them—typically in clusters of three, one each from the capitalist, socialist, and nonaligned worlds—and advocate on their behalf, typically through letter-writing campaigns addressed to officials of the government holding the prisoner.

In the 1970s, Amnesty refined its strategy of aggressive but nonpartisan public advocacy with effective behind-the-scenes lobbying, both nationally and internationally. In 1973, it began its campaign of Urgent Action appeals. Torture (and later abolition of the death penalty) became a special focus. AI played a major role in securing the adoption of the 1975 Declaration on the Protection of All Persons from Being Subjected to Torture and Other Cruel, Inhuman, or Degrading Treatment or Punishment, a decisive step on the way to the 1984 Convention Against Torture. In 1977, it was awarded the Nobel Peace Prize (following the award in 1974 to Sean McBride, the chair of AI's International Executive Committee from 1961 to 1975, for his lifetime of work on behalf of human rights). By 1979, Amnesty International had a global membership of two hundred thousand (up from fifteen thousand a decade earlier).

In the 1980s, Amnesty continued to grow and to penetrate the public consciousness. Emblematic were the series of high-profile fund-raising events that began in 1976 and took their title from the 1979 Secret Policeman's Ball. Begun by Monty Python member John Cleese and involving major stars such as Sting and Eric Clapton, they generated publicity for human rights advocacy among individuals that previously might not have had much interest in the topic. (Bono, the current king of celebrity campaigning for social justice, was in the audience at an early show, which he has identified as a major formative influence.)

With the end of the cold war, Amnesty continued to grow. Perhaps more important, it evolved into an organization with a somewhat broader focus. Today, in addition to the older work on prisoners of conscience, torture, and the death penalty, the organization works on the rights of disadvantaged groups, especially women, children, minorities, indigenous peoples, and refugees, and on eradicating poverty. AI has also devoted considerable attention and resources to expanding membership outside the Western world, symbolized by the fact that since 1992, its secretary-general, the chief executive officer of the organization, has been from the global South (Pierre Sané of Senegal, 1992–2001; Irene Khan of Bangladesh, 2001–2010; and Salil Shetty of India, 2010–).

In early 2011, AI had 2.8 million registered supporters in more than 140 countries, organized into more than fifty country "sections" and a number of "structures" (which are essentially aspiring sections). The highest authority of the organization is the International Council, which meets every two years. Its equivalent of a board of directors is the International Executive Committee, which meets twice a year. An International Secretariat of more than five hundred professionals carries out work in several areas, focused on research, campaigning, communications, and international law and organization. In 2009–2010, it spent approximately £45 million on its various activities.

In addition to the central office in London, AI has fifty international offices, including five in Latin America, six in Asia, six in sub-Saharan Africa, and four in the Middle East and North Africa (Algeria, Israel, Morocco, Tunisia). In early 2011, it was in the midst of six major global campaigns: Demand Dignity (focusing on poverty rooted in injustice and exclusion), Abolish the Death Penalty, Stop Violence Against Women, Counter Terror with Justice, Control Arms (focusing on the global arms trade), and Demand the "Three Freedoms" for Myanmar (focusing on freedom of expression, peaceful assembly, freedom of association, and the plight of prisoners of conscience as well as targeting Burma's ASEAN partners). And in the month of December 2011, AI issued appeals for urgent action on behalf of individuals in Bahrain, Belarus, Chad, China, Colombia, Cuba, El Salvador, Guatemala, Honduras, India, the Maldives, Mexico, Morocco, Russia, Saudi Arabia, Sri Lanka, Sudan, Syria, Turkey, Ukraine, United Arab Emirates, and Zimbabwe and reports or public statements on forced labor in Nepal, mistreatment of Roma in Romania, a decade of US abuses at Guantánamo, the death penalty in Iran, Rwandan refugees in Uganda, Iranian refugees in Iraq, and political repression in the name of security in Saudi Arabia.

2. HUMAN RIGHTS WATCH

Human Rights Watch (HRW) is more than a decade younger than Amnesty International and not a mass-membership organization. Based in New York, its roots are in Helsinki Watch, a group formed in the United States in 1978 to monitor compliance with the 1975 Helsinki Final Act, which included human rights commitments by the countries of Europe on both sides of the Iron Curtain (plus the United States and Canada). Similar watch committees were created in a number of other countries. (They coordinated their actions in the International Helsinki Federation for Human Rights, beginning with eight members in 1982 and growing to forty-four members in 2007, when it was forced to dissolve because of the embezzlement by its former financial manager.) In the United States, however, the Helsinki model was replicated in other regional watch groups— Americas Watch, founded in 1981; Asia Watch (1985); Africa Watch (1988); and Middle East Watch (1989)—which were united under the umbrella of Human Rights Watch in 1988.

HRW carries out research, issues reports (on particular countries and particular topics as well as a respected annual report), and engages in public campaigning and political lobbying. HRW has always had a broader focus than Amnesty International—although with *much* greater attention to civil and political rights than economic, social, and cultural rights. In the 1990s, it significantly expanded its scope to include violations of the laws of war and individual criminal responsibility for war crimes and genocide. (In 1997 it shared the Nobel Peace Prize as a founding member of the Campaign to Ban Landmines.) Over the past decade, it has also focused considerable attention on human rights violations associated with antiterrorism policies and practices and has begun to address economic and social rights seriously, especially rights to health, education, and housing.

For the fiscal year ending June 30, 2011, HRW raised $136 million from contributions, grants, and special projects. In financial terms, its ten principal programs focused on Africa ($5.9 million), Asia ($4.6 million), Europe and Central Asia ($4.1 million), Middle East and North Africa ($3.1 million), Women's Rights ($2.1 million), Health and Human Rights ($2 million), Children's Rights ($1.6 million), International Justice ($1.3 million), the Americas ($1.3 million), and the United States ($1.1 million). (Expenditures on other programs totaled $11.4 million.) These figures represent a major increase over earlier years, in large part as a result of George Soros's $100 million donation to HRW in 2010 (to be disbursed over ten years).

Illustrative of the range of its activities, Human Rights Watch in the last two months of 2010 issued reports on legal reform in Tunisia; crimes against humanity in Syria; immigration law in the American state of Alabama; attacks on lawyers in Ukraine; postelection violence in Kenya; child marriage in Yemen; child labor in gold mining in Mali; violence against lesbians and transgender people in South Africa; impunity for war criminals in Nepal; violence against protesters in Homs, Syria; killing, torture, and disappearances in Mexico's war on drugs; and labor abuses in Chinese state-owned mines in Zambia. As this list suggests, Human Rights Watch understands human rights rather broadly, including not only the established body of international human rights law but also additional rights (particularly protection against discrimination on the basis of sexual orientation or gender identity) and violations of the laws of war and other harm to civilians in armed conflicts.

3. NONPARTISAN ACTION

Human Rights Watch is unusually independent and aggressive in its actions. It thus provides a focus for a broader discussion of bias and legitimacy in the actions of human rights NGOs.

Like other transnational human rights NGOs, the work of HRW is dependent on its ability to obtain and verify reliable information about violations. Its reporting and advocacy thus are shaped not simply by the severity of violations in a country but by its ability to work in that country (or to obtain reliable information from individuals with recent firsthand local knowledge). In addition, as an advocacy organization, it has a special interest in addressing situations where its work may bring concrete results—not to the exclusion of countries where short-term changes are unlikely or even inconceivable, but with special attention to countries that are open or vulnerable to the pressures of publicity. And HRW, like all human rights NGOs, has issues of special organizational concern.

As a result of these political realities, HRW, like all other advocacy groups, has been accused of bias. But rather than factual errors in its reports—which, of course, do occur occasionally (but very rarely)—such complaints typically involve claims, usually by the targeted governments and their partisans, that other countries with equally bad or worse records are not comparably targeted or that the violations identified are somehow "justified" in the case in question.

During the cold war, such complaints were the staple of Communist Party state dictatorships and military dictatorships of both the Right and the Left. Today, when a Robert Mugabe in Zambia or an Alexander Lukashenko in Belarus makes such complaints, they are largely ignored. But particularly in the United States, Human Rights Watch has in recent years been a special target of defenders of Israel's antiterrorism policies and its policies in the Occupied Palestinian Territories. The ensuing debates provide a useful lens on the nature of nonpartisan human rights advocacy.

Nonpartisan does not mean nonpolitical. In fact, human rights advocacy is and must be intensely political. It is principally about how a state treats its own nationals (and others over whom it exercises legal jurisdiction). Demands to stop human rights violations are demands for changes in legal and political practices. When violations are severe and systematic, human rights advocacy in effect demands that a regime either fundamentally transform its character or put itself out of business.

The vital question, then, is whether (political) advocacy for human rights is carried out in a nonpartisan fashion, that is, in a way that is not based on or intended to promote any particular party, person, or cause (other than human rights). Human rights advocates might properly be called partisans for human rights. They claim, though, to pursue their activities in an otherwise nonpartisan fashion. And nonpartisan action is central to the legitimacy and the power of NGO advocates in particular, who have few resources on their side other than their single-minded commitment to human rights.

Let us grant, for the sake of argument, the accuracy of the principal complaints of the "friends of Israel" who condemn Human Rights Watch, that many other regimes with human rights records comparable to and even much worse than Israel's—including most of Israel's enemies—have not been comparably criticized.[2] Let us also acknowledge that the government of Israel claims that many of the practices for which it receives international criticism are undertaken in the name of antiterrorism (which was central to Israeli policy decades before 9/11). But criticisms of inaccuracy are largely unjustified. (While reasonable people may disagree about the reliability of particular sources, virtually every particular claim is sourced, and despite extensive efforts to debunk HRW's reporting, only rare and isolated errors have been identified, most of which have been connected with difficulties in gathering and verifying information imposed by the Israeli government and its military.) And nothing in these facts indicates partisanship in HRW's criticism of Israeli human rights practices.

A few governments engage in human rights violations that they do not seek to justify in any serious fashion. Most, though, claim a higher purpose that justifies "unfortunate" sacrifices being imposed on individuals and groups in their society. Whether such arguments are persuasive is, ironically, a political question—and usually an inescapably partisan one. Human rights advocates self-consciously refuse to engage such issues of partisan politics. Rather, they decry the violations, independent of any and all alleged justifications.

Human rights advocates do not look at all sides of a partisan political conflict. Such "balanced" or "evenhanded" approaches may be appropriate for others. But the job of human rights NGOs is to focus narrowly and single-mindedly on human rights. Period. And that focus is essential to nonpartisan action. If there is a legitimate justification, the government in question can present that to its people, its friends and allies, and the international community.

There is a danger, certainly, of selecting (otherwise legitimate) targets of criticism on partisan criteria. In the case of Human Rights Watch, however, there is no evidence of such partisanship. Its reach is truly global, as reflected not only in its annual report but also in the list of recent reports above. And its work on Israel falls well within its regional and substantive mandates. Furthermore, its extensive work on human rights in the United States, where it is based, shows an admirable willingness to look at human rights violations at home, not only abroad. (The US section of Amnesty International similarly targets American domestic human rights practices—much to the chagrin of many Americans.)

HRW's work on gay, lesbian, bisexual, and transgender rights actually raises more questions about partisanship. (Compare Problem 3.) Such rights are *not* part of established international human rights law. Therefore, targets may respond, with a certain degree of plausibility, that they are being held to standards that neither they in particular nor the international community in general has endorsed. This, for example, has been the response of Iran (when its president and other officials have not foolishly denied the existence of homosexuals in Iran).

This brings us back to the central contribution of the Universal Declaration to human rights advocates, namely, providing almost universally agreed-upon standards of international human rights. NGOs that stay within the substantive scope of the Universal Declaration are protected against charges of partisanship (on the grounds of the substance of their concerns). Those who go beyond settled international human rights law do risk (not il)legitimate charges of attempting to "impose their values" on others. Although the charge of imposition is ludicrous, given that the only power being exercised is that of publicity, advocacy on behalf of disputed values is very different from advocacy on behalf of settled principles of international human rights law.

4. NGO LEGITIMACY

This discussion raises the broad issue of the legitimacy of NGOs and their advocacy. To put it bluntly, who authorized NGOs?

The simple answer is international human rights law. Human rights NGOs, in their typical work of reporting and advocacy, merely draw attention to practices that are, at least on their face, inconsistent with uncontroversial principles of international law. Furthermore, they are simply engaging in the collective exercise of the rights of freedom of expression of their members. Target governments may persecute such organizations and activities in their own territories—they may even criminalize them—but that is simply an expression of the problem to which human rights NGOs are drawing attention.

Yet the picture is not quite that simple. As noted above, human rights advocacy is intensely political. And when external actors criticize governments that have considerable local political legitimacy, the issue of NGO legitimacy may be more than just a smoke screen behind which vicious governments seek to hide.

Here nonpartisanship becomes essential. International human rights law has considerable international, transnational, and national legitimacy in the contemporary world. So long as human rights INGOs operate in a nonpartisan fashion within the confines and on behalf of established international human rights principles, they partake of that legitimacy—particularly when, as is usually the case, their activity is focused on publicizing evidence of violations.

The legitimacy of external actors is further enhanced when their advocacy parallels or supports that of national actors. In democratic and other relatively open regimes, the existence of genuinely nonpartisan local human rights NGOs making parallel arguments enhances the legitimacy of international actors. And where levels of repression do not allow space for local human rights NGOs, indirect evidence that international actors are supporting local advocates serves a similar role.

Human rights INGOs are important and legitimate actors in the global human rights regime. They lack the legal and political authority of states and the international legal authority of multilateral actors. As advocates, however, they have the moral and legal authority of international human rights law behind them. And as long as they engage in truly nonpartisan action within their mandate, they are not merely legitimate but important members of the international community.

PROBLEM 5: HUMAN RIGHTS
OBLIGATIONS OF MNCs

The Problem

Multinational corporations (MNCs) have become immensely powerful actors that are becoming increasingly global in character (not simply multi- or international). Doesn't it make sense, then, to impose direct human rights obligations on MNCs? Why should their immense and growing economic power not be matched with direct human rights responsibilities? Isn't this especially the case because their globalization has restricted the ability of welfare states to provide economic and social rights for their citizens?

A Solution

Such a change would involve fundamentally altering the existing system of national implementation of international human rights. Globalization does pose serious problems for this system, as we will discuss in some detail in Chapter 14. Imposing special direct human rights responsibilities for MNCs, however, is the wrong solution.

Recall the distinction drawn in Chapter 2 between duties not to deprive, duties to protect from deprivation, and duties to provide. *All* social actors, including MNCs, have duties not to deprive. But I can see no reason MNCs should have *special* duties.

It might be argued that MNCs are specially situated to deprive and therefore should be specially obliged. But is that true? Is there any evidence, for example, that *multinational* corporations are worse for human rights than local corporations? Whether we consider wages, working conditions, or environmental practices, local firms can be, and often are, at least as bad as their multinational colleagues. And multinational firms that produce branded goods, because of their relatively high profit margins, often are able to provide better conditions for their workers and neighbors than local commodity producers. (Nike can afford to pay more than manufacturers of house-brand sneakers.) In fact, protecting the value of their brand may demand not merely meeting but exceeding local norms.

This might suggest, though, special human rights not to deprive for *all* firms. But we already do that, in the form of health and safety regulations, minimum-wage legislation, and environmental rules. And there is no special reason to single out commercial firms. Nonprofit organizations, for example, should not be held to lower standards on working conditions or wages. Private individuals have no more of a right to pollute than corporations.

Corporations, both local and foreign, often do use their power in harmful ways, both directly harming their workers and communities and through their influence of local and national governments. The solutions to such problems, however, are standard legal and political solutions, not new human rights duties.

Turning to duties to protect and to provide, direct human rights obligations for corporations, whether national or multinational, are even more problematic. Do we really want corporations protecting our rights? As private, profit-making enterprises, they would seem to be particularly poorly suited to carrying out such duties. Even in their areas of operation, self-regulation is likely to be a recipe for disaster. Some states might be overly exuberant, misguided, or inept in their exercise of their duties to protect. But there is no reason to suspect that firms would systematically do a better job.

As for duties to provide, the best that can be said is that some states may reasonably choose to rely on corporate provision for some economic and social rights. But the reliance of the United States on employer-provided health insurance is hardly a promising model. And the Japanese system of firm-based provision, which worked well in the 1960s, 1970s, and 1980s, has come under considerable strain. Furthermore, even where firms are the first line of provision, states are ultimately responsible.

Nothing I have said is an argument against aggressive efforts at corporate social responsibility. There may even be very good reasons for states to legislate greater corporate social responsibility (for both local and foreign firms). But these are matters of social justice, not human rights duties—which returns us to another central theme from Chapter 2, namely, that not all good things are a matter of human rights.

There may even be good reasons for developing global or regional codes of conduct for MNCs. But it is hardly unproblematic to argue that foreign firms should be held to higher standards than local firms. And although there may be very good reasons for countries to impose certain standards on the international operations of "their" firms—the United States has long done this through the Foreign Corrupt Practices Act, originally adopted in 1977—this would be a matter of social justice and public policy, not a new system for implementing human rights. And we should not overlook the theoretical problem of extraterritorial jurisdiction (however attractive we may find it in this particular case).

Further Problems

Privatization of government functions has been a major area of discussion—in different ways in different regions—for the past few decades. Is there any reason to believe that profit-making businesses are better able to provide human rights than states? Which kinds of rights? What about nonprofit organizations?

Now ask the same questions about *protecting* human rights.

Is the mix between state and nonstate provision one of those areas where we should not merely expect but positively value international variations based on local culture, history, and politics? What, though, are the limits on designing a system of provision that makes unusually heavy use of "private" provision by corporations and not-for-profit providers?

DISCUSSION QUESTIONS

1. Have human rights INGOs been given adequate attention here? States may ultimately make the final decisions. But are their decisions sufficiently influenced by NGOs that NGOs deserve more attention?
2. Is the conventional distinction between human rights NGOs and "development" organizations desirable? Is it defensible? Does it subtly denigrate economic and social rights? Or is there an important distinction to be drawn between advocating for the substance of rights and advocating for rights? (For example, is working on getting people more food necessarily work on the *right* to food?)
3. Is there a better way for NGOs to achieve international legitimacy? Is the issue of legitimacy a truly serious one or primarily a diversion raised by the targets of transnational advocacy?
4. Grant that human rights INGOs have a certain kind of legitimacy. So do states, though. How should we deal with the resulting conflicts? Are there good general rules? Or does it depend on the particular NGO and the particular state?
5. The distinction between *political* and *partisan* that I have drawn may be clear in theory. Is it so clear in practice? How can action addressed against a government really be nonpartisan? Are there multiple senses of *nonpartisan* operating in such discussions?

SUGGESTED READINGS

Chapter 7 of David P. Forsythe, *Human Rights in International Relations,* 2nd ed. (Cambridge: Cambridge University Press, 2006), addresses human rights NGOs. It is a natural place to go first after this chapter. Peter R. Baehr, *Non-governmental Human Rights Organizations in International Relations* (New York: Palgrave Macmillan, 2009), provides a comprehensive analytical survey.

Stephen Hopgood, *Keepers of the Flame: Understanding Amnesty International* (Ithaca, NY: Cornell University Press, 2006), offers an excellent analysis of AI that, although deeply sympathetic to the work of the organization, is often critical of its practice. Ann Marie Clark, *Diplomacy of Conscience: Amnesty International and Changing Human Rights Norms* (Princeton, NJ: Princeton University Press, 2001), is also a valuable study of this iconic organization. William F. Schulz, *In Our Own Best Interest: How Defending Human Rights Benefits Us All* (Boston: Beacon Press, 2001), is an impassioned argument by a longtime advocate.

Philip Alston, ed., *Non-state Actors and Human Rights* (Oxford: Oxford University Press, 2005), and George Andreopoulos, Zehra F. Kabasakal Arat, and Peter Juviler, eds., *Non-state Actors in the Human Rights Universe* (Bloomfield, CT: Kumarian Press, 2006), are the best broad scholarly studies. Although somewhat dated, Claude E. Welch Jr., ed., *NGOs and Human Rights: Promise and Performance* (Philadelphia: University of Pennsylvania Press, 2001), is still worth consulting.

NGO activism, however, is not without its problems. David Kennedy, *The Dark Sides of Virtue: Reassessing International Humanitarianism* (Princeton, NJ: Princeton University Press, 2004), is a brilliant analysis of the pitfalls of advocacy that matches its potent criticisms with a genuine sympathy and commitment to a more just and humane world. Michael Ignatieff's *Human Rights as Politics and Idolatry* (Princeton, NJ: Princeton University Press, 2001) offers a powerful warning about the dangers of excessive self-righteousness and rigidity, again from the perspective of a sympathetic scholar-activist.

11

—◇—

Comparing International Actors and Evaluating International Action

This very brief chapter pulls together the material considered in Part 2. It compares the strengths and weaknesses of multilateral, bilateral, and transnational actors and offers a brief summary evaluation of international action as a whole.

1. COMPARING INTERNATIONAL ACTORS

Multilateral, bilateral, and transnational actors each have certain comparative advantages—and disadvantages. We can assess these with a simple framework in which "power" is understood as a matter of legal authority, material resources, and nonmaterial resources (especially moral authority and prestige).

As a rough first approximation, we can say that multilateral actors have moderately high authority, very modest material resources, and moderately high nonmaterial resources. International and regional organizations that address human rights have charters that give them international legal standing. Furthermore, as organizations whose members are sovereign states, their actions are the collective actions of the member states. The material resources at their disposal to act on behalf of human rights, however, are few and largely restricted to the activities of a relatively small professional staff. Multilateral human rights actors lack both carrots and sticks, that is, money and other material resources that they can dispense to encourage improved levels of compliance. Nonetheless, their legal authority and their record of relatively nonpartisan action give their words a certain weight.

Bilateral actors have relatively low levels of international legal authority. States are, of course, free to express their views and advocate for their interests on all matters of legitimate international concern, including human rights. But foreign states have no special authority as human rights advocates. And the fact that

161

national foreign policy fundamentally involves the pursuit of national interests casts a certain suspicion on bilateral human rights advocacy.

States, however, usually have more in the way of material resources that they can devote to their human rights initiatives. This is particularly true when a state decides to link other goals and instruments of national foreign policy to the human rights practices of its partners. Furthermore, acting on behalf of internationally recognized human rights provides a certain kind of moral authority, especially when international human rights initiatives are sustained over time and when they sometimes take priority over the pursuit of other international actors.

Transnational human rights NGOs, as we saw at the end of the preceding chapter, have no independent international legal authority. They also lack material resources. (Development NGOs, which do have direct or indirect control over considerable sums of money, because of their humanitarian missions typically do not manipulate these resources—in particular, they do not threaten to withhold humanitarian aid—in order to seek to improve human rights practices.) The prestige and moral authority of human rights NGOs, however, often are extremely high, especially for organizations that have a long record of aggressive nonpartisan advocacy. And NGOs are largely independent of the constraints of competing state interests, which limit the range and intensity of international action by states and international organizations.

There is thus a certain complementarity to these three modes of international action. Each type of actor has unique resources at its disposal. Where concerted action is possible, these resources may be combined in ways that make the resulting coordinated action more than the sum of its parts. And when international actors can link up with local partners—as it were, pressuring states from above and below—even more may be possible.

In the end, though, international actors, with a few limited exceptions (most notably the European Court and the UN Security Council), are largely restricted to encouraging the national implementation of international human rights. The material and moral resources at the disposal of international actors, including powerful states, are primarily persuasive. In most instances, then, the international contribution, at least in the short run, is modest at best.

Occasionally, the balance of local forces may be such that international action can tip the scales decisively in favor of human rights. Most often, though, international action, at least immediately, offers more or less effective encouragement of incremental changes in national human rights practices. We should not underestimate the importance of such achievements—individually, cumulatively, and, perhaps most important, in their long-run impact on national and international political environments. Neither, though, should we overestimate their significance.

2. THE PRIORITY OF NATIONAL ACTION

Most human rights issues involve how a state treats its own citizens on its own territory. And the established system of national implementation of international human rights underscores that, in most instances, this is a matter of sovereign national jurisdiction. Human rights advocates, both national and international, may encourage, condemn, cajole, and plead. States, however, ultimately decide.

Furthermore, the long-term fate of human rights depends largely on the citizens whose rights are in question. External actors lack the capacity for the intensive monitoring that is ultimately necessary to make human rights secure. They also lack the immediate incentives that as a practical matter are necessary to engage in the sustained efforts, sometimes at great cost, to force states to respect human rights. And, in the end, external actors lack the power that ordinary citizens have to pressure their governments to respect and implement their international human rights obligations.

In the most repressive environments, external actors may have a decisive role in keeping the idea of human rights alive in national political discussions. In slightly less repressive situations, international actors may be able to provide vital support to isolated or fledgling local human rights advocates. In countries where the overall human rights situation ranges from not too bad to excellent, external actors can often achieve incremental changes in policies and may provide a useful, occasionally even vital, supplement to national actors.

In the end, though, it is up to a free people to defend their own rights. And if they don't do that, international action almost certainly will come to nothing. The fate of human rights ultimately depends on the willingness of right-holders—ordinary citizens, acting individually and collectively—to struggle for those rights. It is the responsibility of right-holders to use their rights, individually and collectively, to demand that their governments respect those rights. National human rights defenders and ordinary citizens hold the real power to realize human rights. Ultimately, they can and must make for themselves a society and a legal and political system where their human rights are respected, implemented, enforced, and enjoyed.

3. A SYSTEM OF INTERNATIONAL ACCOUNTABILITY

Nonetheless, international actors can provide a helping hand—which often is valuable and occasionally decisive. And, for all its limitations, the global human rights regime has created a real system of international accountability. This is a sharp contrast to the almost complete lack of systematic attention to human rights prior to 1945.

Although sovereign states retain a primary responsibility for implementing internationally recognized human rights in their territories, they no longer enjoy the protections of discreet diplomatic silence. Quite the contrary, persistent human rights violators increasingly must act in the light of embarrassing international publicity mobilized by national and international public and private groups. Global, regional, national, and transnational actors have created a web of pressures that makes it almost impossible today for states to avoid a public accounting of their human rights practices.

Although most of the current mechanisms of accountability rely principally on the power of public exposure and scrutiny, the value of publicizing violations and trying to shame states into better compliance should not be underestimated. Even vicious governments may care about their international reputations. For example, in the late 1970s and early 1980s, no less vile a government than the Argentine military regime devoted considerable diplomatic effort to thwart the investigations of the UN Commission on Human Rights. Furthermore, publicity often helps at least a few of the more prominent victims of repression.

The most important impact of all this (largely verbal) international human rights activity, however, probably lies less in its immediate achievements on behalf of victims than in the fact that national and international norms and expectations are being altered. The idea of human rights has a moral force and mobilizing power in the contemporary world that seem hard to resist. And as more and more citizens throughout the world come to think of themselves as endowed with inalienable rights, the demand for human rights continues to cause dictators to flee and their governments to crumble.

The sword often proves mightier than the word, at least in the short run. But the task of human rights advocates, wherever they may be, is the ancient and noble one of speaking the truth of justice to power. And far more often than so-called realists would ever allow, truth can triumph. We should not underestimate the power, especially in the long run, of calling the powerful to account—even in forums that on their face seem sadly, even painfully, weak.

PART THREE

Post–Cold War Issues and Cases

12

Responding to Human Rights Violations in China: Tiananmen and After

The year 1989 was a decisive turning point in modern history—and in the international struggle for human rights. The remarkably quick and bloodless collapse of the Soviet empire, symbolized most dramatically by the opening of the Berlin Wall and by Czechoslovakia's Velvet Revolution, combined with the steady progress of democratization in Latin America and accelerating liberalization in Africa and Asia, marked, if not the "new world order" many Americans trumpeted in the early 1990s, a new era for human rights.

June 4, 1989, however, saw one of the most striking violations of human rights in the past several decades, as Chinese tanks rolled through Tiananmen Square, crushing China's budding democracy movement, which to this day remains violently repressed. But responses to the Tiananmen massacre also reveal a significant maturing of international human rights action, which continued to develop positively throughout the 1990s.

1. CHINA'S DEMOCRACY MOVEMENT

Students have been the heart of China's democracy movement since its symbolic beginning on May 4, 1919, when three thousand students took to Tiananmen Square to protest concessions to Japan at the end of World War I. For more than a thousand years, China's governing elite was composed of Confucian scholar-bureaucrats recruited through a national system of competitive examinations. Beyond their ordinary duties, these officials had an extraordinary right, even obligation, of political remonstrance: in difficult times, they were expected to call on the emperor to live up to the standards of good government that justified his rule—

whether or not the emperor (and other officials) wanted to listen and whatever the personal cost to the remonstrator.

The emperor's authority was seen as resting on a mandate of heaven. Remonstrances recalled to the emperor the duties to his people that accompanied the heavenly grant of power. This provided limited checks and balances in a political system without formal separation of powers. Remonstrances allowed the people, through intellectuals acting as their representatives, to press for reform when they were no longer able to tolerate injustice but were unwilling to resort to riots and rebellions (a recurrent feature of Chinese politics, especially in hard economic times). Widespread protests by intellectuals have long been a recognized sign of political crisis in China. Student protests thus have unusually heavy cultural weight in China.

Human rights problems in contemporary China are rooted in the creation of the People's Republic of China on October 1, 1949, when Mao Zedong and his Chinese Communist Party (CCP) installed a classic Leninist party-state totalitarian regime. Under Communist Party rule, all aspects of life have been controlled by a centralized bureaucracy that enforces rigid conformity with ideological directives. Most internationally recognized civil and political rights are regularly and systematically violated. Remarkable progress has been made in some areas of economic and social rights, especially by abolishing feudal land tenure and social relations. But tens of millions of people died in famines that resulted from state policy decisions in the 1950s. And in recent decades, housing, health care, and social services have become increasingly problematic for the bottom quarter of the population.

The most frightening systematic human rights violations in contemporary China came during the Great Proletarian Cultural Revolution. On July 28, 1966, all universities and schools were closed. In August, the CCP called upon the masses to form cultural revolutionary groups to attack "rightist" elements that had taken a "capitalist road." "Red Guards" spread an arbitrary reign of political intimidation and terror, dispensing "socialist justice" for offenses as minor as a casual critical comment, insufficient revolutionary fervor, or simply because a friend or relative's former job had branded that person a "class enemy."

Many millions of people were accused—and thus almost automatically found guilty—of ideological offenses. At minimum, this meant demeaning forced "reeducation." Most also lost jobs, school places, and housing. Millions suffered forced internal exile or imprisonment, usually accompanied by physical abuse during detention. An unknown number of people were executed.

Repression in contemporary China, however, has been punctuated with interludes of political opening. For example, in May 1956, Mao called for letting a hundred flowers bloom—instead of the single path previously enforced by the CCP. But the party soon returned to its old ways, imprisoning many of the hundred-flowers intellectuals.

Serious public stirrings of a new democracy movement began in April 1976 with national demonstrations in memory of Zhou Enlai, one of the leaders of the Chinese Revolution and through much of the Mao era the second most powerful man in China. Although these demonstrations were violently repressed, Mao's own death in September 1976 touched off an intense power struggle. The result was a new political opening at the end of 1978.

In Beijing, public political debate took place in "big-character" posters on what came to be known as Democracy Wall. Particularly noteworthy was Wei Jingsheng's call for a "fifth modernization"—democracy—to complete the officially proclaimed modernizations in industry, science and technology, agriculture, and defense. Wei called on China to think of progress as involving more than just power and prosperity, to recognize important human and political dimensions beyond economic and military development. But the Democracy Wall movement, like the Hundred Flowers opening, was short-lived. Wei and other leading dissidents were sentenced to long prison terms in 1979.

In the 1980s, under the leadership of Deng Xiaoping, China embarked on a program of sustained economic liberalization. A cheap and disciplined workforce made China a rapidly growing presence in world markets. Markets were also given an expanding role in domestic production and pricing decisions. A thriving industrial economy developed on China's south coast. Furthermore, the government used its control over agricultural marketing to pay farmers more for their produce. Average farm incomes doubled during the decade.

Political reforms, however, continued to be resisted. In December 1986, demonstrations at more than 150 campuses in more than twenty cities called for better living conditions, a free press, and democracy. In mid-January 1987, the authorities cracked down. Fang Lizhi, who was emerging as one of China's leading dissidents, was removed as vice rector of the University of Science and Technology in Hubei. At the same time, the CCP purged its leading advocate of reform, General Secretary Hu Yaobang. The ensuing campaign against "bourgeois liberalization," however, was mild and notably unsuccessful. Debate over democracy, although restricted to private discussions, continued through 1988.

In a country unusually attuned to historical symbolism, China's democracy movement eagerly anticipated the approach of 1989, a most portentous year: the two hundredth anniversary of the French Revolution, the seventieth anniversary of the May 4 movement, the fortieth anniversary of the Chinese Revolution, and the tenth anniversary of the repression of the Democracy Wall movement.

Fang Lizhi kicked off new protests in February 1989 with a letter calling for the release of Wei Jingsheng and other political prisoners. Following the death of Hu Yaobang on April 15, 1989, students defied the government and held their own unofficial memorial, as they had with Zhou Enlai in 1976. Beginning with ten thousand students, their numbers grew to more than one hundred thousand on April 22, the day of the official funeral. This was the start of the Tiananmen democracy movement.

A statement drafted by Fang in December 1988, on the fortieth anniversary of the Universal Declaration of Human Rights, received wide endorsement as the movement developed. Its five proposals indicate the general tenor of demands.

1. Lift the ban on nonofficial publications. . . . The government should not intervene as long as those publications do not advocate violence or spread pornography. . . .

2. Guarantee the right of freedom of association. . . . [W]ith a prerequisite of nonviolence, people, through organizations and parties not in power, have the right to openly criticize the policies of the party in office.
3. Direct elections of county and district leaders . . .
4. Release all political prisoners. . . . Delete the words "crime of counter-revolution" from the code of criminal law. Declare that it is forbidden to charge anyone for reasons of ideology or politics.
5. Separation of party and government.[1]

In the spring of 1989, China's democracy movement was developing into a theoretically coherent call for political opening, focusing on freedoms of speech and association. Practically, it was taking to the streets. And in a symbolic gesture, recalling Qing dynasty (1644–1922) remonstrances, student leaders knelt on the steps of the Great Hall of the People and asked Premier Li Peng to come out to talk. When he refused, they launched a massive boycott of classes on April 24.

The official response was complete rejection of all student demands. A private speech by Deng Xiaoping on April 25 set the tone: "This is not an ordinary student movement but a turmoil. We must take a clear-cut stance, carry out effective measures, and counteract quickly to stop this agitation. . . . This entire episode is a planned, conspiratorial activity."[2] On April 26, the official *People's Daily* published an editorial titled "We Must Oppose the Turmoil with a Clear-Cut Stance."

The protesters, however, seemed inspired rather than intimidated. Although the government would carry out its implied threats in less than six weeks, the surprising resolve of the students provided breathing room. On May 4, more than one hundred thousand students marched to Tiananmen Square. New petitions called for even greater reforms. On May 13, three thousand students began a hunger strike. Held in front of Mao's mausoleum, in the shadows of the monument to the martyrs of the Communist Revolution, it was a gesture of self-sacrifice.

The hunger strike coincided with the visit of Mikhail Gorbachev, the first by a Soviet leader since 1959. For the government, Gorbachev's visit symbolized the end of the Sino-Soviet rift and China's new position in the world. To the students, however, Gorbachev symbolized dramatic reform from within.

Popular support continued to grow. By May 17, as a thousand hunger strikers were hospitalized, more than a million protesters and onlookers jammed the streets in and around Tiananmen Square. Smaller demonstrations were being held in more than twenty cities. The CCP was—from its perspective, ominously—losing its monopoly over civil society.

Totalitarian states maintain control not through direct force but by monopolizing public and private associations, preventing citizens from acting collectively outside of state control. By late spring, increasingly sophisticated and effective autonomous student organizations began to emerge. Press reports on Tiananmen largely ignored official controls. The students also received growing support from workers, businessmen, bureaucrats, and even some soldiers.

China's rulers faced a decisive choice: accept structural political changes or crack down, with violence if necessary. In the fall of 1989, communist leaders in Eastern

Europe did not have the heart or the stomach to shoot their own people. In the late spring of 1989, China's leaders did.

On May 20, 1989, martial law was declared in Beijing. Troops were summoned to remove the protesters. Demonstrators, however, still numbered more than a million. The troops were slowed by mass passive resistance: "The people of [Beijing] took to the streets and erected makeshift barricades. They surrounded the army convoys, sometimes to let the air out of tires or stall engines but more often to argue with or cajole the troops, urging them not to enforce the martial-law restrictions and not to turn their guns on their fellow Chinese."[3]

With absolute party rule at stake, Deng called in new, hardened, and loyal troops. The students, sensing crisis, reduced their numbers in the square. But they did not go quietly. On May 29–30, a statue of the Goddess of Democracy was erected.[4] Defiant declarations and interviews continued. An estimated one hundred thousand people attended what proved to be the final demonstrations on June 2–3.

The army's attack—as shocking as it was inescapable—came on the night of June 3. The government admits killing three hundred unarmed protesters and bystanders. Outside estimates put the number at three times that figure, plus another three hundred killed in Chengdu. In the ensuing repression, thousands were arrested. Thousands more fled underground or overseas. At least dozens, and probably hundreds, were executed. And hopes for human rights and democracy in China lay bulldozed beneath the treads of the tanks of the "People's Liberation Army."

2. INTERNATIONAL RESPONSES TO TIANANMEN

The international response was swift, strong, and coordinated. On June 5, the United States imposed an arms embargo, suspended high-level official contacts, and froze new aid. The European Community adopted similar sanctions on June 27, one day after the World Bank froze $780 million in loans to China. Japan suspended its new five-year aid program, valued at ¥810 billion (roughly $6 or $7 billion, depending on exchange-rate fluctuations). The Group of Seven (G7) annual economic summit in Paris in July also condemned the massacre.

China's political costs are extremely difficult to measure. Its economic costs, however, were demonstrably significant. New commitments of bilateral foreign aid dropped from $3.4 billion in 1988 to $1.5 billion in 1989 and to $0.7 billion in 1990. Assuming a 20 percent annual increase in aid commitments without the disruption of Tiananmen (well below the average 50 percent annual growth for the period 1985–1988), China lost about $11 billion over four years in bilateral aid alone.[5]

Despite numerous small violations, sanctions were widely observed until July 1990, when Japan announced the end of its aid moratorium. Most other countries then began to relax their sanctions more or less rapidly. A series of visits by foreign ministers to Beijing in the spring of 1991 marked China's emergence from diplomatic isolation. The renewal of China's economic boom in late 1991 substantially increased the incentives to abandon sanctions. Official bilateral aid committed in 1992 exceeded the previous record year of 1988. By 1993, most countries other than the United States had returned to business as usual—which included criticism of Chinese human rights practices (especially the treatment of dissidents) but not sanctions.

We can get a good sense of the politics involved by looking at the actions of the two principal bilateral actors, Japan and the United States, and the multilateral response at the United Nations.

A. Japan

Japan opposed more than guarded statements of disapproval, imposing sanctions only under pressure from its allies (especially the United States).[6] This position reflected strong economic interests, regional security concerns, and a genuine belief that isolating China was an inappropriate and unproductive strategy.

Within the limits set by US pressure, Japan consistently advocated what amounted to Reagan-style quiet diplomacy and constructive engagement. On June 5, the day that US sanctions were announced, Japan merely indicated that it was monitoring the situation, regretted the loss of life, and hoped for a quick end to the turmoil. On June 7, the Chinese ambassador was given a note indicating that Japan had no desire to interfere in China's internal affairs (which was China's description not only of sanctions but even of public criticism). Japanese lobbying before and during the Paris G7 summit succeeded in avoiding new collective sanctions. And after the G7 summit, Japan worked both to minimize international sanctions and to end them as quickly as possible.

Peter Van Ness has aptly described Japan's policy as "nominal conditionality."[7] Without allowing Chinese brutality to pass unnoticed, Japanese officials tried to minimize its impact on their relations with China and focused their diplomatic effort on doing the least they possibly could to harm or even offend China.

In September 1989, a Diet (parliament) delegation led by Foreign Minister Ito Masayoshi met with Deng Xiaoping and other top Chinese leaders. In December, Japan renewed cultural exchanges and donated a symbolic $3.5 million to modernize a hospital and a television station. Requests for political asylum were denied. Japanese authorities allowed Chinese embassy and consular officials to harass and intimidate Chinese students in Japan. Students were sent home against their will, despite official pledges made in June and July 1989 to extend lapsed student visas. And the resumption of foreign aid, along with a major new five-year $8 billion agreement at the end of 1990 to exchange oil and coal for technology and equipment, helped to buffer China from continuing Western sanctions.[8]

Much money was to be made in China, and both Japanese firms and their government wanted to make sure that Japan got at least its fair share. But economic engagement was also part of a broader strategy of tying China into cooperative bilateral and regional relationships to enhance regional stability, Japan's overriding geopolitical goal. Japan is deeply committed to the power of cooperative diplomatic engagement and the long-run transforming power of economic development. As an Asian regional power, Japan also had security interests (for example, in Korea and the South China Sea) that could be compromised by Chinese hostility. The Japanese response to Tiananmen thus was a consistent part of a clear general strategy.

B. The United States

The United States represents the other end of the spectrum of international responses. Americans were captivated by the Tiananmen protesters. Popular shock at the massacre produced an unusually strong and long-lasting reaction. As the rest of the world returned to business as usual with China, the United States maintained, and even considered expanding, its sanctions. But divided government a Republican president who preferred engagement and a Democratic Congress that preferred sanctions—led to considerable inconsistency.

In July 1989, four aircraft were delivered to China with navigation systems covered by the arms embargo. Secretary of State James Baker met with Chinese foreign minister Qian Qichen in Paris to discuss the civil war in Cambodia, despite the embargo on high-level contacts. National security adviser Brent Scowcroft and Thomas Eagleburger, the number-two official at the State Department, made a secret visit to Beijing. Secretary Baker's speech at the annual meeting of the Association of Southeast Asian Nations did not even mention China. And in December 1989, Scowcroft and Eagleburger made a second visit to Beijing, the United States sold three communications satellites to China, and President George Bush vetoed a bill to extend the expired visas of Chinese students.

President Bush, however, did criticize China, both publicly and privately. In December 1990, he devoted the bulk of his discussions with the foreign minister, Qian, to human rights. In April 1991, Bush met with the Dalai Lama, thus raising the sensitive issue of (human rights in) Tibet.[9] There was even limited administration support for material sanctions. For example, Bush accepted November 1989 legislation that called for suspending new World Bank loans to China. In April 1991, the United States blocked the sale of parts for a Chinese communications satellite.

In Congress, despite early tough talk, legislation regarding sanctions did not receive a final vote in 1989 or 1990. Nonetheless, with support from and prodding by NGOs, Representative Nancy Pelosi and the Senate majority leader, George Mitchell, led an extended campaign against administration policy that came closest to success in March 1992, when Bush was forced to veto legislation that linked human rights to an extension of China's "most favored nation" (MFN) trading privileges in American markets.

Candidate Bill Clinton criticized Bush's position during the 1992 campaign. As president, on May 28, 1993, he issued an executive order listing seven human rights criteria (including a general provision on observance of the Universal Declaration of Human Rights) that China would be required to meet before he would recommend extending MFN privileges again in 1994. China now faced a credible threat of reduced access to the American market.

Nevertheless, delinkage of trade and human rights began almost immediately. A memorandum in mid-July 1993 by Winston Lord, assistant secretary of state, called for a new strategy of "comprehensive engagement." This became administration policy in September. Top officials from the Departments of State, Defense, the Treasury, and Agriculture visited China. And in November 1993, Clinton met with Chinese president Jiang Zemin at the Seattle summit of leaders from the Asia-Pacific Economic Cooperation forum. The United States was clearly preparing for China's return to full status in the international community.

Meanwhile, with George Bush no longer there to do the work (and take the heat), opponents of human rights conditions on MFN status began to organize. Business mobilized its considerable lobbying skills and power. A bipartisan group in Congress argued that blunt, blanket sanctions like withholding MFN privileges were not an appropriate tool—a view shared by former president Carter and former secretary of state Cyrus Vance. As one administration official put it, denying MFN status was "an atomic bomb. And nobody drops a bomb. What we need is to get usable tools."[10] A growing number of people were also becoming convinced that rapid social change in China was making broad trade sanctions obsolete, even counterproductive. For example, Massachusetts senator John Kerry returned from a trip to China in early 1994 a convert to engagement.

Aggressive Chinese diplomacy also had an impact. Protests and threats were effectively mixed with cooperative gestures. Strategically timed releases of prisoners were a standard tactic. China also made concessions on secondary human rights issues, such as prison labor, and on unrelated issues. For example, China signed the Nuclear Nonproliferation Treaty in 1992. China reached understandings with both the Bush and the Clinton administrations on transferring missiles and missile technology. They opened discussions on piracy of music and software.

Few were surprised, then, when on May 26, 1994, Clinton announced that despite China's failure to meet the conditions of the 1993 executive order, MFN status would be extended unconditionally. "In the end, economics won the day. It wasn't really even close."[11] China's energy market alone was estimated to be worth as much as $150 billion over the coming decade. By the end of the century, $30 billion was to be spent for telephone modernization. Aircraft purchases over two decades were projected to be $40 billion. These were staggering opportunities for profits and jobs.

Trade and investment had never been included in American sanctions (except for military and "dual-use" products). Nonetheless, there was concern that continued human rights friction would harm the competitive position of American firms. For example, German chancellor Helmut Kohl returned from a visit to China in November 1993 with nearly $3 billion in new contracts. And China did prove to be generous after linkage was buried. A business delegation led by the secretary of commerce, Ron Brown, returned in September 1994 with more than $5 billion in contracts. The following February, a visit by Hazel O'Leary, the energy secretary, netted $2 billion in new contracts.

But there was more to the decision than simple greed. The collapse of allied support left the United States with little choice. Trade sanctions are vulnerable to "free riding" and "defection," by which parties that do not abide by sanctions take advantage of those who do. With limited defections (for example, Japan in 1990), sanctions may still affect the target and the costs will remain spread across several cooperating parties. But by 1994, when everyone else had already defected, the United States, not China, was most likely to be harmed by sanctions.

Cooperation on security issues also counterbalanced China's human rights record. In addition to the civil war in Cambodia, missile technology, and nonproliferation, China acquiesced in the UN-authorized attack on Iraq after its invasion of Kuwait. China, in other words, was made to pay—in other areas. Human rights pressures thus brought clear foreign policy gains.

All things considered, the most striking feature of the US response to Tiananmen was its sustained strength, especially given China's economic and military power. Only against South Africa in the 1980s had the United States ever pursued a comparably strong set of human rights initiatives. And never before (or since) has the United States been willing to accept such high political and economic costs on behalf of human rights violations short of genocide.

Some of this can be attributed to the particular details of the case. But part of the explanation lies in the maturing of human rights as an international issue and the improved post–cold war environment for international human rights.

C. The United Nations

China's power largely insulated it from multilateral criticism. The massacre was never the subject of a UN General Assembly resolution. But the subcommission of the Commission on Human Rights did adopt a resolution in August 1989. And Geneva became the site of intensive diplomatic struggle.[12]

The "offending" subcommission resolution read, in its entirety:

> The Sub-Commission on Prevention of Discrimination and Protection of Minorities,
> Concerned about the events which took place recently in China and about their consequences in the field of human rights,
> 1. Requests the Secretary-General to transmit to the Commission on Human Rights information provided by the Government of China and by other reliable sources;
> 2. Makes an appeal for clemency, in particular in favor of persons deprived of their liberty as a result of the above-mentioned events.

Even this (almost shamefully timid) response was denounced by China as "interference in China's internal affairs . . . incompatible with the purposes and principles of the Charter of the United Nations, and contraven[ing] the rules that regulated international relations."[13] And China descended on the Commission on Human Rights the following February with an entourage of forty diplomats committed to preventing even a mention of these "events." A comparably mild resolution was defeated in the commission in February 1990.

Such exertion by a potential target of multilateral human rights criticism is perhaps the strongest evidence that it is not all just hot air and pointless words. If a government that calls up the army to shoot unarmed students is this concerned about oblique criticism by a relatively obscure UN body, shame and reputation cannot be entirely negligible considerations.

But China's power prevailed. A resolution on Tibet was not introduced in the subcommission's 1990 session in return for Chinese agreement not to oppose a resolution on Iraq.[14] In August 1991, the subcommission did narrowly adopt a resolution on human rights in Tibet. This, though, was the final victory for China's critics in Geneva. At the 1992 commission session, a resolution on Tibet was defeated 27–15 (with 10 abstentions). China managed to escape even a vote in the 1992 subcommission. At the 1993 commission meeting, the resolution on China was defeated 22–17–12. The 1993 subcommission resolution on Tibet was defeated 17–6–2. After that, China disappeared from the commission's agenda. And throughout all of this, serious condemnation was never even debated.

3. ASSESSING THE IMPACT OF INTERNATIONAL ACTION

The "bottom line" is that the hold of China's communist dictators was never weakened. Even today, despite looser controls on speech and publication, pleas for political reform remain rare and dangerous. For example, Tiananmen activist Wang Dan was sentenced in November 1996 to eleven years in prison for continuing to call for democracy. In 2003, Li Zhi was sentenced to eight years in prison for criticizing corruption. In 2005, Shi Tao was jailed for ten years for criticizing human rights abuses. In 2008, Liu Xiabao, the 2010 Nobel Peace Prize winner, was detained and the following year sentenced to imprisonment for eleven years. In 2010, artist and social critic Ai Weiwei was placed under house arrest (in part, it seems, to prevent him from attending the Nobel ceremony honoring Liu). And in a change of government tactics, in April 2011 Ai was charged with tax evasion and in June presented with a punishing tax bill of nearly $2 million.

The Dui Hua Foundation has documented more than 24,000 political prisoners since 1980. More than 5,000 of them remained in prison in 2011. And the total is certainly higher.

Nevertheless, international action did have an impact on China. Numerous individual prisoners were released, both in response to general pressure (for example, 573 detainees were released when martial law was lifted in January 1990) and in exchange for particular concessions. For example, in early May 1990, prior to Bush's first MFN decision, China released some 200 detainees. In January 1994, in response to Clinton's moves toward engagement, some prominent Tibetan prisoners were freed. Several thousand lives, perhaps even tens of thousands, were improved because foreign governments were willing to exert political influence and expend political and financial resources on behalf of human rights. International pressure also seems to have been a modest deterrent to new acts of repression, some executions, and mistreatment of some prisoners.

China was also punished for its behavior. It lost several billion dollars, and China's economic boom was delayed by a year or two. Furthermore, the Chinese authorities seemed genuinely stung by international criticisms.

Chinese concessions on security and economic issues were further costs. They were also a benefit to the United States, Japan, and Europe. Although human rights advocates may be reluctant to trumpet such indirect, nonrights benefits of international human rights policies, they cannot be ignored in a broader foreign policy assessment. Rights-abusive governments may be forced to make side payments to third parties even where direct benefits for victims cannot be obtained.

In passing, we should also note that sanctions were not without costs to the sanctioning states. Bilateral foreign aid is usually sufficiently "tied" to donor-country suppliers to produce substantial sales (and thus jobs). Suspending military sales even more clearly forgoes profits and jobs (which are usually well paid and, especially in the United States, often located in politically significant places). After Tiananmen, sanctioning countries accepted modest domestic economic costs to pursue international human rights objectives. Even talk created frictions that had costs for the pursuit of other objectives in relations with China. Human rights remained a serious irritant in Sino-American relations through 1996.

We should also consider the potential moral and political costs of inaction. One's own commitment to human rights requires some sort of action, even if there is scant chance to punish or transform the target state. To fail to act in the case of gross violations would be shameful. Furthermore, considerations of consistency may also require action that one knows is likely to be largely symbolic. And even symbolic action has symbolic value; rarely is it entirely futile.

Finally, I want to suggest that international action subtly but significantly transformed China's normative political environment, both nationally and internationally. Consider the changes in the regime's counteroffensive after Tiananmen.

China initially used "the big lie." For example, one Chinese diplomat claimed that "not a single person had been killed by the army or run over by military vehicles."[15] But even the Chinese leadership seems not to have expected many to accept this account.

Appeals to sovereignty were therefore central. For example, the first issue of the *Beijing Review* published after the massacre described the US response as "flagrant accusations against China regarding something which is exclusively China's affair."[16] But in 1989, few other countries saw criticism of human rights abuses as interference in a country's internal affairs.

A more subtle Chinese argument allowed talk, but only talk. "The two countries may exchange criticisms on issues of human rights . . . but it is not advisable for one to use human rights as a tool to hurt the other."[17] However, all foreign policy manipulates negative and positive incentives, harms and benefits, to alter the behavior of others. In fact, by the late 1980s, diplomatic protests and military and economic sanctions had become an accepted, even an expected, means for expressing human rights disapproval. China was thus forced to back away from extreme claims of sovereign prerogative.

As a result of post-Tiananmen diplomacy, "China [came] to accept human rights as a legitimate part of the international agenda."[18] Chinese defenses thus increasingly emphasized arguments of cultural relativism. For example, China's 1991 Human

Rights White Paper claimed that human rights were indeed being realized in China, particularly subsistence rights, the most important rights of all.

These arguments reject the fundamental principle of the interdependence and indivisibility of human rights (see §2.4). And if the best a government can claim is that after forty years of rule, your people are not starving, the bankruptcy of that government is strikingly illustrated. But here I am interested in the politics, rather than the substance, of these arguments.

Although clearly intended as cynical manipulation of the language of human rights, this change in rhetoric has had subtle positive consequences. Less than twenty years ago, the very term *human rights* was dangerous. Even Chinese scholars of international law writing in English rarely touched on human rights. Today, however, the term is relatively widely used.

Although there are still severe limits on how human rights issues are addressed, those boundaries are not fixed. And arguing over the proper human rights strategy, rather than the very use of international human rights norms, is significant progress. The Chinese have been dragged beyond denial and forced to engage the international human rights regime—with consequences that are hard to predict.

China now operates in a realm of national and international discourse in which human rights are legitimate grounds for argument and action. The result is implicit recognition of a new kind of accountability. That recognition is extremely limited and has been even more reluctantly tendered. But this conceptual opening may prove to be the principal contribution of international responses to the Tiananmen massacre.

4. CONSTRUCTIVE ENGAGEMENT REVISITED

Europe and the United States initially adopted a "classic" strategy of punishment, shame, and isolation. They came around, however, to Japan's strategy of engagement. Is there more to be said for constructive engagement today than its failure in South Africa in the 1980s would suggest?

Engagement has a broad foreign policy justification. Because countries have multiple, cross-cutting policy objectives, it would be self-defeating for them to let any one objective preempt efforts to pursue other objectives. Human rights is but one important issue in Sino-American relations. Therefore, human rights concerns must be integrated with interests such as trade and security into a general bilateral strategy. Comprehensive engagement attempts to maximize linkages and increase overall influence and achievements.

Engagement, however, also has a human rights justification, which is my focus here. Markets, it is often argued, lead those whom they make prosperous to demand civil and political rights. Economic "freedom" leads to calls for political freedom that repressive governments cannot ultimately resist. Therefore, fostering economic development contributes to fundamental political change. Manipulating selfish economic interests thus becomes a way to realize civil and political rights. Economic support that appears to help stabilize repression actually undermines it.

This argument seems suspiciously convenient and a bit too clever. Reliance on automatic mechanisms, even if successful, fails to respond to the psychological and moral need to do what one can, here and now, to resist (or at least respond to) gross and systematic violations of human rights. Waiting for other processes to have a positive human rights impact also consigns those who face a moderately efficient state, unusually ruthless oppressors, or a highly underdeveloped economy to decades of suffering.

But public criticisms and sanctions have never caused structural political change. And in countries such as South Korea, prosperity does seem to have supported demands for political opening. Engagement thus deserves a hearing. However, there must be active engagement in the human rights struggle of people living today—*constructive* engagement rather than passive waiting.

Consider an analogy with peace. Democracies, understood as regimes that respect internationally recognized political rights, almost never fight wars with other democracies. Therefore, if markets produce civil and political rights, they will also produce peace. But no one would seriously suggest handing national security policy over to the Department of Commerce and the International Monetary Fund. While waiting for peace, immediate, concrete security interests and objectives must be addressed. Likewise, we cannot sit back and wait for markets to produce human rights—if we take human rights seriously as a foreign policy objective.

Long-term economic engagement may be a significant background force for human rights. But if engagement is to be a defensible human rights strategy, both sides must be at least minimally engaged in an active, ongoing process of change. For example, target governments must be expected to produce at least the symbolic gestures and incremental changes that public strategies of pressure regularly yield. This requires foreign states to retain and periodically use the reactive and punitive tactics of the 1970s and 1980s.

Likewise, if business involvement is justified in part because it helps human rights, we can legitimately ask for concrete evidence of that help. At the very least, we can ask that firms avoid actively denying human rights—for example, that they try to avoid actively participating in state efforts to suppress free trade unions. During the MFN debate, however, American business opposed even voluntary codes of conduct for firms operating in China. Resisting even such modest measures of responsibility and accountability raises suspicions that profits, not human rights, lay behind the appeal for a return to business as usual in China.

Consider also a full-page ad by a major US company under the title "Staying the Course Benefits Others."[19] The company argued that in the future as in the past, "rather than cut and run from trouble spots, we will work to change them." And this company explicitly pointed to civil and political rights. "Particularly in countries where attention is focused on civil and political reforms . . . great global companies can be a positive force for change." As Caiman J. Cohen of the Business Coalition for US China Trade put it during the 1994 MFN debate, trade is "part of the solution—not part of the problem."[20]

The ad's first example was Indonesia. The "bloodshed and months of turmoil" mentioned were in fact one of the most massive episodes of state terrorism anywhere in the world in the 1960s. But the "change" the company touted was new jobs and the transfer of skills and technology. This did not even address, let alone contribute to ending, systematic violations of civil and political rights. And the same government that murdered several hundred thousand Indonesians—estimates ranged up to a million when this ad appeared—remained in power for more than three decades afterward.

The ad also pointed to Nigeria, which suffered under a succession of military dictatorships over three decades and became a prominent international concern when human rights and environmental activist Ken Saro-Wiwa was executed in 1995. Again, though, the "change" produced was jobs. Although these jobs were a significant benefit to the fifteen hundred Nigerian employees and their families, there was no connection between employment and civil and political reforms.

Multinational corporations that provide good jobs to local workers and are aware of the social consequences of their activities are indeed desirable. But the issue in engagement arguments is the link between the pursuit of profits and political change. For this, treating workers well is irrelevant—especially for firms that see human rights almost entirely as a matter of civil and political, not economic and social, rights. If the best advocates of engagement can point to are regimes that have for decades successfully resisted structural political change, the strategy would seem to be completely bankrupt.

My point is not to criticize business in general, let alone particular firms. It is vital, though, to ask whether business is committed to active constructive engagement or merely passive waiting and hoping.

If businesses are simply pursuing profits, let them argue for the single-minded pursuit of gain. Debate then would focus on when, where, or even whether firms—which, after all, are first and foremost profit-seeking enterprises—should pursue human rights objectives. If they claim to be making a human rights contribution, though, it is fair to ask for the evidence.

We must pose similar challenges to advocates of foreign policy engagement. "Engagement" may easily degenerate into inaction against, or even collusion with, human rights violators. In engaging others, we must not become disengaged from our own values and day-to-day efforts to realize them. Even where we cannot remove murderers from power, we must speak out against them and do what we can to make them pay for their crimes.

5. HUMAN RIGHTS AND
GREAT POWER CHINA

In 1989, China was beginning to be considered a potential great power. In the intervening two decades, it has unquestionably become a great power. For example, Chinese GDP in 1990 was somewhat smaller than Brazil's and less than 4 percent of the global total (which was already a substantial increase from a bit more than 2 percent in 1980). By 2010, Chinese GDP surpassed Japan as the world's second largest and constituted nearly 14 percent of the global total. Per capita GDP, measured in "purchasing parity" terms (which corrects for differences in local prices between richer and poorer economies), jumped to well over four thousand dollars in 2010 from about three hundred dollars in 1990 (and less than two hundred dollars in 1980). And although inequality has increased dramatically, poverty reduction in China has been stunning. In 1980, about 85 percent of the population was classified as poor. By 2010, this number had been reduced to about 15 percent. In just thirty years, more than half a *billion* people were taken out of poverty (although more than a third of the population still lives on less than two dollars a day). About three-quarters of all poverty reduction in the developing world since 1980 has been in China (despite having only about a quarter of the developing world's population).

Human rights thus have moved out of the spotlight in relations with China—partly because repression has been "normalized," partly because of respect for China's achievements in improving living standards, and partly because China as a great power receives the same deference as other great powers. But the fact that it has not dropped entirely off the foreign policy agendas of the United States and many European countries is testimony to the fundamental changes in the international human rights environment over the past few decades. In fact, despite being a great power today, China receives more human rights criticism than it did in the 1970s and 1980s, when its human rights practices were far worse but antagonism toward the Soviet Union earned it effective exemption from international criticism.

Bilateral human rights criticism of China today is, to be sure, merely verbal and usually muted. It is reminiscent of policies in the 1970s elsewhere in the world, which tended to focus on prominent political prisoners—which, because they involve individuals rather than systematic practices of repression, provide an opportunity for external powers to obtain (and targeted governments to provide) direct and concrete, if largely symbolic, results. But China in particular, given its public sensitivity to shame and a deep concern over the respect it feels due to its status, takes even such initiatives very seriously.

For example, it mounted a major diplomatic campaign in response to Liu Xiabao's selection as Nobel laureate. This extended to a minor row with the Netherlands when several individual members of the Dutch delegation to the Beijing International Book Fair, at the suggestion of the Dutch section of Amnesty International, wore tiny lapel pins with an empty chair, a small copy of the statue by Maarten Baas representing the seat left vacant for Liu at the Nobel awards ceremony. This level of sensitivity suggests that even symbolic action is not without purpose—especially in the long run. And even in the short run, as we noted in Chapter 4, victims and their families, friends, and supporters have consistently called for the continuation of such activities, which they have indicated they value.

Furthermore, China has become more enmeshed in the global human rights regime as a result of its rise. Great powers are not just states with a lot of power. They also have special (informal) rights—most notably, a right to be consulted on matters of major international concern. In return, though, they are expected to be "good international citizens" in the minimum sense of formally endorsing important international norms across a wide range of issues, which since at least the end of the cold war includes international human rights norms. China signed the International Human Rights Covenants in 1997 and 1998—actions that were unthinkable just a decade earlier—and ratified the economic and social covenant in 2001. And it has become active (although not constructive) in global and especially regional human rights discussions.

Given China's actual human rights practices, there is considerable cynicism in many of these activities. Nonetheless, as I have suggested a number of times above, over time purely verbal behavior can influence attitudes, ideas, and ultimately even practice. Thus, getting China actively within the global human rights regime—rather than standing defiantly outside, as it did right through the initial aftermath of Tiananmen—is an accomplishment of some real potential long-term significance.

It also seems to be making a modest contribution to internal developments. Human rights advocacy, by that name, still remains rare and dangerous in China. But advocating for particular rights has become possible, particularly at the local level in a growing number of jurisdictions. Environmental activists have been a regular part of the political scene for a decade now. Housing activism has made a dramatic appearance in the past couple of years, as have protests over land in rural areas and over working conditions in many individual factories. And, perhaps most interestingly, it is (usually corrupt) local governments, not the central authorities, that are the biggest impediment to such activities. In fact, the central government and local activists often have a shared interest in local reform—so long as the central government does not perceive reformers as part of an organized group that might suggest elements of an independent civil society. (In other words, freedom of association remains ruthlessly repressed, in standard totalitarian fashion.)

Although activists do not talk publicly about it, the broader human rights context of their actions is an open secret to both the public and the authorities. They draw legitimation for their work from international norms. And those norms provide some limited protection against state retaliation—which is still a very real possibility (although not the near certainty that it was even in the mid-1990s).

In other words, bilateral and transnational human rights advocacy directed at China, and ongoing multilateral human rights activities of a more general nature, provides limited but important support for local advocates in China and does not let the government sweep human rights completely under the rug, as was previously the norm. This is about all that can be realistically expected from international human rights policies directed against a powerful government fully in control of its own country. The "problem" lies in the global human rights regime, and its foundational principle of national implementation, rather than in the inadequacies of international advocacy.

PROBLEM 6: HUMAN RIGHTS AND "ASIAN VALUES"

The Problem

China, once it gave up on denial of the Tiananmen massacre and denunciation of the victims, argued that it had its own distinctive vision of human rights. This fed into a broader argument in the early 1990s, expressed most subtly by a number of Singaporean politicians and public intellectuals, about "Asian values." Asians, the argument went, were more concerned about duties and communities than rights and individuals. And it certainly is undeniable that compared to, say, the admiration for individual assertion in the United States, Asian societies place much more emphasis on harmony, the avoidance of shame and public embarrassment, and deference to family and larger communities. How should Asians and non-Asians respond to such arguments for, as the title of a well-known article put it, Asia's different standard?

A Solution

For all the talk about Asian difference, the past three decades have actually seen a substantial convergence of Asian human rights practices toward Western interpretations of international norms. In the early 1980s, Japan was a rare Asian exception in its unconditional embrace of the full range of internationally recognized human rights and its high level of achievement in realizing those norms in national practice. Today it is increasingly seen as a model for the region—a model that South Korea, Taiwan, and even Singapore already have largely replicated. In the past decade, Indonesia has emerged as a vibrant democracy that is shifting the balance in Southeast Asia. Even Burma (Myanmar) has, as I completed these revisions at the end of 2011, made some limited but promising openings. And China not only is wealthier and more powerful than it was at the time of the Tiananmen massacre, but is freer (although still highly repressive) and has *much* less severe poverty.

Recall the distinction drawn in Chapter 3 between concepts, conceptions, and implementations of human rights. There is no plausible evidence of distinctive Asian *concepts* of human rights. For example, no substantial deletions from or major additions to the Universal Declaration of Human Rights would receive anything close to a consensus among Asian governments today—however much a number of them may claim that for various reasons, international human rights norms do not apply to them now. At the level of statements of the form "Everyone has the right to . . . ," there are no systematic differences between Asia and other regions.

At the level of conceptions as well, it is hard to discern any real *systematic* differences between Asia and other regions. Let us grant that most Asian societies are more family oriented than most Western societies. (Even here I would emphasize that explanations in terms of culture are problematic—two centuries ago, Western societies were equally family centered—and that differences between Asia and Africa and Latin America are not clear.) This might suggest different systems of social provision that rely more on families and less on the state. In fact, though, Singapore is the exception rather than the rule in imposing (limited) legal obligations on children to support their aged parents.

Even at the level of implementations, I am aware of no evidence of *systematic* differences between Asia and other regions. For example, Asian approaches to hot-button issues such as pornography and homosexuality may differ from Western approaches, but they are strikingly similar to those in Africa and the Arab world.

We must be careful not to confuse international human rights norms with Western practice. Westerners who do so are rightly criticized. But so should be those who argue for distinctive Asian values.

This is not to suggest that regional cultural—and historical, and political—differences are irrelevant to human rights practices. Such differences, though, are likely to express themselves principally in how Asians choose to exercise their internationally recognized human rights. For example, an Asian emphasis on consensus and the avoidance of public shame may have an impact on party systems, with a greater tendency to nonideological dominant parties. (Even here, however, South Korea and Taiwan are characterized by robust and even fractious interparty competition and shifting electoral fates of parties, suggesting that we should be careful not to overstate the difference.)

Or consider gender equality, which because it touches everyday life for most people is an unusually sensitive issue. International norms do require that all human rights be available equally to men and women. Therefore, to deny women the right to run for political office is to violate their human rights. They remain free, however, not to run. And voters are at liberty to treat sex as a relevant consideration in casting their ballots. Article 22 of the Universal Declaration recognizes the right of everyone to work and to free choice of employment. Therefore, women cannot be legitimately prevented from working outside the home. They are free, however, to choose not to. And to the extent that that choice is culturally preferred in Asia, it is likely to be made more frequently.

"Free" choice, of course, rarely is without costs in any domain. Human rights focus on ensuring that the state is not directly or indirectly responsible for those costs. At the very least, acts that would be prohibited were they done by men to men must be treated as especially heinous offenses when they are done to women for acting "uppity." And no group can be allowed to use the apparatus of the state to impose rules and roles on any other group that they do not impose on themselves.

Human rights empower those individuals and groups who will bear the consequences to decide, within certain limits, how they will lead their lives. Differences across time and place are thus not merely justifiable but to be expected. For example, we would anticipate that Asian children would give greater weight to the views and interests of their families than would North American children. Confrontational political tactics are likely to be less common (and less successful). There is likely to be less social tolerance of "deviant" behavior of all types.

These examples, however, illustrate individuals exercising the same human rights in different ways, not a different conception of human rights. And they do not suggest the legitimacy of prohibiting "Western" exercises of these rights. A human rights approach rests on the idea that people are probably best suited, and in any case entitled, to choose the good life for themselves. If Asians value family over self, they will exercise personal rights with family consequences in mind. If they value harmony and order over liberty, they will exercise their civil liberties in a harmonious and orderly fashion. Such choices must be respected—but only so long as and to the extent that they are in fact matters of choice.

The above suggests that the Asian-values debate, which continues to rage as the global balance of power shifts toward Asia, really has little to do with human rights. It is (ironically, given the standard account of Asian values) about Asian self-assertion and intended as a public rebuke of Western arrogance—which is very real, especially in the United States. (Consider, for example, American criticisms of corporal punishment in Singapore while defending the death penalty in the United States.)

The Asian-values debate was also about Asians confronting their own relatively poor record of human rights performance. It was simultaneously an insistence that Asians do believe in international human rights norms and an attempt to explain why, nonetheless, regional practice was disappointing and regional multilateral action was nonexistent. It *is* harder in Asia for governments to call one another publicly to account. But that, I would suggest, is a problem—at best an explanation—not an excuse. And Asians are beginning to grapple, very tentatively, with regional multilateral action, as suggested in the ASEAN human rights mechanism noted in §6.4.

Further Problems

Do international human rights standards leave enough room for incorporating Asian (or other foreign) values into national human rights practices? If you think not, what particular examples seem most compelling?

Why shouldn't a government be able to enforce long-established traditions? Does the fact that they have to be imposed by force really make that much difference? Don't laws that protect internationally recognized human rights also have to be enforced and thus in some important sense be imposed? What is the difference?

What will happen to international human rights advocacy as the global balance of power continues to shift to Asia? Suppose that Asian governments follow a path more like Japan than the United States. Should we see this as anything other than an addition to the sum total of global advocacy? Even if the average aggressiveness declines, as more Asian governments speak out, isn't that a net plus? In fact, isn't it likely that more of an Asian sensibility in human rights advocacy could increase its effectiveness, especially if we take into account Asian human rights NGOs?

DISCUSSION QUESTIONS

1. The evidence from Eastern Europe in late 1989 suggests that the Chinese government was basically right in its political assessment: substantial liberalization would have meant the end of Communist Party rule. Does this provide some justification for the Chinese crackdown? Why should some states but not others be allowed to preserve their social and political systems?

2. Why was there so much fuss over the Tiananmen massacre? China had for decades regularly engaged in massive repression yet received only

mild criticism. In the 1950s, tens of millions died as the direct and indirect results of China's "development" policy. And in the Great Proletarian Cultural Revolution of the 1960s, perhaps as many as hundreds of millions had their basic human rights aggressively assaulted. Why were these earlier abuses largely ignored? Why did Tiananmen receive extensive global condemnation?

3. Why should killing several hundred people in order to restore things to pretty much the way they were one year earlier make such a difference? Could one argue that the real failure in international human rights policies toward China lay not in responses to Tiananmen but in acquiescence to decades of massive totalitarian repression, not just before but also after Tiananmen?

4. Who was hurt by economic sanctions? To what extent do sanctions merely victimize innocent people a second time? Consider Iraq in the 1990s, an even more extreme case, where by some estimates thousands of children a month were dying from food shortages caused in significant part by international sanctions. But if we don't impose economic sanctions, aren't we, in effect, giving in to regimes that use their people as hostages? If leading opposition figures request the imposition of sanctions, as was the case in South Africa in the 1980s, that may simplify our problem. But what about cases such as Iraq (or China), where the opposition has been silenced or eliminated?

5. What were the various motives in Japan's response to Tiananmen? In the US response? How would you evaluate these priorities?

6. How long should a country be punished for even a shocking act such as the Tiananmen massacre? At some point, the past needs to be forgotten—not buried, but set aside in foreign policy. How do we know when that is? Are there general standards or guidelines that we might develop or draw on?

7. I suggested that the abandonment of sanctions by US allies largely justified an American return to business as usual. Isn't this troubling? Should we really let others dictate to us when to lift (or impose) sanctions? Aren't we obliged to follow our own judgments? At what cost?

8. Which "bottom line" do you find most persuasive: Did China literally get away with murder, or did it suffer unusually strong and sustained international punishment? Both?

9. Repressive regimes regularly release prisoners or improve their treatment in response to international pressure. This may make us feel that we have achieved something. But just how important is it? Does it amount to just treating symptoms while ignoring causes?

10. What, though, is the alternative? It is clear that outside actors can often make things a lot worse. But how often have they made things systematically better? Can outsiders really do much more than apply Band-Aids to wounds while they wait for deeper social, economic, and political forces to transform local people's tolerance for repression?

11. Should businesses be in the "business" of improving human rights? If you believe that individuals and governments have a responsibility to do something about international human rights, why shouldn't businesses have similar responsibilities? If businesses don't have any international human rights responsibilities, why should states or individuals?
12. If businesses have no human rights responsibilities overseas, why do we impose them on businesses operating domestically? Answer the same question for individual citizens. And then for governments.

SUGGESTED READINGS

Readers interested in further information on international responses to Tiananmen ought to begin with Rosemary Foot, *Rights Beyond Borders: The Global Community and the Struggle over Human Rights in China* (Oxford: Oxford University Press, 2000). This almost perfect book covers foreign policy, the United Nations, and NGO activity carefully and subtly and gives a superb sense of the possibilities for and limits on international human rights action. It is also very readable. Rosemary Foot, "Bush, China, and Human Rights," *Survival* 45 (2003): 167–186, extends the discussion into the post-9/11 era. Those who want just a single chapter can do no better than Merle Goodman, "China," in *Implementing U.S. Human Rights Policy,* edited by Debra Liang-Fenton (Washington, DC: US Institute of Peace Press, 2004).

Roberta Cohen, "People's Republic of China: The Human Rights Exception," *Human Rights Quarterly* (November 1987): 447–549, provides essential background reading that demonstrates how the international responses to Tiananmen were a dramatic change. Elizabeth Economy and Michel Oksenberg, *China Joins the World* (New York: Council on Foreign Relations Press, 1999), and Alastair Iain Johnston and Robert S. Ross, eds., *Engaging China: The Management of an Emerging Power* (London: Routledge, 1999), examine broader changes in China's relations with the external world in the 1990s, focusing primarily on economic and security issues.

The literature on the implications of the emergence of China as a great power is huge. For accounts that emphasize the United States, good places to start include Rosemary Foot and Andrew Walter, *China, the United States, and Global Order* (New York: Cambridge University Press, 2011); Michael D. Swaine, *America's Challenge: Engaging a Rising China in the Twenty-First Century* (Washington, DC: Carnegie Endowment for International Peace, 2011); Aaron L. Friedberg, *A Contest for Supremacy: China, America, and the Struggle for Mastery in Asia* (New York: W. W. Norton, 2011); Richard Rosecrance and Gu Guoliang, eds., *Power and Restraint: A Shared Vision for the U.S.-China Relationship* (New York: PublicAffairs, 2009); and Robert Ross, *US-China-EU Relations: Managing the New World Order* (Hoboken, NJ: Taylor & Francis, 2010). Warren I. Cohen, *America's Response to China: A History of Sino-American Relations,* 5th ed. (New York: Columbia University Press, 2010), is a standard history.

For other dimensions of China's rise, see Zhu Zhiqun, *China's New Diplomacy: Rationale, Strategies, and Significance* (Farnham: Ashgate, 2010); Deng Yong, *China's Struggle for Status: The Realignment of International Relations* (Cambridge: Cambridge University Press, 2008); Lowell Dittmer and George T. Yu, eds., *China, the Developing World, and the New Global Dynamic* (Boulder, CO: Lynne Rienner, 2010); Brantly Womack, *China Among Unequals: Asymmetric Foreign Relationship in Asia* (Singapore: World Scientific, 2010); Wang Yizhou, ed., *Transformation of Foreign Affairs and International Relations in China, 1978–2008* (Leiden: Brill, 2011); and Edward S. Steinfeld, *Playing Our Game: Why China's Economic Rise Doesn't Threaten the West* (Oxford: Oxford University Press, 2010).

Perry Link's *Evening Chats in Beijing: Probing China's Predicament* (New York: W. W. Norton, 1992) is an immensely engaging attempt to capture the political climate of Tiananmen and the ideas and aspirations of many Chinese democrats. Zhang Liang, Andrew J. Nathan, and Perry Link, eds., *The Tiananmen Papers* (New York: PublicAffairs, 2001), provides an inside account of high-level decision making. Stephen C. Angle and Marina Svensson, trans. and eds., *The Chinese Human Rights Reader: Documents and Commentary, 1900–2000* (Armonk, NY: M. E. Sharpe, 2001), provides an excellent selection of primary source material for the whole twentieth century. Those who wish to really wade into the sources might start with the online archive *Tiananmen Square and U.S.-China Relations, 1989– 1993* (Farmington Hills, MI: Gale, 2010).

David M. Lampton, "America's China Policy in the Age of the Finance Minister: Clinton Ends Linkage," *China Quarterly,* no. 139 (1994): 597–621, provides an excellent, detailed, but brief review of Clinton's China policy, focusing on the 1994 MFN decision. The UN response is covered in detail in Ann Kent, "China and the International Human Rights Regime: A Case Study of Multilateral Monitoring, 1989–1994," *Human Rights Quarterly* 17 (February 1995): 1–47. On Chinese participation in international institutions more broadly, see Alastair I. Johnston, *Social States: China in International Institutions, 1980–2000* (Princeton, NJ: Princeton University Press, 2008). David Arase, "Japanese Policy Toward Democracy and Human Rights in Asia," *Asian Survey* 33 (October 1993): 935–952, sets Japan's post-Tiananmen policy in a broader regional context. Michael A. Santoro, *Profits and Principles: Global Capitalism and Human Rights in China* (Ithaca, NY: Cornell University Press, 2000), provides a good discussion of the highly contentious issue of the role of international business.

For an unusually subtle Chinese defense by the director of the Department of American Studies at the Shanghai Institute of International Studies, see Ding Xinghao, "Managing Sino-American Relations in a Changing World," *Asian Survey* 31 (December 1991): 1155–1169. More typically vitriolic and xenophobic official Chinese statements can be found in numerous issues of the *Beijing Review.* For 1989, for example, see the issues of June 12, p. 10; July 3, pp. 9–10; July 10, pp. 18–21; July 17, pp. 18–19; July 31, p. 10; and November 20, pp. 38–40. John F. Cooper, "Peking's Post-Tiananmen Foreign Policy: The Human Rights Factor," *Issues and Studies* 30 (October 1994): 49–73, reviews in detail the evolution of China's response. China's official White Paper is *Human Rights in China* (Beijing: Information Office of the State Council, 1991).

On Asian values, the best general reader is Joanne Bauer and Daniel Bell, eds., *The East Asian Challenge for Human Rights* (Cambridge: Cambridge University Press, 1999). Anthony J. Langlois, *The Politics of Justice and Human Rights* (Cambridge: Cambridge University Press, 2001), is an excellent sympathetic critique that takes the idea of Asian values seriously while strongly criticizing the manipulation of the idea by Asian autocrats. Chapters 1 and 2 provide perhaps the best overview of the nature of the debate available in a single place. Two unusually clear and subtle presentations of the argument for distinctive Asian values are Bilahari Kausikan, "Asia's Different Standard," *Foreign Policy* 92 (1993): 24–41, and Fareed Zakaria, "Culture Is Destiny: A Conversation with Lee Kuan Yew," *Foreign Affairs* 73 (March–April 1994): 109–126.

13

Humanitarian Intervention Against Genocide

The Convention on the Prevention and Punishment of the Crime of Genocide was adopted by the UN General Assembly on December 9, 1948, the day before the Universal Declaration. This reflected the central role of the Holocaust in crystallizing international concern with human rights. But it also marked the creation of a separate legal regime **genocide**, largely divorced from the global human rights regime. For example, genocide is not mentioned in either the Universal Declaration of Human Rights or the International Human Rights Covenants.

The 1990s finally integrated genocide into the international human rights mainstream. The development of a *practice* of armed **humanitarian intervention** was driven by a combination of a new geopolitical environment, in which rivalry between the superpowers no longer prevented humanitarian action, and the unusually brutal character of the "new wars" of the 1990s. These were largely wars within, rather than between, states. They also largely ignored the traditional distinction between civilians and soldiers, often intentionally targeting the civilian population of the other side—even defining those civilians as "the enemy."

Here I will focus on the former Yugoslavia, particularly Bosnia-Herzegovina and Kosovo, which introduced **ethnic cleansing** to the world's vocabulary. I will also discuss more briefly the dramatically contrasting examples of Rwanda and East Timor. Together, they document the acceptance, in barely a decade, of a right to armed humanitarian intervention against genocide. The final case study, Sudan, though, documents the continuing limits on the willingness of the international community to respond to genocide with force.

1. CASE STUDY: BOSNIA

Yugoslavia was created at the end of World War I, an assemblage of the previously independent states of Serbia and Montenegro; the former Austro-Hungarian territories of Slovenia, Istria, Dalmatia, Croatia-Slavonia, Vojvodina, and Bosnia-Herzegovina;

and Macedonia, taken from the Ottoman Empire's last European holdings. Although the dominant Serbs actively discriminated against other ethnic groups, different groups lived together more or less harmoniously (except under Nazi occupation during World War II, when Serbs were targets of genocide by the Ustasha, a local fascist group operating a puppet regime in Croatia).

After World War II, the communists, the strongest force in the resistance to Nazi rule, reorganized Yugoslavia under the leadership of Josip Broz Tito. In a country in which every ethnic group was a minority (roughly two-fifths were Serbs and a fifth Croats), a federal political system granted substantial power to six republics (Serbia, Croatia, Slovenia, Bosnia-Herzegovina, Macedonia, and Montenegro) and two autonomous regions within Serbia (Kosovo and Vojvodina).

For three decades, the system worked tolerably well. In fact, the considerable repressive apparatus of the totalitarian Yugoslav state was used to discourage, and when necessary suppress, claims of superiority by Serbs or separatist demands by non-Serbs. The principal exception was the treatment of ethnic Albanians in the Kosovo region of Serbia, who faced far more discrimination than other ethnic groups in Yugoslavia and were denied the recognition and self-rule that went with federal republic status.

Tito's death in 1980, however, removed the final arbiter from a system with immense potential for squabbling and deadlock. The accumulated inefficiencies of decades of control by nine separate communist bureaucracies (six republics, two autonomous regions, and the federal government) ended the economic growth that had greased the system. By the mid-1980s, Yugoslavia faced a political and economic crisis well beyond the capabilities of its ruling communist functionaries.

A. The Breakup of Yugoslavia

In 1987, Slobodan Milošević seized on Serbian nationalism to consolidate his rapid rise to power in the Serbian republic. Milošević skillfully manipulated memories of Ustasha brutality, fostering hatred of Croats. He also invoked the quasi-mythic grandeur of Serbia's fourteenth-century Nemanjid dynasty. He aimed to paint Muslims, who made up about one-sixth of the country's population, as enemies, successors of the Turks who had defeated medieval Serbia. Milošević also revived and cleverly manipulated the Serbian Orthodox Church to further mobilize hostility toward Croats, most of whom are Roman Catholics or Muslims.

Using tactics made famous by Hitler, Milošević and his front group, the Committee for the Protection of Kosovo Serbs and Montenegrins, organized more than one hundred mass protest demonstrations with average turnouts of more than fifty thousand people. By February 1989, the last vestiges of regional autonomy in Vojvodina and Kosovo were eliminated. In addition, Milošević allies had been installed in Montenegro, leaving him in firm control of half the country.

Kosovo, whose population was 90 percent ethnic Albanian, was particularly severely repressed. Milošević abolished the regional government, imposed Serbo-Croatian as the official language, banned Albanian-language media, and fired six thousand teachers after prohibiting Albanian-language secondary schooling. All of this was presented as "liberating" Serbs from the remnants of the "Turkish yoke." In July 1991, he even confiscated six thousand hectares of land for distribution to Serbian colonists.

The other republics, especially Slovenia and Croatia, had the legal and political power to block this protofascist Serbian imperialism. But this only led Milošević to rely increasingly on extralegal means. For example, arms shipments for the Yugoslav National Army (JNA) "inexplicably" began appearing in Knin, Croatia's principal Serbian city, in the fall of 1990. After negotiations to maintain a loose federal system failed, Slovenia and Croatia, fearing the worst, declared independence on June 25, 1991.

Slovenia was ethnically homogeneous and prosperous. It also did not share a border with Serbia. Although it was invaded by Serbia the day after it declared independence, by early July a cease-fire negotiated by the European Community (the predecessor to the current EU) effectively secured Slovenian independence.

The conflict thus shifted to Croatia, where violence had been escalating since the ethnically Serb region of Krajina had declared autonomy in March 1991 and asked for union with Serbia. Both Croats and Serbs manipulated memories of past discrimination and atrocities—and prepared to inflict new ones.

In the last four months of 1991, Serbs and Croats fought a brutal war that targeted "opposition" civilians no less than opposing armies. The fifteenth cease-fire, reached on January 2, 1992, and supported by fourteen thousand peacekeepers of the United Nations Protection Force in the former Yugoslavia (UNPROFOR), lasted about a year. Serbian separatists, however, controlled one-third of Croatia's territory, which remained under (sporadically violent) dispute until a successful Croatian offensive in the summer of 1995.

With the stalemate in Croatia, international attention turned to an even more brutal conflict in Bosnia-Herzegovina (hereafter referred to as simply Bosnia). Bosnia was in many ways a microcosm of Yugoslavia, itself a republic of minorities. In the 1991 census, 44 percent identified themselves as "ethnic Muslims," 32 percent as Serbs, 17 percent as Croats, and 7 percent as "Yugoslavs" or other. In fact, Bosnia was the only Yugoslav republic without an ethnic majority.

Although Bosnia had been a place of considerable ethnic tolerance, especially in the capital of Sarajevo, when war did come it hit with unprecedented ferocity. And Bosnia's Muslims were particularly vulnerable because they lacked the support of neighboring conationals.

Separatist Serbs gained control of two-thirds of the territory of Bosnia. They perfected and popularized the strategy of ethnic cleansing, introduced by Croatian Serbs the preceding year, which aimed to rid "Serbian" territory of Muslim (and Croat) residents through systematic terror and sporadic murder.

Serbian military action was directed as much at innocent civilians as at opposing soldiers. Relief supplies were blocked. Villages and cities were shelled from a distance when they could not be shot up and burned at close range. Captured men were routinely tortured or murdered, often en masse. Women, children, and the elderly were sometimes shot, often physically abused, but more typically "merely" forced to flee. And Serbian soldiers systematically, on orders from superiors, raped young Muslim women, to degrade them and shame their families.

B. Responding to the Bosnian Genocide

Out of a prewar Yugoslav population of 23 million, about a quarter of a million people were killed and two and a half million left homeless in the various wars of the early 1990s. The international community was often, and in many ways justly, criticized for doing too little, too late. However, it did not sit by and idly watch the genocide, as it had during the cold war in places like Uganda and Cambodia.

The UN Security Council imposed an arms embargo on all parties and placed Serbia under a comprehensive economic embargo. A special war crimes tribunal was created. Peacekeepers were sent to protect civilians and facilitate the delivery of humanitarian assistance. And much of the international community exerted considerable diplomatic and political pressure on Serbia and its Bosnian allies. When a peace agreement was finally signed at Dayton in December 1995, there were fifty thousand UN peacekeepers in the former Yugoslavia, at an annual cost of about $2 billion; three thousand humanitarian workers were in the field; and the Office of the United Nations High Commissioner for Refugees alone was spending $500 million a year on humanitarian assistance.

Initial responses, however, were timid and largely reflected geopolitical concerns, especially keeping Yugoslavia intact. The international community was willing to allow immense suffering to prevent Yugoslavia from becoming a precedent for an even more catastrophic breakup of the Soviet Union—which, it must be remembered, had not yet dissolved. (There was no way of knowing then that its breakup would be anywhere near as peaceful as it ultimately proved to be.) Thus, even Slovenia, despite its democratic credentials and Westward-leaning orientation, was pressured into formally remaining within the increasingly imaginary federal Yugoslavia.

By the time the war entered its Bosnian phase, however, the Soviet Union had already broken up and the European Community had recognized the independence of Croatia and Slovenia. Although geopolitical concerns continued to intrude—for example, politics within the North Atlantic Treaty Organization (NATO), the problem of defining the post–cold war role of Russia, and Russia's political ties to Serbia complicated diplomatic and peacekeeping activities—for the remainder of the conflict the United States, Europe, the United Nations, and even Russia maintained sustained efforts in human rights, humanitarian assistance, peacekeeping, and diplomacy that were without parallel during the cold war.

i. Multilateral Human Rights Agencies

In August 1992, at the first special session in its history, the UN Commission on Human Rights appointed Tadeusz Mazowiecki, former prime minister of Poland, as special rapporteur. Mazowiecki visited Bosnia on August 21–26 and confirmed "massive and grave violations of human rights" throughout Bosnia. A second mission in October concluded that "the Muslim population are the principal victims and are virtually threatened with extermination." A second special session of the commission, held November 30 and December 1, 1992, condemned Serbia, the JNA, and leaders of Serb-controlled areas. Never before had the commission responded with anything even close to such speed. And the vigor of its response was equally striking.

The Security Council also acted (relatively) rapidly and with resolve. An arms embargo and trade sanctions were followed by the creation, in February 1993, of the International Criminal Tribunal for the former Yugoslavia, which by 1996 was actively prosecuting war criminals.

These initiatives, however, responded to, rather than stopped, the genocide. As we have seen, though, the international community has never seriously considered giving coercive enforcement powers to multilateral human rights institutions. Multilateral human rights diplomacy must rely instead primarily on international public opinion, which, at least in the short run, has little effect on shameless butchers. The Commission on Human Rights did just about everything it could. The war crimes tribunal, the first since Nuremberg, was a major innovation. The "problem," in the end, was that most states considered genocide preferable to the "solution" of transferring authority to an international agency that might act, or force them to act, more strongly.

ii. Humanitarian Assistance

Humanitarian assistance aims to cope with some of the most pressing human consequences of war (and other political and natural disasters). Humanitarian workers seek not to prevent violence but to ease the burden on civilian victims. Even these limited tasks, though, undercut the Serbian strategies of pursuing ethnic cleansing in the countryside and strangling Sarajevo. The Bosnian Serbs therefore saw humanitarian assistance as intensely political—which it was, given their strategy—and consistently used all means in their power, including force, to stop international relief from reaching its targets. (Muslim and Croat forces much more irregularly prevented aid deliveries.)

The international humanitarian response in Bosnia was swift, sustained, and relatively effective. All the external parties pressed both the Bosnian Serbs and the Milošević government to allow humanitarian aid to flow. The United Nations used strong diplomatic pressure and (limited) force to deliver aid to more than 2 million people. UN peacekeepers provided intelligence, occasional armed convoys, and a visible, vigilant presence that reduced attacks on civilians.

The suffering in Bosnia was horrible. More than one-third of Bosnia's people were forced to flee their homes. Most of the Bosnian Muslims who did not flee were forced to endure extended Serbian sieges. The more than 200,000 deaths in Croatia and Bosnia were proportionally equivalent to the deaths of about 5 million Americans.

But to have dramatically reduced this suffering, those providing assistance would have had to issue a credible military threat to enter the conflict on the side of Bosnia's Muslims. Leading states simply were not willing to endorse such an option, preferring instead to rely on diplomacy, humanitarian assistance, and sanctions short of the punitive use of force.

iii. Peacekeeping

The soldiers that the UN sent in under the banner of UNPROFOR (the United Nations Protection Force) were peacekeepers. **Peacekeeping** involves interposing neutral forces *with the permission of the belligerents* in order to monitor or maintain a truce or settlement. Peacekeepers are lightly armed and are authorized to use force only for self-defense. The aim of peacekeeping is not to repulse or punish an aggressor. That is a job for collective security enforcement, as in the Gulf War of 1991.

UNPROFOR's mandate was restricted to limiting the extent and severity of the fighting. The international community condemned ethnic cleansing. It was willing to prosecute those responsible once the fighting ended. But it would not take the military steps necessary to end the conflict. Genocide continued—perhaps even occurred—in Bosnia because outside powers were unwilling to fight a war to stop it.

The task of UNPROFOR was less to prevent war (soldiers shooting soldiers) than to prevent war crimes (soldiers massacring civilians). To the Serbs, however, UNPROFOR represented a hostile external world frustrating their objectives, which they were well on their way to achieving when the UN intervened. They thus focused their efforts on subverting UNPROFOR and completing the ethnic cleansing of "their" country. This was a near-certain recipe for disaster.

The compromised mission of UNPROFOR came to be embodied in the institution of United Nations Protected Areas (UNPAs), or "safe areas." First established in 1992 in Croatia, they were extended to Bosnia in 1993. UN strategy increasingly came to focus on excluding the Bosnian Serbs from UNPAs in Srebenica, Goradze, Tuzla, Zepa, and Bihac (as well as Sarajevo, which had been under siege since March 1992).

These enclaves were intended to provide humanitarian refuge for victims of the fighting, temporary frontiers across which "peace" was to be kept, and barriers to ethnic cleansing. The Serbs showed some tolerance for the first of these objectives. They rejected the second and third. The "safe areas" thus were under constant pressure and sporadic attack. In the summer of 1995, they collapsed.

Serbs resumed heavy shelling of Sarajevo at the end of May 1995, provoking retaliatory NATO air strikes. The Serbs counterretaliated by shelling the safe areas. For example, 65 children were killed in a single artillery barrage on the center of Tuzla. In addition, 325 UN peacekeepers were taken hostage. NATO responding by sending 12,500 new troops armed not merely for self-defense but with significant air- and ground-fighting capabilities. The Serbian response was to transform the "safe areas" into killing zones.

In July 1995, Srebenica was overrun, as an appalled and ashamed UN contingent found itself able only to stand by and watch. Adult men were separated from the rest of the refugees, who were sent fleeing. Of the total "protected" population of about 40,000, more than 7,000 were slaughtered and buried in mass graves.

With people now dying as an unintended but very real consequence of the "best efforts" of the international community, the West, and particularly the United

States, finally intervened. NATO air strikes increased in number and severity. Political pressure built up to end the arms embargo, which had helped the Serbs (who received Serbian and JNA weapons) and harmed the Muslims (who had access only to modest quantities of primarily small arms smuggled in with difficulty). NATO's intensified air strikes, coupled with the Croatian victories in Krajina and renewed pressure applied to Milošević (who was being increasingly squeezed by the West), forced the Bosnian Serbs to the negotiating table.

A marathon three-week session at Wright-Patterson Air Force Base in Dayton, Ohio, backed by immense US pressure, produced a peace agreement on December 14, 1995. Throughout 1996, a 60,000-person multilateral Implementation Force supervised the military disengagement. This was followed by a 30,000-person Stabilization Force, which was replaced at the end of 2004 by the European Union Force, which in 2011 had 1,600 troops deployed in Bosnia.

Bosnia today remains in an awkward position, largely propped up by EU financial support. In addition, the EU special representative plays a decisive role in the politics of Bosnia—where ethnic communities, nationally, regionally, and often even locally, still tend to act as separate entities, rather than as parts of a single federal state. But although no one is really satisfied with the situation, it is stable, generally peaceful, and for most parties preferable to the politically plausible alternatives.

iv. Assessing the Bosnian Intervention

Viewed in isolation, Bosnia appears as largely a failure of international action. The international community waited three and a half years to meet Serb force with force. Earlier military engagement might have had high human and financial costs. It almost certainly, though, could have prevented much of the suffering of Bosnia's civilians—and probably would even have reduced the total human, financial, and political costs.

Nonetheless, Bosnia and its people were, quite literally, kept alive. More than 2 million people received humanitarian assistance. International action helped to keep Sarajevo from falling, thus averting an even greater disaster. The arms embargo prevented an even larger bloodbath (especially if one attributes part of the relatively good record of the Bosnian Muslims to their lack of opportunities to exact revenge). And UN peacekeepers sent to the border of Macedonia in December 1992 stopped the fighting from moving east and south.

Taking a comparative perspective, this suggests that Bosnia was not merely a success but a major breakthrough. *Relatively* strong international action came *relatively* rapidly. In the end, armed force was brought to bear. And international action was decisive in ending the conflict. Bosnia marked a crucial step in transforming international responses to genocide.

Precedents, however, are made by later actions that treat them as constraining. They do not automatically cause comparable action in the future. Furthermore, their meaning changes as they become embedded in streams of action. The meaning of Bosnia emerged only as the international community confronted new genocides in Rwanda, Kosovo, and East Timor.

2. CASE STUDY: RWANDA

If Bosnia is the "success story" of the early 1990s, Rwanda was the great, and horribly tragic, failure.

Ethnic conflict in Rwanda was in large measure the creation of Belgian colonial rule. After receiving control over Rwanda from Germany after World War I, the Belgians exacerbated the tensions between the two main groups in the territory, the majority Hutu and the minority Tutsi. After having purged Hutus from the largely Tutsi elite, the Belgians used the Tutsi elite as an instrument of colonial domination, provoking understandable resentment from the Hutu majority.

In 1959, as independence was approaching, Hutu resentment turned into the violent assertion of political dominance. Some 20,000 Tutsis were massacred, and another 200,000 were forced to flee. In the ensuing years, sporadic ethnic violence, with short bursts of genocidal killing (particularly in 1964 and 1974), marked politics in Rwanda, as well as in neighboring Burundi. The staggering scope of the violence that occurred in 1994, however, was unprecedented.

The prelude to genocide began in October 1990 when the Rwandan Patriotic Front, made up primarily of Tutsis living in refugee camps, invaded Rwanda from their bases in Uganda. The Hutu-dominated military government of Juvénal Habyarimana portrayed this as an attempt to (re)impose Tutsi domination and responded with increased repression. A cease-fire to this inconclusive conflict was finally negotiated in the summer of 1992. In August 1993, a fragile peace agreement was signed in Arusha, Tanzania.

Meanwhile, the Habyarimana government and its radical Hutu supporters established a network of Hutu militias (*interahamwe*), which by the spring of 1994 numbered about 30,000. Radio stations, especially the government-controlled Radio Mille Collines, spread increasingly virulent anti-Tutsi propaganda. From the national cabinet down to local mayors, preparations were laid for a massive, organized campaign of violence against Tutsis and political opponents of the regime. The killings began on the night of April 6, 1994, after the plane carrying the presidents of both Rwanda and Burundi was shot down. (Responsibility remains a matter of considerable controversy.)

Individual contingents of the United Nations Assistance Mission in Rwanda (UNAMIR), a peacekeeping forcing observing implementation of the Arusha Accords, tried to shelter some civilians. The formal mandate of UNAMIR, however, restricted the troops to monitoring. In any case, UN peacekeepers themselves quickly became targets. Ten Belgian soldiers were captured on April 7, tortured, and murdered.

Two weeks later, the Security Council unanimously agreed to cut the UNAMIR force from 2,500 to 270, despite estimates that more than 100,000 civilians had already been massacred. Not until April 30, when hundreds of thousands had been killed, did the Security Council even condemn the violence. Even then it pointedly refused to call it a genocide, admitting only that "acts of genocide" had been committed. The United States, as late as June, also continued to refer only to "acts of genocide," wary of the international legal obligation under the genocide convention to respond.

The world stood by and watched while more than 750,000 Rwandans out of a prewar population of about 6,750,000 (proportionally the equivalent of roughly 30 million deaths in the United States) were butchered in a little more than three months. And *butchered* is a brutally accurate term: the machete was the weapon of choice of many of the *génocidaires.* Another 2 million Rwandans fled to Zaire (now the Democratic Republic of the Congo).

All of this was particularly troubling because information was available—in the media, at the United Nations, and in the major governments involved (France, the United States, and Belgium)—that genocide was imminent. In January 1994, the commander of the UN force, General Roméo Dallaire, asked for, but was denied, permission to confiscate the weapons of the *interahamwe.* Throughout February and March, General Dallaire pleaded, with increasing desperation, for reinforcements and a more robust mandate, but the Security Council refused.

As we have noted, the United Nations is an intergovernmental organization, made up of and controlled by its member states. The Security Council is dominated by its five permanent members (China, France, Russia, the United States, and the United Kingdom), each of whom can veto Security Council action. In the case of Rwanda, four of the permanent powers actively opposed UN action. The United States had recently been forced to make a humiliating withdrawal from Somalia and was unwilling to consider involvement in another small, fractious African country. France, which considered itself to have special geopolitical interests in central Africa, was wary of weakening its regional influence. Russia and China had "principled" objections, insisting that the conflict was an internal Rwandan matter. (Britain appeared willing to consider stronger action but had no desire to lead on the issue of Rwanda.) All these political forces conspired against UN intervention. And in a cruel irony, Rwanda happened to occupy one of the ten rotating seats on the Security Council and used this position to try to minimize the scope and severity of the problem.

Because of the low-tech nature of the genocide, even as few as several thousand troops could have stopped much, probably even most, of the killing. However, those states with the knowledge and power to do something chose inaction. In their "defense," few expected anything like the scope of violence that occurred—although a willingness to tolerate tens of thousands of deaths is still shameful. As the tragedy unfolded, though, and appreciation grew of the opportunity for humanitarian action that had been forfeited, a deep sense of shame spread through the international community.

3. CASE STUDY: KOSOVO

When the next major humanitarian crisis arose, in Kosovo in 1998 and 1999, the contrasting lessons of Bosnia and Rwanda weighed heavily on the minds of decision makers and public opinion. In Bosnia, limited but real success had been achieved, despite rather difficult conditions. In Rwanda, relatively modest measures undertaken at modest costs almost certainly would have had immense humanitarian payoffs. Nonetheless, the worst genocide since World War II had been permitted to proceed, largely without international resistance. When the Kosovo crisis presented itself, key international actors, led by the administration of President Bill Clinton in the United States and the government of Prime Minister Tony Blair in Britain, seem to have "learned" from Bosnia and Rwanda that successful humanitarian intervention was both (politically and logistically) possible and (morally, perhaps even politically) necessary.

Kosovo, as noted above, had been a region of Serbia, not a republic of Yugoslavia. This was crucial, because when Yugoslavia (and then the Soviet Union) broke up, it did so according to the old internal boundaries. The model was the decolonization of the Western empires, where new states were created by following old colonial boundaries. Absurd as many of those boundaries were, they had the inestimable virtue of being long established. Anything else would have been a recipe for border wars. The breakup of Yugoslavia was treated as analogous to the dissolution of the Serbian empire, just as the breakup of the Soviet Union was treated as analogous to the dissolution of the Russian empire. Thus, federal republics such as Serbia, Bosnia, and Slovenia as well as Russia, Kazakhstan, and Georgia easily received local and international recognition of their independence. Other internal units, such as Kosovo in Serbia (Yugoslavia) and Chechnya in Russia (USSR), did not.

As discussed above, this left Kosovo's ethnically Albanian population under the increasingly brutal domination of Serbia. Although the Milošević government regularly hinted at its goal of "cleansing" Kosovo, it was not included in the Dayton settlement because Kosovo was neither independent nor a site of widespread fighting. Western leaders would soon regret this calculated concession to Serbia.

Throughout the mid-1990s, the Kosovo Liberation Army carried out sporadic, quite ineffective guerrilla operations that had little popular support. The Serbian government, however, responded with increasingly brutal repression, including attacks on civilians. The Serb massacre of fifty-eight people in Perkazi in February 1998 initiated a spiral of escalation. In the following twelve months, about a thousand people, mostly ethnically Albanian Kosovar civilians, were killed. Perhaps even more ominously, more than four hundred thousand were forced to flee their homes.

Some debate remains about the intent of the Milošević government. The prevailing opinion in much of the West by early 1999 was that ethnic cleansing had begun in earnest. Efforts to get the Security Council to act were nonetheless blocked, primarily by Russia.

The Clinton administration, however, continued to argue, forcefully, that the lessons of Bosnia and Rwanda proved that early action was necessary. Britain and some other European states agreed. The problem was determining who would act, on what rationale, in the absence of Security Council authorization. Rather than act unilaterally, or create an ad hoc coalition, they decided to use NATO, the old cold war alliance against the Soviet Union that had been trying to reinvent itself as a new kind of regional security organization.

A land invasion was ruled out, as the costs, in terms of troops mobilized and lives lost, were anticipated to be more than Western publics would accept. This left only airpower. From March 24 to June 19, 1999, NATO forces carried out an increasingly punishing campaign of aerial bombardments, including repeated attacks on the Serbian capital of Belgrade.

The Serbian authorities took advantage of the attacks to put into action a well-coordinated campaign of ethnic cleansing. About ten thousand people were killed, and nearly a million and a half people were forced to flee their homes. The speed and efficiency of the Serbian actions clearly indicated Milošević's rather elaborate plan, which he had been waiting for the "right" moment to implement.

Three features of the Kosovo intervention deserve special mention. First, it was undertaken as genocide began, or perhaps even before. In Bosnia, intervention occurred when genocide was well under way. In Rwanda, genocide was pretty much over when the international community finally intervened. The intervention in Kosovo marked the first time that international action came early, perhaps even preemptively.

Second, the intervention was undertaken despite the fact that the number of deaths was *relatively* low. The Serbian strategy of ethnic cleansing used exemplary violence to coerce people into fleeing the territory to be cleansed. Part of the motivation seems to have been a calculated attempt to stay under a perceived killing threshold for an international response. The international response, however, recognized and responded to genuine genocide—a violent attack against a people because of who they are—even though "only" less than several thousand people had been killed when the bombings began.

Third, regional powers acted on humanitarian grounds, in the absence of Security Council authorization or any other particularly powerful legal justification. In effect, the "negative precedent" of Rwanda—something has to be done—took priority over the usual requirements of authorization and legality.

4. THE AUTHORITY TO INTERVENE

Who is entitled to intervene on behalf of (potential) victims of genocide? We can distinguish interveners by their mode of action (unilateral or multilateral) and the scope of the community within or for which they act (global or regional).

The authority of multilateral interveners arises from legal, political, or moral recognition by the political communities that the organization or its members represent. Multilateral intervention necessitates the building of political coalitions across states, which, even if it does not entirely eliminate the influence of national selfishness, substantially increases the likelihood of genuinely humanitarian motivation. At the very least, it makes the political self-interests involved somewhat less narrow. When the multilateral forum is the Security Council—which can act only with both a majority of its membership and the consent of the five permanent members—any use of force that is authorized is likely to have a very central humanitarian dimension to it.

Unilateral actors—which include ad hoc coalitions—may or may not have comparable recognition by broader political communities. It is an empirical question whether a great power acting unilaterally intervenes with authority or merely as a result of its superior power. Great powers have engaged in far more *anti*humanitarian than humanitarian interventions. Multilateral intervention thus is the preferred alternative, for practical as well as theoretical reasons.

Unilateral action by a great power with highly mixed motives nonetheless may save lives that would be lost while waiting for a more "pure" multilateral intervention that never comes. (Classic cold war examples include the conflict between India and East Pakistan [Bangladesh] and that of Vietnam in Cambodia.) Furthermore, unilateral actors, being politically autonomous, may be able to intervene when multilateral action is blocked. And when unilateral actors intervene as de facto representatives of both victims and broader regional or international political communities, their actions may acquire considerable informal legitimacy.

The second dimension of this typology, the distinction between regional and global interveners, concerns the appropriate "level" for action within the international system. Regional and global actors may have different capacities and authorities. For example, regional multilateral action may be easier because of greater common interests within the region. Regional actors may also have the advantage of superior knowledge or authority because they are "closer" to the problem. But if a regional organization is dominated by a regional hegemon (for example, Nigeria in the Economic Community of West African States), it may be (perceived as) a captive of that state, undermining its legitimacy.

Let us apply this typology to Kosovo. Global multilateral action was effectively blocked. China and Russia had a deep and relatively "principled" opposition to multilateral intervention. In addition, Russia had much more selfish political interests in its relationship with Serbia.

The Organization for Security and Co-operation in Europe, the most obvious regional actor, lacked the unified political will needed to act in this particular case—let alone the legal authority to use force. A similar political situation also precluded action through either the European Union or the Council of Europe. Furthermore, unilateral action by the United States was definitely unacceptable to most, if not all, of the states of the EU, as well as most states outside of Europe.

Nonetheless, the states of the EU were unwilling—at least after a lot of political lobbying—to stand by and allow genocide to occur in Kosovo. NATO provided a convenient organizational forum for needed action that could not be authorized elsewhere. Faced with a genuine dilemma, the members of NATO decided that intervention was the lesser of two evils.

Assuming that preemptive humanitarian intervention will generally be blocked at the global level, concerned states seem to be left with the uncomfortable alternatives of inaction, unilateral action, or regional multilateral action. This is a recipe for uneven and "selective" responses to humanitarian crises. There are large parts of the world where there is neither a viable regional actor nor a unilateral actor that has the necessary power, legitimacy, and commitment. Selectivity is further increased by the effective exemption of the permanent members of the Security

Council from UN action and a comparable regional exemption of leading local powers such as Nigeria and India (and their allies). Kosovo also raises the specter of what might be called coercive regionalism, in which the target of action is not a member of the intervening "regional" community. Furthermore, the 2005 intervention of the African Union in Sudan—to which we will return—suggests that relying on (ineffective) regional intervention may be a way for global actors to avoid taking difficult or costly action.

But as long as we retain an international system structured around sovereign states—that is, for the foreseeable future—we are not likely to be able to evade these problems of authority and inequality. We are beginning to grapple with them, though, with a certain degree of success. And the UN-authorized intervention in East Timor later in 1999 largely removed doubts that a right to humanitarian intervention was being established as a matter of positive international law.

5. CASE STUDY: EAST TIMOR

The island of Timor was divided during the colonial era into East Timor and West Timor, held respectively by Portugal and the Netherlands. When Indonesia achieved independence, it received (only) the Dutch holdings in the East Indies (including West Timor, but not East Timor). Neither then, nor in 1960, when the United Nations reorganized its decolonization machinery and classified East Timor as a Portuguese colony, did Indonesia claim East Timor.

In 1974, a coup removed the military government in Portugal, the only Western state still holding a substantial colonial empire (most notably Angola and Mozambique). The new regime was both much more sympathetic to decolonization and distracted from, if not positively uninterested in, its tiny holding in the East Indies. Taking advantage of the situation, East Timor declared independence.

Indonesia, however, had other ideas. It invaded East Timor on October 16, 1975. Indonesian rule was viewed as illegal by most countries. It was rejected by most of the local population. Nonetheless, the government in Jakarta attempted to consolidate its rule through often brutal repression, punctuated by special regional development assistance that suggested material benefits would follow from compliance.

Particularly striking was the Dili Massacre of November 12, 1991. Indonesian troops opened fire on peaceful proindependence demonstrators, killing at least 271 and wounding at least another 275. In addition, more than 250 people disappeared. Besides being unusually brutal, the Dili Massacre was widely publicized, mobilizing public opinion in Portugal, where there was still considerable unease over allowing Indonesia to take control so easily, and in Australia, where the government's strong support for Indonesia came under increasing public pressure. And the news coverage, followed by a British television documentary in January 1992 using graphic video footage of the massacre, galvanized international attention in many countries previously uninterested in East Timor's plight (analogous to the impact of the Sharpeville Massacre on international responses to South Africa).

Eventually, international pressure induced Indonesia to permit a UN-sponsored referendum on independence. In the election, held on August 30, 1999, more than three-quarters of the votes favored independence. Indonesia, however, balked. Local "militias," which were already operating with the acquiescence, and often the active assistance, of Indonesian military authorities, went on a sustained rampage that increasingly appeared to have genocidal aspirations. A fifth to a quarter of the population were forced to flee their homes, with thousands tracked down and killed in churches, schools, and public buildings where they sought refuge.

On September 15, 1999, the Security Council unanimously created the International Force for East Timor, an Australian-led force that, in combination with intensive international political pressure and diplomatic activity, restored order and produced Indonesian acquiescence in Timorese independence. On October 25, 1999, the Security Council established the United Nations Transitional Administration in East Timor. A week later, the last Indonesian troops left East Timor. On May 20, 2002, East Timor achieved full independence.

Accurate figures on casualties are difficult to come by. It is likely, though, that at least a hundred thousand people were killed during the quarter century of Indonesian rule. Something on the order of one in every eight people perished in the struggle for Timorese independence.

The technical illegality of Indonesia's occupation of East Timor facilitated such a strong response. Many countries that would have otherwise been reluctant to accept a UN military operation were able to view this as a decolonization issue more than a humanitarian intervention. Leading international actors, however, had Kosovo (and Rwanda) very much in mind. East Timor was widely understood as a turning point, completing the transformation of Bosnia from an isolated exception to a precedent in a continuing stream of customary law formation that in some complex way also included Kosovo.

The power of the emerging norm of humanitarian intervention against genocide is illustrated by the fact that almost all the conventional political and material considerations counseled inaction. Indonesia is a large, strategically located country (the world's largest majority-Muslim country) with considerable oil resources and a strong record of support for, and by, the West. In addition, there were well-founded fears, both within and outside Indonesia, about the susceptibility of the country to secessionist movements, some of which had been carrying on armed struggles for decades. East Timor, by contrast, is small, poor—whatever its oil resources, they are dwarfed by those of Indonesia—and of little material interest to anyone except its own people. Nonetheless, in the end, and with surprisingly little controversy, the major Western powers and the rest of the Security Council agreed to send soldiers to protect the Timorese people and enforce their decision to attain independence—in part because they had an international legal right to independence, but in large measure because the international community was unwilling to allow their forced incorporation to be maintained through genocide.

6. A RIGHT TO HUMANITARIAN INTERVENTION AGAINST GENOCIDE

At the beginning of the 1990s, positive international law clearly did not authorize armed humanitarian intervention, even in response to massive genocide. Not a single intervention against genocide had been widely endorsed as legal. The Security Council had the authority to determine that genocide represented a threat to international peace and security. In practice, though, it never exercised that authority. The standard pattern, right through the end of the cold war, was for the international community to wring its hands in anguish as genocide played itself out in places like East Pakistan (where in 1971 several hundred thousand were killed and some 10 million people put to flight in calculated ethnic violence), Cambodia (where more than a million and a half people—about one-fifth of the total population of the country—died at the hands of the Khmer Rouge between 1975 and 1979), and Uganda (where more than a quarter-million people died during the rule of Idi Amin in the 1970s). Neighboring states, usually with powerful geopolitical interests, sometimes intervened. None of these interventions, however, was accepted as legal. And most were not even presented as primarily humanitarian by the interveners.

By the end of the decade/century/millennium, however, the Security Council had authorized not only humanitarian interventions in Bosnia and East Timor but also peacekeeping operations in Sierra Leone, Liberia, the Central African Republic, and the Democratic Republic of the Congo that had a central humanitarian component. And in the first decade of the twenty-first century, additional operations were conducted in Liberia, Côte d'Ivoire, Sudan, Burundi, Afghanistan, and Haiti. Today we have both a well-established norm and a surprisingly clear pattern of practice of Security Council–authorized humanitarian intervention against genocide. And the example of Kosovo suggests considerable international toleration for genuinely humanitarian interventions taken in response to Security Council inaction.

Nonetheless, the existing right to humanitarian intervention applies only to genocide. There is no evidence to suggest that it is spilling over into other, more common, human rights violations, even in cases of torture and slavery, where national courts are increasingly applying international human rights norms.

This poses a moral paradox: we seem willing to respond to certain kinds of graphic and concentrated suffering but to tolerate substantially greater suffering so long as it remains more diffuse. This paradox is by no means restricted to genocide. Consider, for example, the contrast between the relatively strong international reaction to the Tiananmen massacre, where hundreds of people died in a relatively telegenic way, and the weak reactions to the systematic and severe daily violations of the human rights of hundreds of millions of Chinese citizens. Even more striking is the substantial international willingness to respond to famines but a parallel unwillingness to deal with the far more serious problem of malnutrition.

If we take seriously the interdependence of all human rights, and if we take seriously the idea that human rights are about a life of dignity, not mere life, then the restriction of humanitarian intervention to genocide is highly problematic. There are, however, powerful practical, and even ethical, reasons to restrict humanitarian intervention to genocide.

Psychologically, the restriction acknowledges the realities of mobilizing an international response adequate to consider bearing the considerable costs associated with military humanitarian intervention—especially if that intervention is not to be restricted to high-altitude bombing. Furthermore, a narrow genocide exception reflects the continuing priority of local and national communities. It remains rare—but no longer unheard of—for states and citizens to be willing to bear the costs of rescuing foreigners from the depredations of "their own" governments. An active sense of cosmopolitan moral community remains very, very thin.

We also need to emphasize that the contemporary practice of humanitarian intervention involves (only) a right, not a duty. Although the report of the secretary-general's Independent International Commission on Intervention and State Sovereignty was titled *The Responsibility to Protect,* no such responsibility is recognized in international law.

The international community may have a *moral* obligation to protect victims of genocide. It might even be argued that such a duty is implied by the very structure of the global human rights regime. National implementation of internationally recognized human rights, if it is more than a political compromise with the reality of state power, must assume that states are capable and not unwilling to protect the human rights of their citizens. But this is patently absurd in the case of genocidal regimes. In fact, it appears as a cruel hoax to continue to act on such an assumption. In such cases, it might be argued, residual responsibility reverts to the international community.

Nonetheless, international law recognizes only a right to humanitarian intervention. As with any right, the Security Council may choose not to exercise it; the council is free to intervene, or not, as it sees fit. And the grounds for both acting and not acting may legitimately appeal to a variety of nonmoral considerations, to which we will turn in a moment. First, though, let us look briefly at a case of genocide from the 2000s that challenges the relatively optimistic picture I have painted so far.

7. CASE STUDY: SUDAN

The roots of Sudan's humanitarian crises go back to it colonial creation, which combined a largely Arab and Muslim North with a largely black and Christian and animist South. When the country attained formal independence, on January 1, 1956, Sudan was already in the midst of a civil war between North and South that continued until 1972—only to break out again in 1983, continuing, more on than off, until 2005. About half a million people died in the first phase of the civil war (out of a population of about 10 million at independence). Perhaps another 2 million died in the second phase. Although there was considerable brutality on both sides, most of the suffering was caused by military action by the North that targeted civilians and used the denial of food, even in times of famine, as a standard tactic.

This particular humanitarian disaster was finally brought to an end in 2011. In January, the people of southern Sudan overwhelmingly voted for independence. In July 2011, the new country of South Sudan peacefully seceded—although peace between the two Sudans is hardly secure and perhaps not even likely.

Sadly, though, this solution seems to have been facilitated by the emergence of a new humanitarian crisis, beginning in 2003, in Darfur, the western region of Sudan, which like the South is primarily non-Arab and non-Muslim (although with a much more substantial Arabized minority). The Darfur conflict initially went in favor of the rebels, who handily outmaneuvered the government army (which was stretched thin to begin with by the conflict in the South and another conflict in the East). The government, however, quickly switched to a counterinsurgency strategy based on *janjaweed* militias, composed on local mounted herders armed by the government, supported by government helicopters. Many thousands were killed, and more than 100,000 refugees were put to flight by the time the conflict moved to the forefront of international attention in 2004.

The violence directed at the non-Arab population was reminiscent of Serbian ethnic cleansing in Bosnia and Kosovo. A conscious effort seems to have been made both to limit the killing, which was aimed primarily at causing targeted populations to flee, and to engage diplomatically with critics in order to forestall an effective, full-scale multilateral intervention. But even this "restrained" violence forced more than two and a half million people—40 percent of the prewar population—to flee and killed perhaps a third of a million people (three-quarters of those deaths being from disease among refugees).

The international response was in many ways rapid and robust. In April 2004, Chad brokered a cease-fire. In August 2004, the African Union (AU) sent 150 Rwandan troops to monitor the cease-fire. They were soon joined by 150 Nigerians. The following month, the Security Council condemned the government for its actions in Darfur. In 2005, the AU peacekeeping force was expanded, first to more than 3,000 troops and then to almost 7,000. A peace agreement between the government and some rebels was signed at Abuja, Nigeria, in May 2006. At the end of August 2006, the Security Council authorized a force of more than 17,000 peacekeepers. Numerous efforts at cease-fires and final resolution were undertaken, by both bilateral and multilateral actors, both inside and outside of the region, including prominently the United States. A major NGO response mobilized substantial pressure both on Sudan and especially on Western governments. Charges were even brought in the International Criminal Court against leaders of the violence, including the sitting president of Sudan, Omar al-Bashir. And a new, more promising, peace agreement was signed by all the major parties in Doha, Qatar, in July 2011.

Compared to Kosovo and East Timor, though, these responses were somewhat timid and noticeably unsuccessful. Genocidal violence continued for more than half a decade. And as I write this, at the end of 2011, it is by no means certain that it is finally over. This "setback" for armed humanitarian intervention against genocide can be explained by the intersection of a considerable range of factors.

The United States, already bogged down in wars in Afghanistan and Iraq, was unwilling to lead a more robust response. Without a substantial American commitment, a substantially larger force could not be raised. And even if it had been committed, no other power or group of powers has the logistical capabilities to support it in the field.

Darfur is a huge area (more than 190,000 square miles, roughly the size of Spain) with primitive infrastructure. The substantial majority of the population lived in widely scattered villages in a flat, semiarid terrain. A large and difficult ground operation thus would have been required to provide protection. (A small lightly armed force, such as would have made a huge difference in Rwanda, could not provide protection against mobile militias backed by air support.)

The international politics were further complicated by China and Russia being even more reluctant than usual to permit armed intervention. China had major economic interests, especially oil. And Russia was both locked in its own brutal separatist war in Chechnya and happy to take the opportunity to sell arms to Sudan's government, despite the UN embargo.

The regional environment also undercut stronger action. The AU was more than willing to intervene. But it lacked any substantial moral authority in Sudan. And it lacked the resources to do an effective job. Furthermore, its efforts were undercut by the indirect support that Sudan received from the Arab League.

Furthermore, the government in Khartoum was an astute and effective opponent. It appears to have carefully studied previous interventions. And it had a clear appreciation of the strengths of its position. Khartoum thus calibrated its actions, both internally and externally, to allow it to continue the ethnic cleansing of Darfur.

All of the above suggests that Kosovo and East Timor may have been *relatively* easy cases that created unrealistic expectations. Being forced out of East Timor was deeply embarrassing for the Indonesian government. But it had little material cost—especially because it has not in fact strengthened secessionist movements elsewhere in the country. Indonesia, in other words, was *relatively* open to international pressure and in the end not willing to fight further to keep a territory to which it had a questionable claim in the first place—especially given the internal political changes that were taking place within Indonesia, leading toward its effective democratization over the following several years. Furthermore, the Australian intervention in East Timor was successful, with a force more than one-third smaller than the clearly inadequate force the Security Council authorized for Darfur.

As for Kosovo, the NATO bombing campaign was not foreordained to succeed. In fact, almost up to the moment that it finally succeeded, it appeared to be failing. The loss of Kosovo, although a much more severe blow to Serbia than the loss of East Timor was to Indonesia, was not decisive, given its broader range of objectives, especially closer integration into Europe and the material (and psychological) benefits that would provide. And there was an internal opposition within Serbia that pressed the government to alter its policy.

The government in Khartoum, by contrast, had demonstrated itself willing to carry out decades-long massacres of people that, although technically fellow citizens, it viewed as culturally, ethnically, and racially inferior. It had the oil resources to support such policies, both internally and externally. It brooked no opposition to its rule, which even in the North of the country was highly repressive (although much less violent). It did not care much what the rest of the world thought of its actions. It needed nothing from outside (other than to sell its oil—which proved no problem). And it pursued its policies with considerable skill.

In other words, Sudan shows that a relatively effective and committed government can largely flout the international community, so long as it is willing to inflict sufficient suffering on "its" people. North Korea, Burma, and Zimbabwe present different variants of this pattern—which has no connection at all with genocides in "failed" states such as Somalia and Congo. Politically possible actions simply were inadequate to stop the killing.

But even in Darfur, the international response had a (limited) positive impact. The number of people directly killed numbered "only" several tens of thousands. Horrible as that figure is, it almost certainly would have been much higher had the international community not been watching carefully. And if the Doha agreement proves durable and effective, the conflict will have ended with the government failing to achieve many of its objectives—in significant measure because the international community, even though unable to stop the violence, would not allow it to succeed.

8. JUSTIFYING HUMANITARIAN INTERVENTION

As the above cases illustrate, justifying humanitarian intervention in contemporary international politics involves a complex interaction of morality, law, and politics. The moral case for humanitarian intervention against genocide is relatively unproblematic. In §3.3, I used John Rawls's notion of overlapping consensus to circumvent disputes over foundational theories of human rights. In much the same way, we can see today an overlapping consensus on the use of armed force against genocide. Whatever their differences, most contemporary moral and religious doctrines agree that genocide is the kind of international crime that in principle justifies armed humanitarian intervention. Across a very wide range of common moral theories and principles, *this* kind of suffering cannot be permitted.

Yet states and international organizations are not unencumbered moral agents. They are also subjects of international law and deeply political actors. And international law and politics impose their own standards of justification. Throughout the cold war, morality justified humanitarian intervention against genocide, but international law, emphasizing sovereignty and nonintervention, prohibited it. Today, law and morality largely converge. But as Rwanda and Kosovo illustrate, states still face a problem when the substantive standard of protecting victims of genocide conflicts with the international legal requirement of UN Security Council authorization.

"Justification" becomes even more complicated when we recognize that states are also political actors. National leaders are *supposed* to take into account the political standard of the national interest. In addition to acting in accordance with the demands of law, morality, and humanity, they should consult the interests of their own state (and perhaps the interests of international society).

Political interests may justify inaction that is morally demanded and legally warranted. In fact, it is essential that potential interveners consider the material and political costs, to themselves and others, of undertaking a morally and legally justifiable intervention. No less important, political interests—or at least the absence of competing political interests—may be a crucial final element in reaching a decision to act on moral and legal justifications.

How we balance these competing standards is, of course, a matter of intense controversy, both in general and in any particular case. But justifying humanitarian intervention requires that we take into account the full range of relevant moral, legal, and political principles—making "justification" a remarkably complex matter in many cases.

9. TYPES OF JUSTIFIABILITY

At least six senses of "justification" are regularly appealed to in cases of humanitarian intervention. The intervention may be what I call authorized, permitted, contested, excusable, tolerable, or justified but failed.

The simplest case is full *authorization*: The intervention fully meets the substantive demands of all the relevant standards. East Timor is an example.

An intervention is *permitted* when it is neither authorized nor prohibited. Most standard understandings of the principle of nonintervention suggest that humanitarian intervention would rarely, if ever, fall into this category. Sovereignty is a foundational legal concept of the society of states. In the absence of clear legal authority to contravene prima facie sovereign rights, we have, at best, a case of competing standards.

Such cases involve what I call *contested* justifications: different standards point in different directions. Almost all interventions are likely to be contested in the sense that someone other than the target objects on some ground. Here I am interested only in contested justifications that arise from conflicting principles that have wide and deep endorsement within international society.

"Authorization," as I have defined it, requires that *all* relevant standards be satisfied. In "contested" cases, however, intervention is *both* (positively) "justified" and (positively) "unjustified." For example, the Independent International Commission on Kosovo described that intervention as illegal but legitimate.

Two kinds of contested cases deserve special mention. The first arises when the intervention is judged "unjustified," all things considered, but is nonetheless *excusable*. Typically, the excuse appeals to a conflicting but subordinate standard. Consider stealing food to feed one's family. Although the law clearly prohibits theft, the moral obligation to one's family may bear considerable weight as a mitigating factor even in a court of law, especially at the time of sentencing. Competing standards make us disinclined to say that the action is simply unjustified, even if it is appropriately punished.

Some interventions may be judged "justified" in a significantly weaker sense of the term, which I call (merely) *tolerable*. An "excusable" intervention involves *intentionally* producing some positively desirable state of affairs through the use of unacceptable means. In contrast, a (merely) "tolerable" intervention either produces a good result largely unintentionally or is simply the lesser of two evils. For example, if we interpret the Vietnamese intervention that removed Pol Pot and the Khmer Rouge from power in Cambodia as an effort to impose a quasi-imperial regional hegemony through force, it was, at best, merely tolerable.

Compare this to the arguably excusable Tanzanian intervention that overthrew Idi Amin in Uganda in 1979. Although clearly unjustifiable according to positive international and regional law, it did remove a barbarous regime, at relatively modest cost (assuming that we need not attribute the later atrocities of the second Obote regime to the Tanzanians). Furthermore, narrow self-interest seems to have played a relatively small part in the decision to intervene. As a result, Tanzania was not sanctioned, except verbally (and even that rather lightly). In fact, it received considerable informal and popular support. Its behavior was treated as excusable, and in some sense perhaps even commendable. Many people interpreted the NATO intervention in Kosovo in these terms, especially after it succeeded.

With merely tolerable acts, though, the underlying principle (for example, conquest of a neighbor) cannot be widely endorsed. Although we should not deny their positive humanitarian consequences, neither should we give much credit to those who produced these results. They are very much like fortunate accidents.

This points to still another set of competing standards, namely, intentions and consequences. The rationale for undertaking an action is important to our evaluation. Results, however, also matter. In the best of all worlds, humanitarian aims will underlie an intervention that has positive humanitarian consequences. But good results need not arise from good intentions. Good intentions are no guarantee of humanitarian consequences. And results that are both seriously bad and due to the negligence of the intervener may even overwhelm the initial justification for intervention.

In other cases, however, the intervener will do everything "right" yet still fail to achieve humanitarian results. To hold that failure alone makes an intervention unjustified would hold interveners up to second-guessing that not only is unfair but would also tend to deter desirable justifications. Therefore, I suggest that such interventions be classed as *justified failures*.

Mixed motives provide still another sort of conflict of standards. Humanitarian interventions typically are costly, both financially and in the risks to which they expose soldiers. States may occasionally accept such risks for purely humanitarian reasons. A number of states are even coming to see preventing or stopping systematic gross human rights violations as part of their national interest. But purely moral motives have been, and are likely to remain, rare.

Nonhumanitarian motives, however, do not necessarily reduce the justifiability of an intervention. Some political motives do not conflict with either humanitarian norms or international law. And even when they do, we need to *balance* the competing considerations. So long as there are significant humanitarian motivations, interventions undertaken with mixed motives often will be contested or excusable.

Inconsistency raises the final conflict of standards that I consider here. Critics often present the impure as trumping the pure: because one did not intervene in A, which is in all essential ways similar to B, intervening in B is somehow unjustified, or at least suspect. Such an argument, however, reflects an absurd perfectionism that would paralyze states not just in cases of humanitarian intervention but in almost all areas of endeavor.

Inconsistency arguments do have real force when they point to blatant partisanship: for example, supporting a practice among friends but intervening when an enemy does the same thing. Consistency per se certainly is desirable, for all kinds of political, psychological, and perhaps even moral reasons. But as Peter Baehr nicely put it, "One act of commission is not invalidated by many acts of omission."[1] Inconsistent need not mean unjustified.

10. A NEW CONCEPTION OF SECURITY

The developing international practice of humanitarian intervention reflects not only the growing spread and deepening penetration of international human rights norms but also new post–cold war conceptions of security. Traditionally, "security" in international relations referred to *national* security, and in particular the security of the state. National security has typically been seen as having primarily military and economic dimensions: protecting one's own territory from attack; projecting power abroad in the pursuit of other vital interests; protecting jobs, incomes, and production capabilities at home; and pursuing economic objectives overseas.

Thus understood, there is no necessary or even obvious connection between security and human rights. Indeed, ruling regimes have frequently seen (national) security and human rights as competing concerns. Scholars and activists in peace studies, conflict resolution, and human rights have long challenged this understanding. In the past two decades, states and international organizations have also begun to consider new visions of security that are much more complementary to human rights.

As we saw in Chapter 4, the juntas that ruled Argentina during the Dirty War could, with apparent seriousness, use "security" to justify the arbitrary murder of between ten and twenty thousand citizens. And such claims resonated with a significant proportion of the governments of the world, including that of the United States. Today, though, even making such a claim would be difficult. And the number of governments that would give serious consideration to such arguments is more like a few handfuls, in contrast to the many dozens of thirty years ago.

"Security" that leaves citizens subject to massacre by their own government no longer passes the "straight face" test. Our conception of security has been expanded to include a minimal level of personal security against one's government, at least in the case of genocide. National security has in no way retreated. But conceptions of human security have gained a real foothold, in multilateral organizations, in governments, and among national and transnational publics.

DISCUSSION QUESTIONS

1. How do you interpret the rapid switch from ethnic tolerance to violent ethnic mobilization in the former Yugoslavia? Clearly, we are not dealing with "primordial" animosities, especially in the case of Serbs and Croats, who had no significant political contact with one another until the twentieth century. But what do you imagine the relative mix was between deep but repressed animosities and the opportunistic manipulation of differences that led to social and political discrimination? Which explanation is more frightening?

2. Is there any moral or theoretical significance in the sharp discrepancy in responses to genocide and responses to other kinds of human rights violations? What *dangers* are posed to international human rights policies when we respond forcefully only to unusually photogenic suffering? In thinking about this issue, consider the analogy of relatively strong international responses to famine but much more modest responses to the more serious problem of malnutrition.

3. In recent years, there has been much talk of a clash of civilizations and the development of anti-Islamic attitudes in the West, especially in the United States. How does Bosnia fit into such arguments? Some have charged that the West did not do more because the Bosnians were Muslims. Others have pointed to the responses in Bosnia and in Kosovo to show how the West was able to distinguish between politicized Islamists and ordinary adherents of one of the world's great religions. Which reading seems more correct?

4. The former Yugoslavia has been used in arguments about the place of race in contemporary Western foreign policies. Here the comparison is with Rwanda. Did the West do more to stop genocide in Croatia and Bosnia because the victims were white than in Rwanda, where the victims were black? What other explanations might there be? Is it as simple as the fact that the killing in Rwanda was over quickly? Remember the length of time it took to get the West seriously involved in Bosnia.

5. Bosnia and Rwanda illustrate a willingness to respond to genocide *after* it has occurred. Why is there no comparable international willingness to respond to *prevent* genocide? Is Kosovo the exception that proves the rule?

6. The war crimes tribunal for the former Yugoslavia, the parallel process for war crimes in Rwanda, and the creation of the International Criminal Court have finally introduced an element of personal international legal responsibility to human rights violations, at least in the case of genocidal warfare. This is obviously of great symbolic significance. But what is its practical value? In the particular cases? In the future? In answering these questions, try to recall the earlier discussions of the role of normative transformation and the relative strengths and weaknesses of individual petition procedures.

7. What *are* the lessons of Sudan? To what extent does Darfur undercut the progress of the 1990s? Is this a question that can be answered confidently before we know what comes next?

8. Do I present an unfair treatment of nationalism? What about the "good" side, embodied in values such as patriotism? More generally, aren't there values in groups and group loyalties that I have systematically undervalued in the highly individualistic account in both this and the preceding chapter?

9. Isn't there a paradox, or worse, in my criticism of nationalism and my acceptance of states as the basis of the international human rights system?

10. Why isn't the principle of humanitarian intervention spilling over to human rights violations other than genocide? Is this good or bad?

11. Would the world be a better place if there were a responsibility to protect victims of genocide? What would the *costs* be? What about protection for victims of other human rights violations? Again, consider both benefits and costs.

12. Is justification for humanitarian intervention really as complex as suggested in this chapter? Isn't it more a simple case of choosing between the obvious moral obligation to act against genocide and the unwillingness to pay the costs of discharging that obligation?

13. Is the linkage between humanitarian intervention and changing conceptions of security as clear as suggested at the end of this chapter? As significant? How much of a difference does it make to say that a government cannot massacre its own citizens in great numbers, while pretty much anything else it does is overlooked? Isn't that the lesson not just of the cases considered in this chapter but of China as well? And even of the leading cold war cases? As long as you can repress your people without resorting to mass murder, doesn't sovereignty still protect even incredibly vicious states? Consider, for example, North Korea. Is it any less deserving of humanitarian intervention than Serbia or Indonesia? Isn't it actually much more "deserving"? Consider the question again, taking nuclear weapons out of the picture.

SUGGESTED READINGS

Readers looking for good introductory book-length discussions have a number of choices. Two of the best are Thomas G. Weiss, *Humanitarian Intervention: Ideas in Action*, 2nd ed. (Cambridge: Polity Press, 2012), and Aidan Hehir, *Humanitarian Intervention: An Introduction* (Houndmills, Basingstoke: Palgrave Macmillan, 2010).

Although this chapter focuses its attention narrowly on international responses to genocide, readers are likely to be interested in further sources on the broader issue. Adam Jones, *Genocide: A Comprehensive Introduction,* 2nd ed. (New York: Routledge, 2011), is a good starting point. Dinah L. Shelton, ed., *Encyclopedia of*

Genocide and Crimes Against Humanity (Detroit: Macmillan Reference, 2005), is an authoritative three-volume reference work. Dale C. Tatum, *Genocide at the Dawn of the Twenty-First Century: Rwanda, Bosnia, Kosovo, and Darfur* (New York: Palgrave Macmillan, 2010), covers most of the cases considered in this chapter in more detail. Cathie Carmichael, *Genocide Before the Holocaust* (New Haven, CT: Yale University Press, 2009), provides historical background.

William A. Schabas, *Genocide in International Law: The Crime of Crimes,* 2nd ed. (Cambridge: Cambridge University Press, 2009), is authoritative. Ronald C. Slye and Beth Van Schaack, *International Criminal Law: Essentials* (New York: Aspen Publishers, 2009), and David Luban, Julie R. O'Sullivan, and David P. Stewart, *International and Transnational Criminal Law* (New York: Aspen Publishers, 2010), tackle the issue from the perspective of international criminal law more broadly.

Those with an interest in moral and political theory should profit from consulting Terry Nardin and Melissa S. Williams, eds., *Humanitarian Intervention* (New York: New York University Press, 2006); John K. Roth, ed., *Genocide and Human Rights: A Philosophical Guide* (Houndmills, Basingstoke: Palgrave Macmillan, 2005); and Larry May, *Genocide: A Normative Account* (Cambridge: Cambridge University Press, 2010).

Two brief readings stand out for thinking ethically about the broad issue of humanitarian intervention. The essential starting point is Michael Walzer, *Just and Unjust Wars* (New York: Basic Books, 1977), 53–63, 101–108. This classic book lays out a strong ethical-legal defense of sovereignty (as a reflection of the rights of individual and communal self-determination) and then argues no less powerfully for a limited right to humanitarian intervention in cases of enslavement or massacre that shock the moral conscience of mankind. Terry Nardin, "The Moral Basis of Humanitarian Intervention," *Ethics and International Affairs* 16 (2002): 57–70, is also essential reading, contrasting more statist defenses such as Walzer's with an alternative tradition that makes direct appeals to substantive principles of natural law and justice.

Much recent debate has been structured around *The Responsibility to Protect,* the report of the International Commission on Intervention and State Sovereignty (available online at http://www.iciss.ca/members-en.asp), which can be read as an effort both to codify the normative progress of the 1990s and to begin a conversation over a more robust doctrine of armed humanitarian intervention. For recent discussions of the responsibility to protect (R2P), see Cristina G. Badescu, *Humanitarian Intervention and the Responsibility to Protect: Security and Human Rights* (New York: Routledge, 2011); Philip Cunliffe, ed., *Critical Perspectives on the Responsibility to Protect: Interrogating Theory and Practice* (London: Routledge, 2011); Ramesh Thakur, *The Responsibility to Protect: Norms, Laws, and the Use of Force in International Politics* (London: Routledge, 2011); James Pattison, *Humanitarian Intervention and the Responsibility to Protect: Who Should Intervene?* (Oxford: Oxford University Press, 2010); and Alex J. Bellamy, *Responsibility to Protect: The Global Effort to End Mass Atrocities* (Cambridge: Polity Press, 2009).

There is now an immense international legal and political literature on humanitarian intervention. J. L. Holzgref and Robert O. Keohane, eds., *Humanitarian*

Intervention: Ethical, Legal, and Political Dilemmas (Cambridge: Cambridge University Press, 2003), and Jennifer M. Welsh, ed., *Humanitarian Intervention and International Relations* (Oxford: Oxford University Press, 2004), provide excellent statements of most leading mainstream perspectives. Nick Wheeler's *Saving Strangers: Humanitarian Intervention in International Society* (Oxford: Oxford University Press, 2000) is perhaps the best single book on the topic considered as an issue in international relations. It is particularly strong on cold war–era practice and its transformation in the 1990s. Brendan Simms and D. J. B. Trim, eds., *Humanitarian Intervention: A History* (Cambridge: Cambridge University Press, 2011), provides historical context for contemporary practice.

On the broader UN role in armed humanitarianism, see Edward Newman, Roland Paris, and Oliver P. Richmond, eds., *New Perspectives on Liberal Peacebuilding* (Tokyo: United Nations University Press, 2009); William J. Durch, ed., *Twenty-First-Century Peace Operations* (Washington, DC: US Institute of Peace and the Henry L. Stimson Center, 2006); and Mats Berdal and Spyros Economides, eds., *United Nations Interventionism, 1991–2004* (Cambridge: Cambridge University Press, 2007).

Among more critical perspectives, David Chandler's *From Kosovo to Kabul: Human Rights and International Intervention* (London: Pluto Press, 2002) is notable. He offers a spirited reading of the rise of so-called humanitarian interventions as an expression of American hegemony. David Rieff is a prolific journalist who has long been an insightful critic of armed humanitarianism. Two good examples of his work are *At the Point of a Gun: Democratic Dreams and Armed Intervention* (New York: Simon & Schuster, 2005) and *A Bed for the Night: Humanitarianism in Crisis* (New York: Simon & Schuster, 2002). Aidan Hehir, *Humanitarian Intervention After Kosovo: Iraq, Darfur, and the Record of Global Civil Society* (Houndmills, Basingstoke: Palgrave Macmillan, 2008), challenges the idea that a fundamental transformation took place in the 1990s.

Samantha Power, *"A Problem from Hell": America and the Age of Genocide* (New York: Basic Books, 2002), is a well-written, thoughtful, and engaging, even gripping, account that includes extended case studies of Bosnia, Rwanda, and Kosovo. Norrie MacQueen, *Humanitarian Intervention and the United Nations* (Edinburgh: Edinburgh University Press, 2011), focuses on Africa, the Balkans, and East Timor.

On the Kosovo intervention, Albrecht Schnabel and Ramesh Thakur, eds., *Kosovo and the Challenge of Humanitarian Intervention: Selective Indignation, Collective Action, and International Citizenship* (Tokyo: United Nations University Press, 2000), is the essential starting point. This remarkable volume not only covers broad issues such as sovereignty, citizenship, and responsibility but also includes a dozen excellent brief chapters on the foreign policies of the great powers as well as many smaller powers. The other essential source is the report of the Independent International Commission on Kosovo, available online at http://www.reliefweb .int/library/documents/thekosovoreport.htm.

The literature on Bosnia is extensive, but there is no obvious place to start, as with the volume on Kosovo by Schnabel and Thakur. Among the more useful books are Sabrina P. Ramet, *Balkan Babel: The Disintegration of Yugoslavia from the*

Death of Tito to the Fall of Milosevic, 4th ed. (Boulder, CO: Westview, 2002); Tom Gallagher, *The Balkans After the Cold War: From Tyranny to Tragedy* (London: Routledge, 2003); Paul Mojzes, *Balkan Genocides: Holocaust and Ethnic Cleansing in the Twentieth Century* (Lanham, MD: Rowman & Littlefield, 2011); and Gerard Toal and Carl Dahlman, *Bosnia Remade: Ethnic Cleansing and Its Reversal* (New York: Oxford University Press, 2011). Misha Glenny, *The Balkans: Nationalism, War, and the Great Powers, 1804–1999* (New York: Viking, 2000), is a very readable volume that places the conflict in a broad historical setting. Jon Western, "Bosnia," in *Implementing U.S. Human Rights Policy,* edited by Debra Liang-Fenton (Washington, DC: US Institute of Peace Press, 2004), is a good brief account of the American response.

On Rwanda, Michael Barnett, *Eyewitness to a Genocide: The United Nations and Rwanda* (Ithaca, NY: Cornell University Press, 2002), is excellent on the role of the United Nations. Christian P. Scherrer, *Genocide and Crisis in Central Africa* (Westport, CT: Praeger, 2002), places the genocide in a broader regional context. Mahmood Mamdani, *When Victims Become Killers: Colonialism, Nativism, and the Genocide in Rwanda* (Princeton, NJ: Princeton University Press, 2001), provides an excellent account of the development of ethnic conflict, showing very clearly that there was nothing "primordial" about it. See also Lee Ann Fujii, *Killing Neighbors: Webs of Violence in Rwanda* (Ithaca, NY: Cornell University Press, 2009).

For a good brief account of American (in)action, see Alison Desforges, "Rwanda," in *Implementing U.S. Human Rights Policy,* edited by Liang-Fenton. More broadly, see Linda Melvern, *A People Betrayed: The Role of the West in Rwanda's Genocide* (London: Zed Books, 2009); Andrew Wallis, *Silent Accomplice: The Untold Story of France's Role in the Rwandan Genocide* (London: I. B. Tauris, 2006); and Roméo Dallaire, with Brent Beardsley, *Shake Hands with the Devil: The Failure of Humanity in Rwanda* (New York: Carroll & Graf, 2005), by the UN commander in the field who saw the genocide coming, pleaded for additional forces, and was ignored.

On East Timor, the Final Report of the Commission for Reception, Truth, and Reconciliation in East Timor (available online at http://www.easttimor-reconciliation .org/ and http://www.ictj.org/cavr.report.asp) is a good place to start for further reading. See also Geoffrey Robinson, *"If You Leave Us Here, We Will Die": How Genocide Was Stopped in East Timor* (Princeton, NJ: Princeton University Press, 2010); Joseph Nevins, *A Not-So-Distant Horror: Mass Violence in East Timor* (Ithaca, NY: Cornell University Press, 2005); and Michael G. Smith and Moreen Dee, *Peacekeeping in East Timor: The Path to Independence* (Boulder, CO: Lynne Rienner, 2003).

14

Globalization, the State, and Human Rights

It is difficult to talk about international relations today for more than a few minutes without at least raising the issue of globalization. (The other unavoidable issue is terrorism, the subject of the next chapter.) What are the implications of globalization for human rights?

Globalization is a web of interconnected processes that challenge the political, economic, and cultural primacy of the state. Because the global human rights regime relies primarily on the national implementation of internationally recognized human rights, this suggests that globalization is undermining the principal mechanism for implementing and enforcing human rights, especially economic and social rights.

1. GLOBALIZATION

Globalization is generally understood literally to mean the creation of structures and processes that span the entire globe. People, goods, and ideas increasingly move and interact across—even irrespective of—national territorial boundaries. Markets, politics, and culture become transnational, even global, rather than national.

Globalization has involved the spread of capitalist markets and the growing transnational integration of systems of production and distribution. Understood in this sense, though, globalization goes back at least to the maritime expansion of the West that began in the late fifteenth century. Karl Marx provided the classic analysis of globalization thus understood. His account of colonialism emphasized the progressive economic and social changes introduced by capitalist markets no less than the brutalities of capitalist imperialism. Marx also emphasized the internationalist perspective of the working-class movement, which he saw as a response to the transnational logic of capital accumulation.

Other aspects of globalization also have roots running back centuries. For example, today's telecommunications revolution, involving high-speed digital networks

219

with ever-growing bandwidth, has a lineage that stretches back not just through television, radio, telephone, and telegraph but to steamships, railroads, and clipper ships. The globalizing spread of ideas and practices of electoral democracy and individual human rights builds on the centuries-old spread of sovereign territorial states and the incorporation of the entire globe into what was originally the European-states system.

Nonetheless, it is plausible to suggest that the pace of change has accelerated, with important qualitative differences that have become evident in the decades on either side of the year 2000. Political action above, below, outside, around, and even without much concern for the state is much more of a practical reality for a much greater number of individuals and groups, in a much greater number of arenas and areas of concern, than it has been for at least the preceding century or two—which in many ways looks like the era of the nation-state.

Change is particularly striking when we look beyond global flows of goods and services to globalizing changes in ideas and identities. The growing transnational consolidation of capitalist markets has been accompanied by the spread of market ideologies and their enforcement by multilateral agencies and multinational banks and corporations. (The global financial crisis has only moderated public expressions of enthusiasm for markets, not fundamentally altered the pressures to comply with their demands.) The spread of American or Western economic and political power has been matched by the spread of initially Western economic and political ideas and models—including human rights. Revolutions in communication and transportation have even begun to alter our understandings of how we conceive of ourselves and the communities in which our lives are embedded and how we relate to government.

Sovereign states may have been the optimal size for economic, political, and social organization in the nineteenth and twentieth centuries. Today they are too small. Ever larger and stronger business enterprises are adopting a truly global form and outlook, causing even powerful states to lose control over aspects of their economies and polities that they have been accustomed to dominating. Regional and international organizations increasingly influence, and sometimes even make, decisions that once were unquestionably the province of states. Transnational nongovernmental organizations now exert powerful and sophisticated pressures on states (and businesses) on issues such as human rights and the environment.

At the same time, globalization often makes the state too large. Local and regional autonomy has become a common theme, especially (but not only) in Europe. Spain has perhaps gone the furthest among nonfederal states in devolving spending and decision making to regional authorities, not just in the Basque and Catalan regions but throughout the country. Consider also the creation of the Scottish and Welsh Parliaments in the United Kingdom, the emergence of the Northern League as a powerful political force in Italy, and the revival of regional languages such as Breton in France and Frisian in the Netherlands. In many countries of the global South as well, demands for greater autonomy are often focused on an intrastate region rather than creating a separate state. "Localization" has become another dimension of globalization.

In fact, the local and the global are increasingly linked without the intermediation of the state. Multinational business provides the most obvious example. But new information and transportation technologies also allow the disenfranchised to leap over their own (often hostile or indifferent) states. For example, Alison Brysk has shown how indigenous peoples in the Americas are able to interact with their colleagues and allies across the globe, dramatically improving their bargaining position vis-à-vis their own state.[1] This is a striking example of what Margaret Keck and Kathryn Sikkink call the "boomerang" model of transnational advocacy: local actors direct information and appeals to transnational colleagues, foreign states, and regional and international organizations, who respond by mobilizing external pressure on resistant states.[2]

Some of these new flows of structures, processes, and opportunities are empowering. The spread of human rights ideas, and their rise to global preeminence in the post–cold war era, can be seen as an element of globalization. More prosaically, individuals and groups with shared interests increasingly are able to interact, in real time, over immense distances, without regard to the boundaries between (or the interests of) states. The Internet and modern transportation networks have allowed a growing number of communities in the global South to exploit the benefits of agricultural and craft cooperatives, fair-trade products, and alternative crops such as miniature vegetables for high-profit markets in developed countries. Mobile phones allow even small entrepreneurs in poor countries to make connections with customers and suppliers that open up previously unimagined possibilities for business and a better life for themselves and their families. Even antiglobalization protests have been significantly facilitated by new communications and transportation technologies.

However, other global flows that circumvent the state have a much darker side. Consider, for example, burgeoning transnational criminal enterprises, transnational human trafficking, sex tourism in Southeast Asia and the Caribbean, and the growing market in private "security" services. There is also an ominous side to the ability of large global firms to accumulate wealth and power that escapes national or international regulation.

No single chapter can even begin to approach anything close to the full range of human rights issues posed by globalization. Here I focus on one, namely, the challenge that economic globalization poses to the liberal democratic welfare state and to economic and social human rights.

2. STATES AND HUMAN RIGHTS

As we have seen, international human rights treaties create obligations for states to respect, protect, and implement the rights of *their own* citizens (and foreigners under their jurisdiction). International human rights norms have made a state's national human rights practices a legitimate area of *noncoercive* international action. International enforcement of these obligations, however, remains largely prohibited. The human rights of nonnationals are largely matters for "their own" states to secure. States have neither a right nor a responsibility to implement or enforce the human rights of foreigners on foreign territory, with extremely limited exceptions such as genocide (and perhaps torture and slavery). Even international supervision of national human rights practices is extremely restricted.

States can do, have done, and will continue to do many nasty, even horrible, things to "their" citizens. In the 1970s and 1980s, such abuses were the focus of most human rights advocates. That made considerable sense then. Globalization, however, suggests that we might do well to focus more on the essential role that states play in implementing and protecting human rights.

Most people enjoy their internationally recognized human rights, particularly when they require coercive enforcement, as a result of action taken by "their own" state. Even Europe's strong and effective regional human rights regime, as we saw in §6.1, is largely a supplement and spur to national action. In fact, the struggle of dispossessed groups has typically been a struggle for full legal and political recognition by the state, and thus inclusion among those whose rights are protected by the state. Human rights advocacy is in may ways aimed at transforming the state from predator to protector of rights.

This is no less true of economic and social rights than civil and political rights. Classical economists across the political spectrum, from Adam Smith to Karl Marx, stressed that market systems of production and distribution, by freeing productive forces from political constraints, have immensely liberating potential. But Smith no less than Marx also recognized that these same productive forces (and those who control them) are typically indifferent to the fates of individuals unable to compete successfully in the predatory world of capitalist competition. Historically, the only mechanism that has been able to protect individual rights in market systems has been the state.

Thus, a human rights perspective on the state is neither statist nor antistatist. Rather, human rights advocates seek to promote a particular type of state. The struggle for economic and social rights has in many ways been a struggle to transform the state from the protector of a dominant economic and political elite into a guarantor of basic rights and equal concern and respect for all.

Globalization threatens "good" states as well as "bad" states. If liberal democratic welfare states are undermined by globalization—and if we fail to create alternative mechanisms for implementing and enforcing human rights—then the substantial achievements of the human rights movement since the end of World War II will be at risk.

3. MARKETS AND WELFARE STATES

The state envisioned by contemporary international human rights norms is liberal; that is, its legitimacy rests on protecting the human rights of its citizens. It is democratic, in the sense that it is committed to universal political participation and, within the limits of the human rights of all, vests political power in "the people." It is also a welfare state, with extensive economic and social obligations to all citizens. And in practice, these economic and social rights can be widely and sustainably provided only to the extent that markets are central to the national economy (which itself is integrated into a global market-based economy).

The inefficiencies of command economies almost always swamp any equity benefits, at least in the medium and long runs. Although countries such as Cuba and Sri Lanka did achieve notable short- and medium-run success during the cold war, in the long run neither growth nor equity has proved to be possible within a command economy. A considerable degree of economic efficiency, and thus reliance on markets, is necessary for *sustainable* progress in implementing economic and social rights.

This important lesson, though, does not justify excluding or even dramatically restricting the role of the state in the economy. States have at least two vital economic roles. They must facilitate the operation of markets, in order to create growth. And they must redistribute resources and opportunities, to ensure that growth contributes to the enjoyment of economic and social rights by all.

Markets, by design, distribute the benefits of growth without regard for individual needs and rights (other than property rights). Markets seek economic efficiency, maximizing the total quantity of goods and services produced with a given quantity of resources. Markets promise to produce more overall, not more for all.

Market distributions take into account only economic value added, which varies sharply across individuals and social groups. Free markets thus *necessarily* produce gross economic inequalities. The poor tend to be "less efficient"; as a class, they have fewer of the skills valued highly by markets. Their plight is then exacerbated when political disadvantage reinforces a vicious rights-abusive cycle. Efficient markets improve the lot of some—ideally even many—at the cost of (relative and perhaps even absolute) deprivation of others. And that suffering is concentrated among society's most vulnerable elements.

Advocates of markets admit that some are harmed in the short run. Everyone, though, is supposed to benefit in the long run from the greater supply of goods and services. "Everyone," however, does not mean each and every individual. Rather, economists refer to the *average* individual, an entirely abstract entity. And even the average person is assured of significant gain only at some point in the future. Here, now, and in the near future, many real, flesh-and-blood, individual human beings and families suffer. Even worse, because markets distribute the benefits of growth without regard to short-term deprivations, those who suffer "adjustment costs"— lost jobs, higher food prices, inferior health care—acquire no special claim to a future share of the collective benefits of efficient markets.

Markets may rely on individual initiative. But they ground a collectivist, "utilitarian" political theory. Markets are justified by arguments of collective good and aggregate benefit, not individual rights (other than, perhaps, the right to economic accumulation). Free markets are an economic analogue to a political system of majority rule without minority rights. The welfare state, from this perspective, is a device to ensure that a minority that is disadvantaged in or deprived by markets is still treated with minimum economic concern and respect. Only when the pursuit of prosperity is tamed by economic and social rights—when markets are embedded in a welfare state—does a market-based economy merit our respect.

Without welfare states (or other comparable redistributive mechanisms), there is no necessary connection between market-led growth and development and the enjoyment of economic and social rights. This fact is now fully accepted; it is the basis of the welfare states that Westerners take for granted. All existing liberal democracies use the welfare state to compensate (some of) those who fare less well in the market.

In fact, one of the great human rights achievements of the past century has been the humanization of capitalist markets by welfare states. State regulation of hours, wages, and working conditions is widely accepted (in theory at least) in most countries throughout the world. Furthermore, the citizens of most states—not simply those with developed market economies—consider their governments to be obliged to provide minimum levels of subsistence, housing, health care, and social services to those unable to acquire them through family or market mechanisms.

Individuals who are harmed by the operation of social institutions (markets and private property rights) that benefit the whole are entitled to a fair share of the social product their participation has helped to produce. The collectivity that benefits in the aggregate has an obligation to look after individual members who are disadvantaged in or harmed by markets. The welfare state guarantees *all* individuals certain economic and social goods, services, and opportunities, irrespective of the market value of their labor.

The welfare state today, however, is under assault from economic globalization. As an international division of labor continues to develop, leading to a growing separation between locales of production and consumption, firms are increasingly free to move "offshore," in whole or in part, in order to escape the higher costs imposed by welfare state guarantees of economic and social rights. States, by contrast, for all their power, remain largely tied to and limited by a particular territory. The resulting threats to economic and social rights are perhaps most evident in the developed market economies of western Europe, where benefits have already begun to erode. In much of the developing world, welfare states face additional attacks from internationally mandated and managed structural adjustment programs, which in addition to targeting waste and inefficiency also typically target social welfare expenditures.

Consider the changing role of the International Monetary Fund (IMF). Originally created to supervise a global financial regime based on fixed exchange rates—which were intended to *increase* national economic control in order to better realize welfare state policies—the IMF today serves principally to enforce the ever-widening penetration of market mechanisms, with little concern for social welfare. Thus, whereas John Ruggie aptly described the postwar international economic order as "embedded liberalism"—market mechanisms embedded within a political commitment to liberal democratic welfare states—the reigning ideology today is more (neo)classically liberal, pursuing market efficiencies with relatively limited regard to welfare.[3]

4. MARKET DEMOCRACY AND
AMERICAN FOREIGN POLICY

Since the end of the cold war, there has been a powerful convergence of markets, human rights ideas, and political power behind the idea of "market democracy," a vision of national and international political legitimacy that is arguably a central part of the process of globalization in the early twenty-first century. Markets and democracy certainly are "good things," especially when contrasted to the alternatives of command economies and authoritarian or totalitarian rule. They are not, however, the same good things as human rights. We have already seen that in the case of markets. And the same is true of democracy, as we saw in Problem 1 in Chapter 2.

A. Democracy, Democratization, and Human Rights

Democracy answers the question of *who* should rule. Democracy empowers the people and seeks to realize their collective good. Human rights, by contrast, address *how* governments should rule. Human rights empower autonomous individuals. They seek to ensure that personal and societal goals, including democratically defined goals, are pursued within the confines of guaranteeing every individual certain minimum goods, services, and opportunities.

Human rights define the range within which democratic decision making is allowed to operate. Human rights are fundamentally nonmajoritarian. They are concerned with each rather than all. They aim to protect every person, against majorities no less than against minorities. Human rights ordinarily take precedence over the wishes of the people, no matter how intensely even the vast majority of society desires to abuse some individual or group. In fact, in procedurally democratic states, where the majority is relatively well positioned to care for its own rights and interests, the *principal* function of human rights is to limit democratic decision making.

The post–cold war world has seen the continued spread and deepening of electoral democracy. For the first time in history, the majority of people on this planet live under democratically elected governments. This momentous achievement is a source of legitimate satisfaction. We must not, however, overestimate its human rights significance. In particular, we must not confuse decreased tolerance for old forms of repressive rule with support for, let alone institutionalization of, rights-protective regimes. We can distinguish three levels of political progress toward respect for internationally recognized human rights.

Liberalization involves a decrease in human rights violations and an opening of political space for at least some previously excluded groups—roughly, progress in civil and political rights short of democratization. China has undergone periodic limited liberalizations. Poland liberalized in the 1980s, initially under the pressure of Solidarity, before it democratized in 1990. South Korea liberalized in the 1980s before establishing electoral democracy in the 1990s.

By *democratization,* I mean the process of establishing electoral democracy, which involves a qualitative leap beyond liberalization. When "soft" authoritarian regimes allow truly fair and open elections (not just once, or if they win), the political system is fundamentally transformed.

A *rights-protective regime* both makes the protection of internationally recognized human rights a central element of its mission and, through extensive, intense, and sustained effort, has achieved considerable success in realizing this aspiration. This is *liberal* democracy. If one insists on using the language of democratization to describe transitions from electoral to liberal democracy, one might talk about the "deepening" of democratization—although it is respect for human rights, rather than for the will of the people, that deepens.

Note that only the second of these three processes is centrally connected with democracy understood in the core sense of rule of the people. The distinction between electoral and liberal democracy concerns not who rules but how (within what limits). Liberalization, too, is concerned with the limits on government rather than who rules.

Nonetheless, "democratization" is often used to cover all three kinds of change, on the assumption that they are phases of a single, largely linear process of development. Political development, however, is not "naturally" driven toward a single end. Resistance to authoritarian rule is often not a transition to democracy, or anything else, but a reaction against injustice. Regimes that have liberalized often resist democratization. Even fair and moderately open elections may produce governments that violate human rights.

One of the most disturbing lessons of democratization in eastern Europe and central Asia since the end of the cold war, as in much of Africa in the 1960s and 1970s, is that many people see voting as a device for acquiring prosperity and a sense of control rather than a way to ensure widespread protection of human rights. Even more disturbing are the cases where the majority seeks electoral power to oppress a minority—or a minority hijacks the electoral process to oppress the majority.

Electoral democracy may be a necessary condition for liberal democracy. Liberalization and electoral democracy may even foster liberal democracy by allowing human rights advocates political space and opportunities. But there is no natural, inescapable evolution. Electorally democratic governments may use their power in ways that violate, threaten, or fail to defend internationally recognized human rights. Especially in times of crisis or disillusionment, electoral democracy may even be prone to populist, protofascist demagoguery.

Elections are only a device. They have very different meanings in different political contexts. All other things being equal, it is a good thing if leaders are freely chosen and speak for the people. What is most important, though, is whether human rights are secure. Only when supported by rights-protective political attitudes and institutions will elections lead toward deeply liberal democratic regimes.

The danger, especially in US foreign policy, is that we will forget that democratization is, at best, a good start on realizing human rights. Americans seem inclined to the convenient but dangerous illusion that once elections have been held, the struggle for human rights—or at least our part in the struggle—is largely over. In fact, as recent events in Iraq have shown, the struggle really begins then.

B. Market Democracy and Economic Rights

Turning to questions related to market democracy, Americans too often forget how heavily the US government is involved in regulating markets and attempting to counteract the social inequities they produce. Not even Ronald Reagan proposed returning to anything even approximating a true free-market economy. Twentieth-century liberal democracies were distinguished from "free-market capitalism" by redistributive policies that protect individual rights and seek social justice. And even contemporary American advocates of free markets only want to reduce, not eliminate, state intervention and regulation. (For example, Senator Rand Paul speaks for almost no one other than mine owners when he calls for abolishing federal mine safety regulations and regulators.)

Despite all the gaps in its coverage, the United States is a huge welfare state. For example, workers and employers together are taxed one-seventh of an employee's income just to fund a single social welfare program: state-supported old-age pensions (Social Security). Even Americans, who are more individualistic and antistatist than most Europeans, see their welfare state as an essential part of the American political ideal.

In American foreign policy, however, all one hears about is markets. When dealing with countries still shaped by the legacy of command economies, the allure of the market is perhaps understandable. However, American advocacy of markets in the former Soviet bloc and the Third World ignores their significant human costs. There is a disturbing parallel with cold war anticommunism: excessive focus on the "problem" (communism; command economies) yields inattention to the "unintended" consequences of the "solution" (dictators; markets).

This is particularly true for American support of IMF-imposed structural adjustment programs. Structural adjustment almost always has immediate and detrimental short-term effects on the enjoyment of economic rights by large segments of the population. Reductions in state spending on education and health, retrenchments in public-sector employment, reductions in real wages, and programs to privatize land leave the poor even more vulnerable than they were before. In addition, the political unpopularity of often-punitive cuts in social services may disrupt the pace and process of political liberalization and democratization.

I do not mean to suggest that even punishing structural adjustment is always the wrong course of action, all things considered. Each country is unique. There are difficult trade-offs that need to be made between competing goals and time frames. Furthermore, practice shows that program implementation is at least as important as program design in determining human rights consequences. But such problems need to be confronted, seriously and directly, rather than brushed aside with appeals to the general virtues of markets.

Neither do I mean to belittle the problems faced in implementing economic and social rights or the contribution of properly regulated markets. Markets, to repeat, are necessary. It is essential, though, to give equal emphasis to the fact that they are not sufficient.

I do not even want to deny that some countries may face a tragic choice between growth and equity. But where victims of market-driven growth truly cannot be prevented (at a reasonable cost), they must be acknowledged, and mourned. Instead, in their enthusiasm for sweeping away the old, Americans too often seem not to see, let alone be troubled by, the problems in the new.

5. AN ALLIANCE OF STATES AND HUMAN RIGHTS ADVOCATES?

If the welfare state is increasingly unable to ensure economic and social rights for all, regional or global institutions might seem to present an obvious "solution." The problem, of course, is that there is little evidence of the imminent emergence of global redistributive institutions. Virtually all states, including even relatively well-to-do and committed liberal democratic welfare states, remain extremely reluctant to transfer substantial authority to global political institutions.

Nonetheless, interstate mechanisms are not necessarily doomed to failure. For example, the harmonization of social policies in the European Union can be viewed as a collective regional effort to reduce the incentives of individual states to compete for jobs by dismantling the welfare state. Europe, however, looks very much like the exception that proves the rule. And even the Europeans seem uninterested in using the Organization for Economic Cooperation and Development, or some new institution, to spread cooperation on social policy across a wider range of developed market economies. The eurozone crisis of 2011 (and I suspect 2012) even suggests a deep reluctance to bear substantial costs on behalf of other EU members.

Transnational actors offer another potential mechanism for revitalizing economic and social rights. Human rights NGOs, trade unions, women's groups, environmentalists, indigenous peoples, and a host of other groups in "civil society" share a common interest in (re)asserting welfare state control over global markets and multinational business. Civil society actors, however, are at an extreme disadvantage, both because of their relative lack of economic and political resources and because they face far greater problems in forming national and transnational alliances. In addition, although not as territorially bound as states, they are usually less mobile than the businesses against whom they are pitted.

The current international situation with respect to economic and social rights has parallels to conditions in western Europe in the mid-nineteenth century, where business had the upper hand and skillfully used its resources to protect its interests. Contemporary multinational businesses also have the advantage of being able to play country against country—and in the United States, because of its federal system, state against state. Those seeking to strengthen the welfare state, by contrast, face the daunting task of (re)establishing control. Multinational businesses need only evade regulation.

Advocates of economic and social rights, however, have resources of their own, including national electoral power and advanced communications technologies that increase their capabilities for national and transnational organization. Furthermore, unlike in the nineteenth century, they can draw on the moral force of authoritative international human rights norms and the accumulated experience of many decades of welfare state policies.

In addition, advocates of internationally recognized economic and social rights share a common interest with at least some government elites in controlling transnational business. Especially in highly institutionalized liberal democratic welfare states, human rights advocates and states share a deeply rooted desire to temper the efficiency of markets with rights-based concerns for at least minimally equitable distributions of social goods, services, and opportunities. Of course, state elites often seek control over business for their own selfish, even predatory, purposes. But even then their shared desire to gain greater control over corporate practices and profits provides the basis for at least tactical political alliances with human rights advocates.

Once again, the issue is not the state per se but the *type* of state. Transnational business is using economic globalization to press for a state that gives greater emphasis to markets, the domain of social action where their power and skills are greatest. Human rights advocates and allied elements of civil society are seeking to use their electoral, organizational, and moral power on behalf of welfare states. Thus, the fate of human rights is likely to depend, in the early twenty-first century as in the late nineteenth and early twentieth centuries, on who controls the state and how they use that control. In those countries where human rights advocates are maintaining or strengthening their position, an alliance with the state may prove the best way to reestablish the social control over markets necessary to ensure economic and social rights for all.

In the era of globalization, however, no individual state acting alone is able to impose new regulations, or even hold on to its former ability to control "its own" firms. They must cooperate, regionally and internationally, if they are to have a chance of humanizing global markets. And they must forge new alliances with national and transnational civil society actors. Whether this is practically possible, however, is by no means clear.

My enemy's enemy is my friend, the old rule of realist international politics, applies today to states and human rights advocates. Whatever their past animosities, today they face a new common enemy. The future of human rights just might be determined by their ability to develop new forms of cooperation that protect the state as an essential mechanism for realizing human rights—at least until new mechanisms are created, which still seems, at best, very far off in a speculative future.

A central purpose of human rights advocacy has always been to empower people to force "their" state to treat them as they deserve to be treated. This has meant shaping states into instruments to protect, rather than ignore or even trample on, the human rights of their citizens. Today, this increasingly requires states and citizens to stand up to, and attempt to exert control over, transnational and global, not merely national, forces. If not, then much of the hard-won human rights progress of the twentieth century is at risk.

PROBLEM 7: WEST, SOUTH, AND MARKET REDISTRIBUTIONS

The Problem

Globalization is beginning to erode the capacity of Western welfare states to provide economic and social rights at the levels at which their populations have become accustomed. Other factors, including demographic changes and politically motivated overcommitments to beneficiaries, are also part of the explanation. But the new global division of labor has undoubtedly reduced the number of well-paid, low-and moderately skilled jobs available in developed market economies. This simultaneously creates new demands for benefits and restricts the ability of states to fund those benefits by taxing increasingly peripatetic firms.

But is this really a global human rights problem, all things considered? Aren't the same global market forces dramatically raising incomes in numerous countries in the global South? In fact, given the much greater marginal utility of improvements for poor people in the global South than the losses likely to be suffered by middle-class beneficiaries in the West, isn't the net human rights impact of economic globalization positive?

A Solution

The extension of market efficiencies to regions previously suffering under closed or command economies certainly is a good thing for economic and social rights. It creates new goods, services, and opportunities that can be mobilized to better provide economic and social rights for a much greater segment of the population (and perhaps also improve their capacities to demand and enjoy civil and political rights as well). But there is no *automatic* mechanism that ensures that the losses of relatively privileged workers in the West will be transformed into improved economic and social rights for large numbers of people in the global South.

We must not confuse a transfer of resources from West to South with improvements in the enjoyment of economic and social rights in the South. The crucial question is how those transferred resources are distributed in particular southern countries. Were most of the benefits to go to a small elite—which is a particularly plausible possibility in the case of mineral and timber resources—the net effect might even be negative.

In addition, some portion of the resources lost by Western workers is going into the pockets of Western and non-Western capitalists, not southern workers. Much depends on questions such as wage rates and working conditions in the new countries of production and tax and spending policies of their governments. And those are a function of both local conditions and the possibility of firms moving their production to more "business-friendly" environments.

On balance southern workers in many countries have dramatically improved their living conditions as a result of the new global division of labor. This has been most striking in several rapidly growing Asian countries. But it is increasingly true in other regions as well. For example, over eight of the past ten years, Africa grew more rapidly than Asia (including Japan). And even when governments have not been particularly concerned with redistribution or directly providing economic and social rights, in numerous countries their people are enjoying better food, better housing, better health care, and better protection against economic fluctuations. (Remember that private provision is central, even the norm, for many economic and social rights, even in the West.)

This has been dependent on the fact that, so far at least, globalization has been a highly positive sum game; that is, it has increased the total pie, not just redistributed it. For example, real global GDP, measured in 2005 dollars, increased from about $29 trillion in 1990 to almost $50 trillion in 2010. Some significant part of this growth can be attributed to the increasing globalization of production. And that has made available the aggregate resources necessary to support widespread improvements in the enjoyment of economic and social rights.

Any deterioration in the enjoyment of any human rights by anyone anywhere is a legitimate matter of concern for human rights advocates—not to mention the people whose rights are at issue. Nonetheless, these particular losses of Western workers—which, especially in Europe, have so far been extremely modest—would seem, on balance, to be a matter of relatively low concern in a broad, global human rights assessment.

Further Problems

We should not, however, confuse averages, or even the norm, with every case. Consider, for example, Nigeria, which has largely squandered its immense oil wealth in a kleptocratic orgy by a tiny elite. Economic globalization can be, but need not be, a boon to human rights. This is another way of saying that markets are a necessary but not sufficient condition for sustained improvements in economic and social rights.

Furthermore, it is not obvious that sacrifices by Western workers, either to date or in the future, are *necessary* for the improvement of economic and social rights in the global South. "Fair trade" rather than "free trade" *might* be a better formula for improving human rights for all.

Finally, the prospect of global firms being able to redirect a growing percentage of the benefits of national and international markets to themselves needs to remain a major concern of human rights advocates. In the long run, mechanisms comparable to national welfare states will be necessary to ensure that capitalism does not revert to the gross inequalities and inequities that led *all* developed market economies to establish highly redistributive welfare states. As the world begins to work itself out from the global recession of the late 2000s, this may prove to be the most important issue it faces for the future of economic and social rights.

DISCUSSION QUESTIONS

1. What exactly do you mean by *globalization* when you use the term? Is it a recent or a long-standing process? What are its dimensions? Is the global spread of human rights itself a phenomenon of globalization?

2. Human rights advocates typically focus on states as a threat to human rights. This chapter suggests that globalization is forcing human rights advocates to emphasize the role of the state as protector. Has there really been a change? Hasn't the role of the state as protector always been central?

3. Is the welfare state really such a wonderful achievement? Is globalization making a positive contribution by freeing economic initiative from the shackles of excessive welfare state regulation? Can't we see the shift in the balance of power away from states produced by globalization as basically a positive trend? Why do advocates of liberal democratic welfare states want the state in our lives economically but out of our lives in other domains?

4. How would you evaluate the distinction drawn between liberalization, democratization, and creating a rights-protective regime? Applying this distinction and the post–cold war history of the former Soviet bloc, what does it say about Iraq? About the broader process of "democratization" that the war in Iraq has allegedly triggered? Am I correct that this distinction is especially important for Americans, who tend to focus on the formalities of democratization, often to the exclusion of the real substance of protecting human rights?

5. Are markets, from a human rights point of view, really just the lesser evil? Am I correct in suggesting that questions of economic, social, and cultural rights have in recent years often gotten lost in the rush toward market-oriented economic reforms? Even if that is true, is this a necessary first step toward sustained progress on economic, social, and cultural rights? If so, how can we ensure that progress continues?

6. Why are Americans, who claim to be so individualistic, so attracted to democracy and markets, which are fundamentally collective systems of political justification? What kind of individualism is it that Americans really value?

7. Which is the biggest threat to human rights: globalization (markets), states, or terrorism? Does your answer depend on where you live? On which rights you are considering?

SUGGESTED READINGS

Perhaps the best discussion of human rights and globalization available is Rhoda E. Howard-Hassmann, *Can Globalization Promote Human Rights?* (University Park: Pennsylvania State University Press, 2010). Her answer to the title question is a strong but qualified yes—if the efficiencies of global markets can be harnessed to human development in ways comparable to those used by liberal and social democratic welfare states in the twentieth century. An article-length version of Howard-Hassmann's argument is also available: "The Second Great Transformation: Human Rights Leapfrogging in the Era of Globalization," *Human Rights Quarterly* 27 (February 2005): 1–40. A similar and in many ways complementary argument is developed in David Kinley, *Civilising Globalisation: Human Rights and the Global Economy* (Cambridge: Cambridge University Press, 2009). For a much more negative assessment, see Neve Gordon, ed., *From the Margins of Globalization: Critical Perspectives on Human Rights* (Lanham, MD: Lexington Books, 2004). For a balanced assessment of structural adjustment, see M. Rodwan Abouharb and David Cingranelli, *Human Rights and Structural Adjustment* (Cambridge: Cambridge University Press, 2007).

Good and generally wide-ranging discussions can be found in the following books: Wolfgang Benedek, Koen De Feyter, and Fabrizio Marrella, eds., *Economic Globalisation and Human Rights* (Cambridge: Cambridge University Press, 2007); Janet Dine and Andrew Fagan, eds., *Human Rights and Capitalism: A Multidisciplinary Perspective on Globalisation* (Cheltenham: Edward Elgar, 2006); Jean-Marc Coicaud, Michael W. Doyle, and Anne-Marie Gardner, eds., *The Globalization of Human Rights* (Tokyo: United Nations University Press, 2003); and Alison Brysk, ed., *Globalization and Human Rights* (Berkeley and Los Angeles: University of California Press, 2002).

On the huge topic of the movement to establish human rights obligations for corporations, good introductions are available in Chapter 3 of Allison Brysk, *Human Rights, Private Wrongs* (New York: Routledge, 2005), and Chapter 8 of David P. Forsythe, *Human Rights and International Relations*, 3rd ed. (Cambridge: Cambridge University Press, 2012).

On the ethical dimensions of the topic, good places to start are Thomas Pogge, ed., *Freedom from Poverty as a Human Right: Who Owes What to the Very Poor?* (Oxford: Oxford University Press, 2007), and Daniel E. Lee and Elizabeth J. Lee, *Human Rights and the Ethics of Globalization* (New York: Cambridge University Press, 2010). Among the more interesting sustained explorations I would single out David Miller, *National Responsibility and Global Justice* (Oxford: Oxford University Press, 2007), and Thomas Pogge, *World Poverty and Human Rights: Cosmopolitan Responsibilities and Reforms* (Cambridge: Polity Press, 2008).

For interesting discussions that link democracy, globalization, and human rights, see Deen K. Chatterjee, ed., *Democracy in a Global World: Human Rights and Political Participation in the 21st Century* (Lanham, MD: Rowman & Littlefield, 2008), and Nicolas Guilhot, *The Democracy Makers: Human Rights and International Order* (New York: Columbia University Press, 2005).

15

(Anti)Terrorism and Human Rights

This chapter examines not terrorism or antiterrorism per se but their consequences for international human rights. More particularly, I will focus on the impact on US foreign policy. Although this somewhat exaggerates the picture—US policy has been altered more than that of other Western countries—it does so in an instructive way, given the leading American role in the development and prosecution of "the war on terror." I will argue that whatever its justifications and achievements with respect to terrorism, "the war on terror" has provoked a one-dimensional ideological campaign that has marginalized human rights much as during the cold war—but much less widely, less intensely, and for a much shorter time.

1. HUMAN RIGHTS IN POST-COLD WAR AMERICAN FOREIGN POLICY

Assessing the impact of 9/11 requires a baseline of comparison. The preceding dozen years had witnessed a significant increase in the priority accorded to democracy and human rights objectives. In addition, a stream of unilateral and multilateral practice in the 1990s established an international right to humanitarian intervention against genocide.

Although there is little controversy about the existence of these changes, their cause is a matter of contention. How much was due to their rise in the hierarchy of US foreign policy interests? How much was due instead to the demise of (anti)communism, which opened space for the pursuit of other interests? The evidence since September 11 suggests that it was more the latter.

Consider a simple three-interest model of foreign policy. Let us assume that foreign policy comprises security interests, economic interests, and "other" interests. In general, security trumps everything else. Economic interests usually (though not always) take priority over "other" interests. Occasionally, economic interests may even compete with (secondary) security concerns. "Other" interests generally come last. This, I would suggest, is a pretty good first approximation of the outlines of the foreign policy priorities of the United States (and most other countries as well).

The place of an interest within this hierarchy (and within the hierarchy of "other" interests) may change either absolutely or relatively; that is, the (absolute) value attributed to it may change, or the (absolute) value of another interest above or below it may change, leading to a change in the *relative* value (which has remained absolutely constant). I suggest that the increased attention to human rights and democracy in post–cold war American foreign policy was largely relative rather than absolute. Although there may have been a modest absolute increase in the value attributed to human rights, the most important post–cold war change was a dramatic contraction in the scope of security concerns, which opened space for increased attention to human rights.

Compare this to the absolute change in the place of human rights in American foreign policy that took place in the 1970s and 1980s. In the Carter and first Reagan presidencies, debate raged over whether human rights were an appropriate foreign policy concern. A decade later, debate focused on what place human rights should be given in particular cases and their importance relative to other foreign policy interests. Human rights had become entrenched on the American foreign policy agenda as a largely nonpartisan objective. Across the entire mainstream of the political spectrum, which had shifted clearly to the right throughout the decade, human rights had become an accepted, and valued, objective of American foreign policy.

Although the post–cold war changes in American international human rights policy built on this entrenchment of human rights, the dramatic reduction in geopolitical impediments to the pursuit of human rights objectives was more important. In what was often called a unipolar world, there were many fewer security concerns to interfere with the pursuit of human rights objectives. The American (and international) reaction against the 1989 Tiananmen massacre, discussed in Chapter 12, is perhaps the clearest indication of the new geopolitical space for international human rights concerns.

No less important than the changes in the international power structure was the ideological space opened by the demise of communism. During the cold war, protecting "democracy" and "the free world" regularly was deemed to require tolerating (or even actively supporting) human rights violations directed against the "enemies of freedom." With the end of ideological rivalry, which had been at the heart of much of the American support for repressive regimes of the Right, the "threat" posed to "friendly" dictators largely evaporated (in places such as Guatemala and El Salvador) or, when we looked more carefully, could no longer be found (in places like Uruguay and Zaire).

With the definition of democracy liberated from the tyranny of anticommunism, the United States not only developed a renewed emphasis on elections but increasingly came to see that real democracy required an active and effective independent civil society. As civil society promotion programs expanded, important conceptual and practical linkages were forged between human rights and democratization agendas. Whatever the shortcomings in program design, and for all the restrictions imposed by competing interests, this was a major advance in the sophistication and potential impact of US human rights diplomacy.[1]

These progressive trends were significantly reinforced by the collapse of dictatorships of the Right and Left alike. Attention shifted, in part, from the largely reactive and remedial emphasis on stopping systematic and often brutal repression, and aiding its victims, toward a more positive emphasis on helping to build a human rights culture. Once the old dictators were gone, it became increasingly clear that the work of building rights-respecting societies and rights-protective regimes had only begun. This new attitude tended to be expressed primarily in the language of democracy and democratization. In the United States, this was reflected bureaucratically in the change of the name of the State Department's Bureau of Human Rights and Humanitarian Affairs to the Bureau of Democracy, Human Rights, and Labor.

In its least-attractive dimensions, this sometimes led to a fetishistic pursuit of elections. American policy has also often confused political liberalization (that is, reductions in or even elimination of old forms of repression) with democratization, in a naive belief that all progressive political change lies on a path that leads to democracy. But in its more attractive dimensions—which were not entirely lacking during the Clinton years, and even during the first Bush administration— it involved a vision of human rights that went well beyond the simplistic cold war– era vision of stopping torture, freeing political prisoners, and "throwing the rascals out."

2. THE RETREAT OF HUMAN RIGHTS

Some of the changes discussed in the preceding section have become deeply entrenched, most notably the acceptance throughout the political mainstream of human rights as a legitimate concern of American foreign policy. The relative priority attached to international human rights objectives, however, remains a matter of controversy. The argument above suggests that the post–cold war rise of human rights and democracy as objectives of American foreign policy was vulnerable to a reinflation of security concerns. In this section, I suggest that since September 11 we have indeed seen democracy and human rights partly eclipsed by a new geopolitical vision and a new ideological crusade that have striking analogies to their cold war predecessors.

Consider the transformation of Pakistan, in the official American representation, from a retrograde military dictatorship—and one that, in addition, was a major supporter of international terrorism, the preceding decade's most flagrant violator of the nonproliferation regime, and a bellicose threat to regional security in South Asia—to a leading American ally. And despite the lack of any substantial human rights improvements or any progress toward real democracy in Pakistan, the American embrace continued, far beyond what the war in Afghanistan demanded.

Much more generally, governments have taken advantage of the rhetoric of antiterrorism to intensify their attacks on domestic and international enemies. This was particularly true in the first few years following 9/11. Russia and Israel provide perhaps the most tragic examples of the war on terrorism run amok.

In Chechnya, intensified Russian military action certainly owed much to the seemingly interminable nature of that terrible conflict.[2] Russia, however, was emboldened by the language and logic of a global war on terrorism, calculating, correctly, that appeals to antiterrorism today provide partial insulation from international criticism.[3] The muting and partial disabling of humanitarian criticism have certainly not caused Russian brutality, but they have facilitated it.

In Israel, the Sharon government responded to the flood of vicious terror bombings in 2002 with a vengeance that reflected not only its own inclinations but also American toleration for a most brutal war on terrorism.[4] Assassination and collective punishment have become standard operating procedure. The indignities and human rights violations that have long characterized military occupation have intensified in number and severity. Perhaps most brutal were policies consciously aimed at destroying the Palestinian economy and making every Palestinian civilian suffer, both economically and through the denial of personal liberties,[5] for the actions of a tiny group of extremists and the unwillingness or inability of Palestinian authorities to control them.

The terrorist threats Russia and Israel face are very real. But that is no justification for a response that itself relies on systematic human rights violations and terrorist tactics.[6] The United States and its allies, however, have backed off their criticism of Russia—the words are still there, but they lack much conviction anymore.[7] And the United States, Israel's principal ally, has done little to impede its slide into policies that can only accurately be described as state terrorism.

Like anticommunism during the cold war, antiterrorism has become less a material interest of foreign policy than a crusade against evil to be pursued without too much concern for the ordinary restraints of law and conventional limits on the use of force. Where the conflict has been militarized, the classic just-war restrictions have eroded or been ignored: noncombatants are directly targeted, proportionality is ignored, and the very idea of innocent civilians is undermined by direct and indirect attributions of collective responsibility and guilt. Where the struggle is carried out through the institutions of "law and order" and the internal security forces, human rights are the price exacted not just from terrorists but from peaceful political opponents, members of groups that are feared or despised, and ordinary individuals accidentally or arbitrarily caught up in the security apparatus.

These relatively dramatic examples, which involve the positive enabling of rights-abusive policies, are matched by a modest and uneven but real decline in American attention to human rights and democracy promotion. Although the United States remains committed to human rights and democracy, these objectives have moved toward the background in a number of particular cases. The decline has been substantially less dramatic in the past few years than during the cold war. (An analogy with the impact of the war on drugs on US policy in the Andean region is closer to the mark.) Nonetheless, the decline has been real and important.

Support for these changes has by no means been restricted to the political Right. In fact, the most striking fact has been the participation in or tolerance for this shift in policy by moderates and liberals, who are generally inclined toward pursuing international human rights objectives. The Bush administration's antiterrorism policy received strong bipartisan support. Its domestic dimensions provoked sustained (although limited) criticism from prominent mainstream political figures. Criticism of its international dimensions, however, has been restricted primarily to human rights NGOs and figures on the fringes of the political mainstream.

Nevertheless, even the Bush administration did not mount a general attack on human rights and democracy objectives, which have remained goals of American foreign policy. One need not be overly charitable to suggest that this reflects genuine commitment to these values. At the very least, it indicates that important domestic and international constituencies continue to take them seriously. (Hypocrisy is effective only to the extent that it taps into widely and genuinely held values.)

In an important sense, then, the relative decline of human rights in American foreign policy has been largely unintended. The explicit aim has been not to harm or even slight human rights but rather to pursue security objectives that are deemed to be more important. This does not, however, in any way lessen American responsibility. The negative human rights consequences have been very real, were easily anticipated, and are now well known. The lack of intent, though, is important for thinking about the prospects for reversing these trends.

If the decline in the position of human rights in American foreign policy has been largely relative, then any revival—much like the initial post–cold war increase in the prominence of international human rights concerns—will depend on space being opened by the retreat of competing security objectives. A return to a more active, assertive, and consistent international human rights policy must wait for the reopening of the political space currently preempted by the war on terrorism. In the final section of this chapter, I will suggest that we are seeing the beginnings of such a reopening.

3. HUMAN RIGHTS, SECURITY, AND FOREIGN POLICY

A defender of the war on terror might argue that the story I have told so far is a simple one of competing foreign policy objectives: major security interests have appropriately pushed human rights and democracy promotion to the sidelines. I suggest, however, that the actual dynamic has been rather different. In this section, I focus on qualitative substantive changes in the understanding of security—that is, the American tendency to conceive new threats in moralized terms and to respond with an irrational exuberance for a militarized crusade.

Up to this point I have talked of "security" as if its meaning was obvious and constant. Protecting the national territory from invasion may fit this description. However, most other security interests are more thoroughly constructed and variable. Consider a simple three-variable model. What is to be secured—the state (national security) or citizens (personal security)? Where does the threat lie—externally or internally? And what is the nature of the threat—material or moral/ideological?

The relatively constant and uncontroversial dimensions of "security" address external material threats to the state. Security thus understood is indeed plausibly seen as an appropriately overriding concern of foreign policy. Without national security from external material threats, all other interests and values are at risk. As we move away from this relatively simple case, however, "security" becomes more obscure and its priority more contentious. In addition, its conceptual and normative relationships to human rights vary considerably.

Although the security of individual citizens has strong connections with human rights, state security is not necessarily connected to individual human rights; it depends on the character of the state being protected and the means used to secure it. To oversimplify, human rights are about protecting citizens from the state (see, however, §4.2). National security is about protecting the state from its (perceived) enemies. Those enemies may themselves be citizens. And even when the enemies are primarily external, the rights of citizens may need to be sacrificed in order to carry out defensive measures.

An antagonistic relationship between (national) security and human rights is especially likely when security is seen in moral rather than material terms and to the extent that threats are perceived to lie in internal subversion. This was a common perception during the cold war. With "security" understood almost exclusively as a matter of *national* security (which was understood to have a significant ideological dimension), US foreign policy was extremely tolerant of regimes that systematically sacrificed the human rights of their citizens to the (alleged) imperatives of protecting the nation from communist attack and subversion. The cases we have considered in this book—Central America (§8.2), the Southern Cone (§8.3), and South Africa (§8.4)—are just a few of literally dozens of instances.

The post–cold war redefinition of American security interests in less ideological terms has eliminated the American incentive to court repressive regimes in order to keep them out of the communist camp. At the same time, it undermined the principal rationale for repression by rightist dictatorships. Taken together, these changes greatly reduced the antagonism between human rights and security in American foreign policy.

In other words, not only were security concerns reduced in number, but the concept of "security" changed. Russia still posed most of the same material threats in 1995 that it did in 1985; the end of the cold war, and the dramatic decline in the Russian threat, did not coincide with a substantial reduction in Soviet military power. Rather, the ideological threat posed by communism disappeared with glasnost and new thinking, the collapse of the Soviet bloc, and the dissolution of the Soviet Union.

In addition, there was a partial move toward a conception of security with more of a personal dimension—or in the language that became popular in the 1990s, "human security" (compare §13.10). Human security never displaced national security on the American foreign policy agenda. It did, however, acquire a significant place. This is perhaps most evident in the rise of armed humanitarian operations that received strong American support, from Somalia and Bosnia through Kosovo and

East Timor (see Chapter 13). More broadly, the concept of peace building (not just peacekeeping) was added to the international security lexicon, and a human rights dimension was incorporated into a number of postconflict peacekeeping operations.

Terrorism has modestly increased the material threat to the United States. The biggest change, however, has been in the other dimensions of security. The war on terrorism has led to a significantly more ideological vision of security—a theme pursued in greater detail in the next section. The focus on personal security has receded in favor of a renewed emphasis on national security. And the internal dimensions of security have moved to the forefront, as expressed in the language of homeland security. As during the cold war, security and human rights are again increasingly coming to be seen as competing rather than reinforcing concerns.

4. THE AXIS OF EVIL

The implication of the preceding section is that human rights and democracy promotion have lost out less as a result of carefully considered trade-offs of competing interests and more due to a decision to reorient American policy around an ideological crusade. In this section, I suggest, by examining the case of the "axis of evil," that this has introduced a substantially irrational element into American policy. I also argue that the new crusade against terrorism has facilitated dangerous trends in American foreign policy, particularly the demonization of enemies and a tendency to act unilaterally.

One striking consequence of the post-9/11 environment was the rhetorical creation, in 2002, of the Iraq–Iran–North Korea "axis of evil." There were in fact no policy connections among these three countries that would plausibly make them an axis. Quite the contrary, Iran and Iraq have been bitter enemies, and North Korea is not closely linked to either of the other two regimes. This new enemy was constructed out of a hodgepodge of very different (and largely unrelated) concerns—most notably terrorism, proliferation, regional security, and general anti-Americanism. The glue that held together this disparate set of issues and countries was the general antiterrorist hysteria in American policy. No rational assessment of American interests would suggest that American policy ought to focus on these three regimes. This is true even in the narrow case of a well-designed war on terrorism.

Terrorists sponsored by these three regimes had not directed their activities against the United States or the US military. In fact, nationals of these countries—in sharp contrast to those of Saudi Arabia, for example—were not involved in the terrorist attacks on Americans. The global role of these three countries makes them no more deserving of special attention. Other states, including American allies, are equally culpable. Syria, for example, has been as active in the Middle East as Iran. The devastation wreaked by Pakistani-supported Kashmiri terrorists has been at least as significant as anything caused by terrorists supported by the axis of evil—not to mention the long-standing Pakistani support for the Taliban, prior to its post-9/11 about-face.

Much the same is true of the other "crimes" of these regimes. Consider proliferation. North Korea has indeed been guilty of breaching international nonproliferation norms, as well as particular agreements with the United States. But our "ally" Pakistan was the most flagrant proliferator of the 1990s, in a regional security context at least as unstable as that of the Korean peninsula. (There is also evidence suggesting that Pakistan contributed to North Korea's nuclear program.) Iraq's nuclear ambitions were in fact effectively thwarted by international sanctions and monitoring. And Iran, although a legitimate proliferation concern, is not an imminent threat to the United States and has been less than clear in its expression of its intentions.

From a human rights perspective, these problems might be forgivable if these "evil" states were the world's leading human rights violators. A strong case can be made that North Korea and Saddam Hussein's Iraq belonged on any "top ten" list. But the inclusion of Iran in such company is absurd. Revolutionary Iran is in many regards an extremely unappealing regime. The situation, however, was and remains far worse in America's leading ally in the region, Saudi Arabia.

Throughout most of the 2000s, Iran was one of the few countries in the region with a vibrant opposition and real hope for reform—although these were violently crushed in 2009. Despite substantial censorship and a serious problem of legal and political attacks on opposition journalists, Iran was one of the few countries in the region with a substantial cadre of opposition journalists. State-supported vigilante violence is a recurrent, and growing, problem, but opposition political figures face fewer threats to their personal security than in most of the rest of the region. And women's rights are further advanced in Iran than in most Arab countries; certainly compared to Saudi Arabia, Iran, especially Tehran, is a paradise for women's rights.

US policy sacrificed the chance to facilitate the process of reform in Iran, which was vibrant during the Bush administration. Quite the contrary, the bellicose words and actions of the United States made life more difficult for reformers. Rather than recognize the positive (if limited) changes in Iran, the United States chose to single out Iran for special attack. It even sacrificed opportunities to pursue convergent interests cooperatively, most notably in Afghanistan and Iraq.

There has been, in effect, a choice to keep Iran as an enemy rather than either help to reform it or try to settle outstanding issues. And the Bush administration chose to make Iran not just an ordinary enemy, but a demonized one. This certainly was facilitated by the earlier demonization of revolutionary Iran following the hostage crisis. But that was more than two decades earlier. The redemonization of Iran, as part of the axis of evil, was largely driven by the hysteria of the war on terror. (The Iranian government, for its own political reasons, seems at least equally intent on casting the United States as a demonized enemy—further suggesting that none of this is conducive to reform or the expansion of human rights.)

5. THE WAR AGAINST IRAQ

One might describe the focus on the axis of evil as silly. Certainly, the idea that these three second- or third-rate powers are the appropriate focal point for the foreign policy of "the world's only superpower" is patently ludicrous. This silliness has had serious negative consequences—most directly for reformers and human rights in Iran, and more generally in the turn of American attention away from human rights. But the consequences pale before those associated with the war on Iraq.

Like the axis of evil itself, the justification for the invasion of Iraq was cobbled together out of a variety of disparate concerns, including weapons of mass destruction, terrorism, "regime change," a history of animosity, and regional security. Like the general charge against the axis of evil, the particular elements of the charge against Iraq are problematic. And the combination was held together with a lot of post-9/11 hysteria.

The threat of weapons of mass destruction was largely imaginary. Iraq's contribution to international terrorism (before the US invasion and occupation) was not notable. There is no hint elsewhere in American foreign policy that even the most vicious behavior of a government is legitimate grounds for a military invasion. And Iraq was no serious threat to its neighbors, having been effectively hobbled by the first Gulf war and a decade of international sanctions.

In addition to the disorder, death, and destruction that have characterized "liberated" Iraq, the United States has embarked on a series of direct violations of human rights and humanitarian law. Abu Ghraib has entered the popular lexicon as a symbol of sadistic political brutality. Clearly, such excesses are not part of official American policy. But many have argued that they have been facilitated, even encouraged, by American policies and practices that suggest that human rights and the rule of law often must be sacrificed to the fight against terror.

Guantánamo has been carved out as a netherworld where neither American nor international (nor Cuban) law applies and where issues of innocence, proof, responsibility, and proportionality are deemed irrelevant. "Extraordinary renditions"—kidnapping suspected terrorists, transporting them across international boundaries, and delivering them into the hands of "friendly" security services that regularly practice torture—reflect a cynical evasion of even the most rudimentary principles of the rule of law. Although President Bush insisted, with apparent sincerity, that the United States neither practices nor tolerates torture, Vice President Cheney and his staff campaigned for months against legislation that codified this claim (and existing American legal obligations under the torture convention). And the list goes on, with the consequence that even America's closest Western allies have strongly condemned American lawlessness and violations of human rights.

I do not mean to suggest that the war on terrorism directly caused the invasion of Iraq. Rather, it enabled a shift in policy, most notably toward unilateralism and the demonization of enemies. It also helped to hold together the various justifications that were used to build the political coalitions that backed the war. Without the paranoia over terrorism, it is hard to imagine the Bush administration marshaling the national and international support needed to launch the war against Iraq.

6. THE WANING OF THE WAR?

As I was revising this chapter, we commemorated the tenth anniversary of 9/11—just a few months after the "death" of Osama bin Laden. (It would appear to be churlish for Americans to call his assassination what in human rights terms it clearly was: arbitrary execution; murder by the American government.) The Obama administration has been a disappointment to civil libertarians and human rights advocates (although whether for lack of effort or resistance by Congress and American society is a matter of considerable debate). Nonetheless, the atmosphere has changed. There is a growing lack of enthusiasm for the extreme measures of the Bush administration, even among their continuing supporters. After a decade, it is hard to sustain the sense of crisis that was essential to early American excesses. Even those who continue to defend the past American use of "enhanced interrogation techniques" show little enthusiasm for their use in the future.

One can debate how much this new atmosphere is due to the success of the war on terror. For our purposes here, though, the key point is that a less pressing "terrorist threat" opens the possibility for the reincorporation of antiterrorism into a rational and coherent American foreign policy.

Wars—especially moralized wars—discourage rational calculation. There is something unseemly about inquiring into the costs or consequences of combating evil, resolutely, whatever the cost. But when we leave the domain of weighing costs and benefits, we leave behind rational calculation. We did that during the cold war. We did it again in the early years of "the war on terror." The seeming waning of that war may signal the return of rational calculation to American foreign policy.

This does not mean always choosing human rights over antiterrorism. It does, however, mean taking seriously the demands of human rights, calculating calmly an efficient and effective antiterrorism policy, and insisting that foreign policy be based on a sober assessment of real costs and benefits. This—rather than ideological crusades irrespective of cost—can only be good both for American foreign policy and for international human rights.

PROBLEM 8: THE ABSOLUTE
PROHIBITION OF TORTURE

The Problem

International human rights law bans torture absolutely. As Article 2(2) of the Convention Against Torture puts it, "No exceptional circumstances whatsoever . . . may be invoked as a justification of torture." In other words, whatever the cost, torture should not be employed. My experience suggests, though, that few people really believe this—really believe, for example, that if torturing one person could unquestionably save the lives of thousands, tens of thousands, or millions of people (from, say, a chemical or nuclear weapon in the middle of a large city) that the right thing to do, all things considered, would be to let a large number of innocent people die needlessly. Such intuitions suggest that the absolute prohibition on torture ought to be replaced by a more nuanced policy.

A Solution

An absolute prohibition, I will argue, is less problematic than its alternatives. To paraphrase Churchill on democracy, it is the worst policy except for all the others that have been tried. And there are other ways to accommodate legitimate concerns about the perverse unintended consequences of an absolute ban.

Essential to such an argument is the empirical fact that it is extremely rare that torturing a single individual can, with a high probability, save the lives of very large numbers of innocent people. (There may be actual cases where this has been true, but I know of none. And it is telling that, despite the intense debate over this issue during the past decade, there is no widely known historical case where these conditions have been met.) The force of the argument for permitting torture, however, is undercut by decreases in the number of people "saved," decreases in the likelihood of "success," and increases in the amount of torture required.

A familiar legal maxim states that hard cases make bad law. This is particularly true when the cases are extremely rare. Philosophers may value such cases because they sharply pose a dilemma arising from conflicting principles. Law, however, is at its best when it provides general regulations of broad applicability.

This is especially true because the social utility of torture in all but the "perfect" case is likely to be, at best, both modest and highly speculative. Certainly, this is true of all the cases we know about over the past decade. (And I at least doubt that the cases we have not heard about are any different. Were there really a big and dramatic success for torture, especially by the United States, is it really plausible that it has been kept secret?) And the strong temptations to abuse any explicit exceptions make the case for an absolute prohibition powerful, *even on grounds of social utility.*

But what about that "perfect" case? If you really "know" (have a very well-founded belief) that a single individual has information necessary to save the lives of a great number of people, have a reasonable belief that she can be forcibly compelled to reveal that information in time, and there really is no other plausible option, what do you do? I suggest that the proper course of action is to torture her—and then face the consequences, pleading extenuating circumstances as an excuse.

Recall the discussion in §13.9 of different types of justification. With an absolute prohibition, torture will never be "authorized" in the strong sense that all relevant norms provide justification. The justifiability of torture will always be, at best, contested. But it may be "excusable," in the sense that a prima facie unjustifiable act is, all things considered, defensible, perhaps even the best possible choice given the circumstances.

Treating torture as, at best, excusable ensures that each instance will be examined in a context in which the burden of proof has been placed on the torturer. Legislating exceptions will not provide the same kind of scrutiny and leaves the burden of proof more obscure, perhaps even on the side of the victim. And a justification of excusable (at best) properly presents every instance of torture as, at best, a tragic infringement of basic values and human rights. It may be the right thing to do, all things considered. But that is only the lesser of evils.

This is another way of saying that rights are trumps—but only prima facie trumps. There is always a possibility of exceptions, all things considered. But law and policy should not be based on rare and dangerous cases. Such cases are better dealt with individually, on an ad hoc basis, should they actually arise.

Further Problems

Grant that there ought to be an absolute prohibition on torture. What *other* internationally recognized human rights merit such an absolute prohibition? Is torture unique, or close to unique? If so, why? If not, what are we to do when multiple absolute prohibitions conflict?

Now grant that there ought *not* to be an absolute prohibition on torture. What other internationally recognized human rights should have legislated exceptions? Of what sort? On what grounds?

Consider now the possibility that this whole discussion is misformulated in the sense that every right has within it a set of implicit limitations and exceptions. The problem then becomes specifying what those limitations and exceptions are. Suppose that this analysis is theoretically correct. Is it practically viable in the absence of any authoritative statement of those limits and exceptions? If there were a more robust international human rights jurisprudence, would this be a potentially practical way to deal with these issues?

The argument for excusing violations of an absolute prohibition is that it is less dangerous than legislating exceptions. But is excusing torture in rare, truly "necessary" cases going too far? Does it lead us down a slippery slope?

PROBLEM 9: (ANTI)TERRORISM
AND CIVIL LIBERTIES

The Problem

"The war on terror" has had domestic as well as international consequences for human rights. Most of the more serious abuses at the hands of American officials have taken place overseas. Nonetheless, personal liberties—especially privacy and due process rights, but also the free exercise of religion, freedom of association, and even freedom of speech—have been curtailed. The dramatic expansion of surveillance and the removal of some standard legal safeguards in terrorism cases have come at a cost to human rights that even their defenders usually acknowledge. Has it been worth it? Is it still worth that cost today?

A Solution

Once more we face an issue of trade-offs—that is, a question of relative weights. And the issue is empirical, not theoretical. How much additional security has been purchased? What is the real cost of the (modest but real) domestic limitations on personal liberties? I want to suggest that American policy has overrated the benefits, undervalued the costs, and acted out of convenience rather than necessity.

As we saw in Chapter 2, rights are trumps. And one of their principal functions is to remove issues from the domain in which simple calculations of social utility rightly determine public policy. If privacy and due process were not basic rights, one might plausibly argue that even minor improvements in homeland security would justify their limitation. But they *are* basic rights. Therefore, those who would claim justifiable infringement must show both a very large benefit and a pressing necessity.

About three thousand Americans have died from terrorism since 9/11, roughly three hundred people a year. This is roughly the same number of people who die annually from drowning in a bathtub. Twice as many people die annually from *accidental* gunshot wounds. Thirty times as many are killed by drunk drivers. Two hundred times as many people die each year from air pollution. Yet we have no war on guns or air pollution—and certainly would not accept restrictions on basic human rights to prevent some portion of these deaths from occurring.

Furthermore, the connection between restricting civil liberties and protecting people against terrorism is unclear at best. And arguments that they are *necessary* to produce the positive results attributed to them are rarely even made. Instead, it is argued that enhanced surveillance techniques have foiled, and will continue to foil, some not negligible number of significant terrorist plots and that new legal rules have produced, and will produce, more successful prosecutions of terror suspects. But this just is nowhere near enough to justify infringing basic human rights.

Certain limited sacrifices of civil liberties might be justified in some circumstances. The United States over the past several years, however, does not seem to be such a case.

Further Problems

If we grant an antiterrorism exception, why should similar arguments not apply to other types of security? For example, from gun violence? Or from felons that we know have a high probability to reoffend? And why not apply the same arguments to certain nonsecurity goals?

Isn't there, though, a qualitative difference between terrorism and other kinds of threats? Suppose that there is. Just what is it? And how much of a sacrifice of human rights does it justify? On what grounds?

Even if antiterrorism policies are justifiable in themselves, do they lead us down a slippery slope? If not, what prevents it?

DISCUSSION QUESTIONS

1. How much has the world changed since 9/11? For Americans? Europeans? Muslims? Arabs? Israelis? Palestinians? Iraqis? Pakistanis? Afghanis? Africans? Latin Americans? East Asians?

2. Is it true that human rights became permanently entrenched in American and broader Western foreign policies in the 1990s? If the war on terrorism drags on, is it not likely to undercut further the progress of the 1980s and 1990s? What if dramatic acts of terrorism become an annual event in the United States? A monthly event? Just how deep does the commitment to international human rights really go?

3. Is there any evidence that human rights are making a comeback in foreign policy as the initial shock of 9/11 wears off? Is there a difference between the United States and other Western countries?

4. Should we really care all that much about the treatment of terror suspects? Or those who are reliably known to be terrorists? Why should terrorists be entitled to the protections of the rules they seek to overthrow?

5. Are terrorists really forcing us to conceptualize human rights and security as competing concerns? Can a war on terror be effective while respecting the full range of internationally recognized human rights for all? If not, what is the problem with limited, targeted infringements of internationally recognized human rights? Isn't this precisely the sort of emergency that justifies overriding the prima facie priority of human rights?

6. What about the *domestic* human rights impact of the war on terror? How significant are the restrictions on human rights that have been imposed since 9/11 in places like the United States and Britain? Aren't they actually very modest, and probably justifiable (even if controversial)? Certainly, they shouldn't be seen in the same light as the cynical abuses of the language of antiterrorism by, say, the Russians in Chechnya, should they?

7. Grant that the world has become a worse place for human rights since 9/11. Isn't blaming the United States tantamount to blaming the victim?

SUGGESTED READINGS

On the general issue of terrorism and human rights, there are a number of good wide-ranging books, including Andrea Bianchi and Alexis Keller, eds., *Counterterrorism: Democracy's Challenge* (Oxford: Hart, 2008); Richard Ashby Wilson, ed., *Human Rights in the "War on Terror"* (Cambridge: Cambridge University Press, 2005); and Thomas G. Weiss, Margaret E. Crahan, and John Goering, eds., *Wars on Terrorism and Iraq: Human Rights, Unilateralism, and U.S. Foreign Policy* (New York: Routledge, 2004). On the question of how much things have changed for human rights since 9/11, see Michael Goodhart and Anja Mihr, eds., *Human Rights in the 21st Century: Continuity and Change Since 9/11* (Houndmills, Basingstoke: Palgrave Macmillan, 2011).

For comparative studies of national antiterrorism policies, see Mary L. Volcansek and John F. Stack Jr., eds., *Courts and Terrorism: Nine Nations Balance Rights and Security* (Cambridge: Cambridge University Press, 2011); Kent Roach, *The 9/11 Effect: Comparative Counter-Terrorism* (New York: Cambridge University Press,

2011); and Alison Brysk and Gershon Shafir, eds., *National Insecurity and Human Rights: Democracies Debate Counterterrorism* (Berkeley and Los Angeles: University of California Press, 2007).

On the broad issue of trade-offs between human rights and security in the context of combating terrorism, see Christian Walter, ed., *Terrorism as a Challenge for National and International Law: Security Versus Liberty?* (Berlin: Springer, 2004); M. Katherine B. Darmer, Robert M. Baird, and Stuart E. Rosenbaum, eds., *Civil Liberties vs. National Security in a Post-9/11 World* (Amherst, MA: Prometheus Books, 2004); Wolfgang Benedek and Alice Yotopoulos-Marangopoulos, eds., *Antiterrorist Measures and Human Rights* (Leiden: Martinus Nijhoff, 2004); and Michael Freeman, *Freedom or Security: The Consequences for Democracies Using Emergency Powers to Fight Terror* (Westport, CT: Praeger, 2003).

On American abuses of prisoners, good starting points are David P. Forsythe, *The Politics of Prisoner Abuse: The United States and Enemy Prisoners After 9/11* (Cambridge: Cambridge University Press, 2011), and Laurel E. Fletcher, Eric Stover, Stephen Paul Smith, et al., *The Guantánamo Effect: Exposing the Consequences of U.S. Detention and Interrogation Practices* (Berkeley and Los Angeles: University of California Press, 2009). On torture in the United States and US foreign policy, see Karen J. Greenberg, ed., *The Torture Debate in America* (Cambridge: Cambridge University Press, 2006), and Karen J. Greenberg and Joshua L. Dratel, eds., *The Torture Papers: The Road to Abu Ghraib* (Cambridge: Cambridge University Press, 2005).

Notes

Chapter One

1. Article 29 indicates that people also have duties to their community that set parameters for the exercise of rights. Article 30, the final article, states that nothing in the Declaration may be interpreted as justifying any act that aims at the destruction of any of the enumerated rights in the Declaration.

2. Note that the 1948 Convention on the Prevention and Punishment of the Crime of Genocide is not included in this list. International law has technically defined genocide as a sui generis crime outside of the body of human rights law, narrowly and technically defined. For most purposes, though, the reader can adopt the wider ordinary language sense of human rights that includes not only genocide but also what international law calls war crimes and crimes against humanity, which are separate bodies of international law.

3. The least ratified treaty is the torture convention, with 149. The most ratified, the children's rights treaty, has 193 of a possible 195 parties (excluding only Somalia and the United States). The 2006 Convention on the Rights of Persons with Disabilities is coming to be seen in many circles as part of this core. In December 2011 it had 107 parties. (The treaties on migrant workers and enforced disappearances are also often considered to be "core" treaties, but that seems to me a mistake given their relatively narrow scope.)

Chapter Two

1. This is not exactly correct. Although children are human beings, they usually are not thought to have, for example, a right to vote, on the grounds that they are not fully developed. But once they reach a certain age, they must be recognized as holding all human rights equally. Similarly, those who suffer from severe mental illness are often denied the exercise of many rights—but only until they regain full use and control of their faculties. Furthermore, both children and those with severe mental disabilities are denied the protection or exercise of only those rights for which they are held to lack the necessary requisites. They still have, and must be allowed to enjoy equally, all other human rights. And in the case of children, the 1989 Convention on the Rights of the Child seeks to clarify this special status, including rights to special protections.

2. Henry Shue, *Basic Rights: Subsistence and Affluence in U.S. Foreign Policy* (Princeton, NJ: Princeton University Press, 1996; originally, 1980), 51–64.

3. In what follows, I focus on the "external" dimensions of sovereignty, that is, sovereignty as it appears in the relations of states. Here the emphasis is on the absence of any superior (sovereign) above the state and thus on the sovereign equality of states. The "internal" dimensions of sovereignty concern the supreme authority of the state within its territory. Here the focus is on the legal and political superiority of the state over other actors. In the contemporary world, internal sovereignty is usually seen as resting on the state acting in the name and interests of the people: "popular sovereignty."

4. For an extended discussion of this idea, see Hedley Bull, *The Anarchical Society* (New York: Columbia University Press, 1977).

5. Robert Gilpin, "The Richness of the Tradition of Political Realism," in *Neorealism and Its Critics,* edited by Robert O. Keohane (New York: Columbia University Press, 1986), 305; Hans Morgenthau, *Politics Among Nations,* 2nd ed. (New York: Alfred A. Knopf, 1954), 9.

6. George F. Kennan, "Morality and Foreign Policy," *Foreign Affairs* 64 (Winter 1985–1986): 206; George F. Kennan, *Realities of American Foreign Policy* (Princeton, NJ: Princeton University Press, 1954), 48; George F. Kennan, *The Cloud of Danger: Current Realities of American Foreign Policy* (Boston: Little, Brown, 1977), 45.

7. Herbert Butterfield, *Christianity, Diplomacy, and War* (London: Epworth Press, 1953), 11.

8. Robert J. Art and Kenneth N. Waltz, "Technology, Strategy, and the Uses of Force," in *The Use of Force,* edited by Robert J. Art and Kenneth N. Waltz (Lanham, MD: University Press of America, 1983), 6.

Chapter Three

1. Henry Shue, *Basic Rights: Subsistence, Affluence, and U.S. Foreign Policy* (Princeton, NJ: Princeton University Press, 1996; originally, 1980), 29–34.

2. Dunstan M. Wai, "Human Rights in Sub-Saharan Africa," in *Human Rights: Cultural and Ideological Perspectives,* edited by Adamantia Pollis and Peter Schwab (New York: Praeger, 1979), 116.

3. Hung-Chao Tai, "Human Rights in Taiwan: Convergence of Two Political Cultures?," in *Human Rights in East Asia: A Cultural Perspective,* edited by James C. Hsiung (New York: Paragon House, 1985), 77, 79.

4. Fouad Zakaria, "Human Rights in the Arab World: The Islamic Context," in *Philosophical Foundations of Human Rights,* edited by UNESCO (Paris: UNESCO, 1986), 228; Abul A'la Mawdudi, *Human Rights in Islam* (Leicester: Islamic Foundation, 1976), 10.

5. Khalid M. Ishaque, "Human Rights in Islamic Law," *Review of the International Commission of Jurists* 12 (1974): 32–38.

6. Manwoo Lee, "North Korea and the Western Notion of Human Rights," in *Human Rights in East Asia,* edited by Hsiung, 129, 131.

7. Jack Donnelly, *Universal Human Rights in Theory and Practice*, 2nd ed. (Ithaca, NY: Cornell University Press, 2003; 3rd ed. forthcoming 2013), §6.4 (2nd ed.), §6.3 (3rd ed.).

8. Robert E. Goodin et al., *The Real Worlds of Welfare Capitalism* (Cambridge: Cambridge University Press, 1999).

9. Other "examples," such as pornography and homosexuality, miss the mark. Tolerance of neither is required by international human rights norms. Where they are allowed, they involve particular conceptions of the rights to free speech and nondiscrimination that are permitted but not mandated by international human rights norms.

Chapter Four

1. Marcelo Cavarozzi, "Political Cycles in Argentina Since 1955," in *Transitions from Authoritarian Rule: Latin America*, edited by Guillermo O'Donnell, Philippe C. Schmitter, and Laurence Whitehead (Baltimore: Johns Hopkins University Press, 1986).

2. Quoted in Amnesty International USA, *Disappearances: A Workbook* (New York: Amnesty International USA, 1981), 9.

3. Guatemala was the first country to use disappearances systematically as a means of repression, in the 1960s. The practice seems to have been introduced into South America through the example of the Brazilian military in the late 1960s. For a good general introduction, see ibid.

4. Americas Watch, *Truth and Partial Justice in Argentina: An Update* (New York: Americas Watch, 1991), 6. In Uruguay, however, as we will see, most of the disappeared reappeared. Chile fell somewhere in between. But the basic strategy was similar in the three countries.

5. Ian Guest, *Behind the Disappearances: Argentina's Dirty War Against Human Rights and the United Nations* (Philadelphia: University of Pennsylvania Press, 1990), 41.

6. V. S. Naipaul, *The Return of Eva Perón* (New York: Vintage Books, 1981), 170, 162.

7. Lawrence Weschler, *A Miracle, a Universe: Settling Accounts with Torturers* (New York: Pantheon Books, 1990), 145.

8. John Simpson and Jana Bennett, *The Disappeared: Voices from a Secret War* (London: Robson Books, 1985), 225.

9. Ibid.

10. Quoted in ibid., 66.

11. In fact, one of the tragic ironies in Uruguay was that the Tupamaros had already been destroyed before the coup. In Chile there was no guerrilla threat at all.

12. Lawyers' Committee for International Human Rights, *The Generals Give Back Uruguay* (New York: Lawyers' Committee for International Human Rights, 1985), 57; Weschler, *A Miracle, a Universe*, 112; Inter-Church Committee on Human Rights in Latin America, *Violations of Human Rights in Uruguay* (Toronto: Inter-Church Committee on Human Rights in Latin America, 1978), 7; Martin Weinstein,

Uruguay: Democracy at the Crossroads (Boulder, CO: Westview Press, 1988), 44, 52; David Pion-Berlin, *The Ideology of State Terror: Economic Doctrine and Political Repression in Argentina and Peru* (Boulder, CO: Lynne Rienner, 1989), 101.

13. Simpson and Bennett, *The Disappeared*, 110.

14. See Americas Watch, *The Vicaria de la Solidaridad in Chile* (New York: Americas Watch, 1987).

15. Lawyers' Committee for International Human Rights, *The Generals Give Back Uruguay*, 32–35.

16. See Weschler, *A Miracle, a Universe*, 173–236.

17. Hannah Arendt, *The Human Condition* (Chicago: University of Chicago Press, 1958), 241.

18. Zbigniew Herbert, "Mr. Cogito on the Need for Precision," quoted in Weschler, *A Miracle, a Universe*, 191.

Chapter Five

1. Comprehensive information on activities of the council is available at http://www2.ohchr.org/english/bodies/hrcouncil.

2. http://www.ohchr.org/EN/HRBodies/UPR/Pages/UPRMain.aspx is the official website. For a broader range of information on the process, see http://www.upr-info.org/.

3. See http://www2.ohchr.org/english/bodies/chr/special/index.htm.

4. See http://www.ilo.org/global/lang-en/index.htm.

5. See http://www.unesco.org/new/en/unesco/.

6. See http://www.icc-cpi.int/Menus/ICC.

Chapter Six

1. See http://www.coe.int/.

2. See http://www.echr.coe.int/echr/Homepage_EN.

3. The case law and jurisprudence of the European system can be searched through the powerful HUDOC database at http://www.echr.coe.int/ECHR/EN/Header/Case-Law/HUDOC/HUDOC+database/.

4. See http://www.coe.int/t/commissioner/default_en.asp.

5. See http://www.osce.org/.

6. See http://europa.eu/. On human rights in particular, see http://europa.eu/pol/rights/index_en.htm.

7. See http://europa.eu/institutions/inst/justice/index_en.htm.

8. See http://www.oas.org/en/iachr/.

9. See http://www.corteidh.or.cr/index.cfm?&CFID=666614&CFTOKEN=69520161.

10. See http://www.corteidh.or.cr/casos.cfm?&CFID=829208&CFTOKEN=26959705.

11. See http://www.achpr.org/.

12. See http://www.african-court.org/en/home/.

13. For a recent overview, see Mervat Rishmawi, "The Arab Charter on Human Rights and the League of Arab States: An Update," *Human Rights Law Review* (2010): 169–178, http://hrlr.oxfordjournals.org/content/10/1/169.full.

14. The South Asian Association for Regional Cooperation includes all states in the geographic region. But the rivalry between India and Pakistan has made it a largely ineffective organization. And although particular human rights issues are addressed regionally (especially child welfare), there is no authoritative regional declaration. In fact, the 1991 Colombo Declaration, which outlines the priorities of the organization, has no section on human rights and explicitly subordinates democracy, human rights, and the rule of law to development initiatives.

15. Cecilia Medina Quiroga, *The Battle of Human Rights: Gross, Systematic Violations and the Inter-American System* (Dordrecht: Martinus Nijhoff, 1988), 312.

16. For a detailed—and fascinating, even gripping—account of Argentina's efforts in the United Nations, see Ian Guest, *Behind the Disappearances: Argentina's Dirty War Against Human Rights and the United Nations* (Philadelphia: University of Pennsylvania Press, 1990), pt. 2.

Chapter Eight

1. Liisa Lukkari North, "El Salvador," in *International Handbook of Human Rights*, edited by Jack Donnelly and Rhoda E. Howard (Westport, CT: Greenwood Press, 1987), 125–126.

2. Jeane J. Kirkpatrick, "Dictatorships and Double Standards," *Commentary* 68 (November 1979).

3. The Committee of Santa Fe, *A New Inter-American Policy for the Eighties* (Washington, DC: Council for Inter-American Security, 1980), 37.

4. See, for example, Americas Watch Committee and the American Civil Liberties Union, *As BAD as Ever: A Report on Human Rights in El Salvador* (New York: Americas Watch Committee and the American Civil Liberties Union, 1984).

5. Americas Watch, *Annual Report, June 1984–June 1985* (New York: Americas Watch, 1985), 4.

6. Cynthia Brown, ed., *With Friends Like These: The Americas Watch Report on Human Rights and U.S. Policy in Latin America* (New York: Pantheon Books, 1985), 20. Compare with the Watch Committees and Lawyers' Committee for Human Rights, *The Reagan Administration's Record on Human Rights in 1986* (New York: Watch Committees and Lawyers' Committee for Human Rights, 1987), 49, 92–99, and *The Reagan Administration's Record on Human Rights in 1987* (New York: Watch Committees and Lawyers' Committee for Human Rights, 1988), 106. On the Reagan administration's systematic misrepresentation of the facts, see Americas Watch, *Managing the Facts: How the Administration Deals with Reports of Human Rights Abuses in El Salvador* (New York: Americas Watch, 1985).

7. Christopher Coker, *The United States and South Africa, 1968–1985: Constructive Engagement and Its Critics* (Durham, NC: Duke University Press, 1986), 105.

8. Quoted in Charles Cooper and Joan Verloren van Themaat, "Dutch Aid Determinants, 1973–85: Continuity and Change," in *Western Middle Powers and Global*

Poverty: The Determinants of the Aid Policies of Canada, Denmark, the Netherlands, Norway, and Sweden, edited by Olav Stokke (Uppsala: Almquist and Wiksell International, 1989), 119.

9. Jan Egeland, *Impotent Superpower—Potent Small State: Potentialities and Limitations of Human Rights Objectives in the Foreign Policies of the United States and Norway* (Oslo: Norwegian University Press, 1988), 3, 5.

10. Ibid., 15.

11. *Statements and Speeches* 82/12 (Ottawa: Bureau of Information, Department of External Affairs), quoted in Rhoda E. Howard and Jack Donnelly, *Confronting Revolution in Nicaragua: U.S. and Canadian Responses* (New York: Carnegie Council on Ethics and International Affairs, 1990).

12. Egeland, *Impotent Superpower,* 23.

13. Norway and the Netherlands are usually the world's two leading aid providers on a per capita basis; for most of the past thirty years they contributed eight to ten times more per capita than the United States.

Chapter Nine

1. See http://www.state.gov/g/drl/rls/hrrpt/.

Chapter Ten

1. See http://www.amnesty.org/.

2. The Israel-based organization NGO Monitor, which describes itself as "Israel's most prominent watchdog of human rights groups" (http://www.ngo-monitor.org), is a leading source of such arguments.

Chapter Twelve

1. Fang Lizhi, "Declaration to Support Democratic Reform in Mainland China," *World Affairs* 152, no. 3 (1989–1990): 136–137.

2. *World Affairs* 52, no. 3 (1989–1990): 138.

3. Jonathan D. Spence, *The Search for Modern China* (New York: W. W. Norton, 1990), 742.

4. The statue, however, was a late and rather desperate gesture calculated to appeal to the United States more than to the Chinese people. Any Chinese who would have responded positively to this ostentatiously foreign symbol certainly were already mobilized behind the students.

5. Assuming a growth rate of one-third raises the cost to more than $15 billion. China also lost access to about $1 billion in World Bank loans for the better part of a year. Assessing the impact on private funding is more complex. Commercial borrowing was stagnant from 1987 through 1992. Direct foreign investment stagnated from 1988 through 1990, grew some in 1991, and then took off dramatically in 1992. Nicholas R. Landy, *China in the World Economy* (Washington, DC: Institute for Inter-

national Economics, 1994), tables 3.6 and 3.7. Structural economic and legal factors lie at the root of these lulls, which predate Tiananmen. Nonetheless, most observers had expected a surge in foreign investment in late 1989 and 1990. This seems to have been delayed until 1991–1992, at a cost to China of another few billion dollars.

6. The discussion of Japanese policy here draws heavily on K. V. Kesavan, "Japan and the Tiananmen Square Incident," *Asian Survey* 30 (July 1990): 669–681; and David Arase, "Japanese Policy Toward Democracy and Human Rights in Asia," *Asian Survey* 33 (October 1993): 935–952.

7. Peter Van Ness, "Australia's Human Rights Delegation to China, 1991: A Case Study," in *Australia's Human Rights Diplomacy,* by Ian Russell, Peter Van Ness, and Beng-Huat Chua (Canberra: Australian National University, Australian Foreign Policy Papers, 1992), 83.

8. Actual Japanese loan disbursements to China, however, did drop from a high of $670 million in 1989 to $539 million in 1990 and to $424 million in 1991 (almost exactly the 1987 level), in contrast to the large increases anticipated when the new five-year aid plan was approved in August 1988. See Landy, *China in the World Economy,* table 3.5b. Thus, even Japan's most reluctant sanctions had immediate and direct economic costs to China of perhaps $2 billion.

9. China considers Tibet an integral part of its territory. Others consider it an occupied country. In either case, Tibetan culture and religion have been under sustained and often violent attack for more than a half century.

10. Quoted in Bruce Stokes, "Playing Favorites," *National Journal,* March 26, 1994, 714.

11. Thomas Friedman, in the next day's *New York Times,* quoted in David M. Lampton, "America's China Policy in the Age of the Finance Minister: Clinton Ends Linkage," *China Quarterly,* no. 139 (1994): 597.

12. Ann Kent, "China and the International Human Rights Regime: A Case Study of Multilateral Monitoring, 1989–1994," *Human Rights Quarterly* 17 (February 1995): 17.

13. Quoted in ibid., 13.

14. Ibid., 21.

15. Ibid., 12.

16. "U.S. Interference Protested," *Beijing Review* 32 (June 12–25, 1989): 10. Note that the scheduled June 12–18 issue did not appear.

17. Ding Xinghao, "Managing Sino-American Relations in a Changing World," *Asian Survey* 31 (December 1991): 1168.

18. Kent, "Multilateral Monitoring," 21.

19. *Economist,* October 26, 1996. For the curious, the firm was Mobil.

20. Quoted in Stokes, "Playing Favorites," 713.

Chapter Thirteen

1. Peter R. Baehr, "Controversies in the Current International Human Rights Debate," *Human Rights Review* 2, no. 1 (2000): 32n75.

Chapter Fourteen

1. Alison Brysk, *From Tribal Village to Global Village: Indian Rights and International Relations in Latin America* (Stanford, CA: Stanford University Press, 2000).

2. Margaret E. Keck and Kathryn Sikink, *Activists Beyond Borders: Advocacy Networks in International Politics* (Ithaca, NY: Cornell University Press, 1998).

3. John Gerard Ruggie, "International Regimes, Transactions, and Change: Embedded Liberalism in the Postwar Economic Order," *International Organization* 36 (Spring 1982): 397–415.

Chapter Fifteen

1. For a good general overview of the work of the 1990s, see Marina Ottaway and Thomas Carothers, eds., *Funding Virtue: Civil Society Aid and Democracy Promotion* (Washington, DC: Carnegie Endowment for International Peace, 2000).

2. For an overview of the human rights situation in Chechnya, see Human Rights Watch, *Russia: Abuses in Chechnya Continue to Cause Human Suffering,* January 29, 2003, http://www.hrw.org/press/2003/01/russia012903.htm; and *Human Rights Situation in Chechnya,* April 2003, http://www.hrw.org/backgrounder/eca/chechnya /index.htm. For current (although in some cases not entirely nonpartisan) information, see http://www.watchdog.cz/.

3. "Since it launched a military operation in Chechnya in 1999, Russia's leaders have described the armed conflict there as a counter-terrorism operation and have attempted to fend off international scrutiny of Russian forces' abusive conduct by invoking the imperative of fighting terrorism. This pattern has become more pronounced since the September 11 attacks, as Russia sought to convince the international community that its operation in Chechnya was its contribution to the international campaign against terrorism. . . . World leaders, until then critical of Russia's conduct in Chechnya, did little to challenge these claims." *Human Rights Situation in Chechnya,* April 2003, http://www.hrw.org/backgrounder /eca/chechnya/index.htm.

4. Information on Israeli human rights violations is highly politicized. B'Tselem, the Israeli Information Center for Human Rights in the Occupied Territories, is perhaps the best neutral source. See http://www.betselem.org.

5. For a powerful illustration of this phenomenon in microcosm, see B'Tselem, *Al-Mawazi, Gaza Strip: Intolerable Life in an Isolated Enclave,* March 2003, http:// www.betselem.org/Download/2003_Al_Mwassy_Eng.pdf.

6. Political assassinations—if not terrorism, then extrajudicial executions—have become a regular part of the Israeli response to terrorism. In Chechnya, torture has become so pervasive that in the summer of 2003, the European Committee for the Prevention of Torture issued a rare public statement (http://www.cpt.coe.int /documents/rus/2003-33-inf-eng.htm), following strongly worded criticism by the Parliamentary Assembly of the Council of Europe in the spring.

7. For appeals by human rights NGOs calling on Western states to be more vocal on the issue of Chechnya, see http://www.hrw.org/press/2003/06/russia062003 .htm, http://www.hrw.org/press/2003/05/russia053003.htm, and http://www.reliefweb .int/w/rwb.nsf/0/5404f2f0528bc31949256cb6000da38f?OpenDocument.

Appendix:
Universal Declaration of Human Rights

GENERAL ASSEMBLY RESOLUTION 217A (III), 10 DECEMBER 1948

Whereas recognition of the inherent dignity and of the equal and inalienable rights of all members of the human family is the foundation of freedom, justice and peace in the world,

Whereas disregard and contempt for human rights have resulted in barbarous acts which have outraged the conscience of mankind, and the advent of a world in which human beings shall enjoy freedom of speech and belief and freedom from fear and want has been proclaimed as the highest aspiration of the common people,

Whereas it is essential, if man is not to be compelled to have recourse, as a last resort, to rebellion against tyranny and oppression, that human rights should be protected by the rule of law,

Whereas it is essential, to promote the development of friendly relations between nations,

Whereas the peoples of the United Nations have in the Charter reaffirmed their faith in fundamental human rights, in the dignity and worth of the human person and in the equal rights of men and women and have determined to promote social progress and better standards of life in larger freedom,

Whereas Member States have pledged themselves to achieve, in co-operation with the United Nations, the promotion of universal respect for and observance of human rights and fundamental freedoms,

Whereas a common understanding of these rights and freedoms is of the greatest importance for the full realization of this pledge,

Now, therefore,

The General Assembly

Proclaims this Universal Declaration of Human Rights as a common standard of achievement for all peoples and all nations, to the end that every individual and every organ of society, keeping this Declaration constantly in mind, shall strive by teaching and education to promote respect for these rights and freedoms and by progressive measures, national and international, to secure their universal and effective recognition and observance, both among the peoples of Member States themselves and among the peoples of territories under their jurisdiction.

Article 1.   All human beings are born free and equal in dignity and rights. They are endowed with reason and conscience and should act towards one another in a spirit of brotherhood.

Article 2.   Everyone is entitled to all the rights and freedoms set forth in this Declaration, without distinction of any kind, such as race, colour, sex, language, religion, political or other opinion, national or social origin, property, birth or other status.

Furthermore, no distinction shall be made on the basis of the political, jurisdictional or international status of the country or territory to which a person belongs, whether it be independent, trust, non-self-governing or under any other limitation of sovereignty.

Article 3.   Everyone has the right to life, liberty and the security of person.

Article 4.   No one shall be held in slavery or servitude; slavery and the slave trade shall be prohibited in all their forms.

Article 5.   No one shall be subjected to torture or to cruel, inhuman or degrading treatment or punishment.

Article 6.   Everyone has the right to recognition everywhere as a person before the law.

Article 7.   All are equal before the law and are entitled without any discrimination to equal protection of the law. All are entitled to equal protection against any discrimination in violation of this Declaration and against any incitement to such discrimination.

Article 8.   Everyone has the right to an effective remedy by the competent national tribunals for acts violating the fundamental rights granted him by the constitution or by law.

Article 9.   No one shall be subjected to arbitrary arrest, detention or exile.

Article 10.   Everyone is entitled to full equality to a fair and public hearing by an independent and impartial tribunal in the determination of his rights and obligations and of any criminal charge against him.

Article 11.   1. Everyone charged with a penal offence has the right to be presumed innocent until proved guilty according to law in a public trial at which he has had all the guarantees necessary for his defence.

2. No one shall be held guilty of any penal offence on account of any act or omission which did not constitute a penal offence, under national or international law, at the time when it was committed. Nor shall a heavier penalty be imposed than the one that was applicable at the time the penal offence was committed.

Article 12.   No one shall be subjected to arbitrary interference with his privacy, family, home or correspondence, nor to attacks upon his honour and reputation. Everyone has the right to the protection of the law against such interference or attacks.

Article 13.   1. Everyone has the right to freedom of movement and residence within the borders of each state.

2. Everyone has the right to leave any country, including his own, and to return to his country.

Article 14. 1. Everyone has the right to seek and to enjoy in other countries asylum from persecution.

2. This right may not be invoked in the case of prosecutions genuinely arising from non-political crimes or from acts contrary to the purposes and principles of the United Nations.

Article 15. 1. Everyone has the right to a nationality.

2. No one shall be arbitrarily deprived of his nationality nor denied the right to change his nationality.

Article 16. 1. Men and women of full age, without any limitation due to race, nationality or religion, have the right to marry and to found a family. They are entitled to equal rights as to marriage, during marriage and at its dissolution.

2. Marriage shall be entered into only with the free and full consent of the intending spouses.

3. The family is the natural and fundamental group unit of society and is entitled to protection by society and the State.

Article 17. 1. Everyone has the right to own property alone as well as in association with others.

2. No one shall be arbitrarily deprived of his property.

Article 18. Everyone has the right to freedom of thought, conscience and religion; this right includes freedom to change his religion or belief, and freedom, either alone or in community with others and in public or private, to manifest his religion or belief in teaching, practice, worship and observance.

Article 19. Everyone has the right to freedom of opinion and expression; this right includes freedom to hold opinions without interference and to seek, receive and impart information and ideas through any media and regardless of frontiers.

Article 20. 1. Everyone has the right to freedom of peaceful assembly and association.

2. No one may be compelled to belong to an association.

Article 21. 1. Everyone has the right to take part in the Government of his country, directly or through freely chosen representatives.

2. Everyone has the right of equal access to public service in his country.

3. The will of the people shall be the basis of the authority of government; this will shall be expressed in periodic and genuine elections which shall be by universal and equal suffrage and shall be held by secret vote or by equivalent free voting procedures.

Article 22. Everyone, as a member of society, has the right to social security and is entitled to realization through national effort and international co-operation and in accordance with the organization and resources of each State, of the economic, social and cultural rights indispensable for his dignity and the free development of his personality.

Article 23. 1. Everyone has the right to work, to free choice of employment, to just and favourable conditions of work and to protection against unemployment.

2. Everyone, without any discrimination, has the right to equal pay for equal work.

3. Everyone who works has the right to just and favourable remuneration insuring for himself and his family an existence worthy of human dignity, and supplemented, if necessary, by other means of social protection.

4. Everyone has the right to form and to join trade unions for the protection of his interests.

Article 24. Everyone has the right to rest and leisure, including reasonable limitation of working hours and periodic holidays with pay.

Article 25. 1. Everyone has the right to a standard of living adequate for the health and well-being of himself and of his family, including food, clothing, housing and medical care and necessary social services, and the right to security in the event of unemployment, sickness, disability, widowhood, old age or other lack of livelihood in circumstances beyond his control.

2. Motherhood and childhood are entitled to special care and assistance. All children, whether born in or out of wedlock, shall enjoy the same social protection.

Article 26. 1. Everyone has the right to education. Education shall be free, at least in the elementary and fundamental stages. Elementary education shall be compulsory. Technical and professional education shall be made generally available and higher education shall be equally accessible to all on the basis of merit.

2. Education shall be directed to the full development of the human personality and to the strengthening of respect for human rights and fundamental freedoms. It shall promote understanding, tolerance and friendship among all nations, racial or religious groups, and shall further the activities of the United Nations for the maintenance of peace.

3. Parents have a prior right to choose the kind of education that shall be given to their children.

Article 27. 1. Everyone has the right freely to participate in the cultural life of the community, to enjoy the arts and share in scientific advancement and its benefits.

2. Everyone has the right to the protection of the moral and material interests resulting from any scientific, literary or artistic production of which he is the author.

Article 28. Everyone is entitled to a social and international order in which the rights and freedoms set forth in this Declaration can be fully realized.

Article 29. 1. Everyone has duties to the community in which alone the free and full development of his personality is possible.

2. In the exercise of his rights and freedoms, everyone shall be subject only to such limitations as are determined by law solely for the purpose of securing due recognition and respect for the rights and freedoms of others and of meeting the just requirements of morality, public order and the general welfare in a democratic society.

3. These rights and freedoms may in no case be exercised contrary to the purposes and principles of the United Nations.

Article 30. Nothing in this Declaration may be interpreted as implying for any State, group or person any right to engage in any activity or to perform any act aimed at the destruction of any of the rights and freedoms set forth herein.

Glossary

American exceptionalism is the belief that the United States is culturally and politically different from, and usually superior to, other countries. It can be traced to the colonial period and the biblical image of the city on the hill. In the area of human rights, it tends to be expressed in the common American view that the United States in some important sense defines international human rights standards.

Anarchy, the absence of political rule, is characterized by the lack of authoritative hierarchical relationships of superiority and subordination. In international relations, anarchy refers to the fact that there is no higher authority above states. Anarchy, however, need not involve chaos (absence of order). Thus, international relations has been called an anarchical society, a society in which order emerges from the interactions of formally equally sovereign states.

Apartheid, an Afrikaans term meaning "separateness," was the policy of systematic, official racial classification and discrimination in South Africa. Building on a long tradition of racial discrimination, white South African governments in the 1950s and 1960s developed an unusually extensive, highly integrated system of official discrimination, touching virtually all aspects of public life and many aspects of private life as well. The policy was officially renounced following a (whites-only) plebiscite in March 1992.

Civil and political rights are one of two principal classes of internationally recognized human rights. They provide protections against the state (such as rights to due process, habeas corpus, and freedom of speech) and require that the state provide certain substantive legal and political opportunities (such as the rights to vote and to trial by a jury of one's peers). They are codified in the International Covenant on Civil and Political Rights and in Articles 1–15 and 18–21 of the Universal Declaration of Human Rights (see Table 1.1).

Cold war is the term used for the geopolitical and ideological struggle between the Soviet Union and the United States following World War II. It began in earnest roughly in 1948, waxed and waned over the following forty years, and finally ended with the collapse of the Soviet bloc in 1989.

Cosmopolitan and **cosmopolitanism** refer to a conception of international relations that views people first and foremost as individual members of a global political community ("cosmopolis") rather than as citizens of states.

Disappearances are a form of human rights violation that became popular in the 1970s. Victims, rather than being officially detained or even murdered by the authorities or semiofficial death squads, are "disappeared," taken to state-run but clandestine detention centers. Torture typically accompanies disappearance, and in some countries the disappeared have also been regularly killed.

Economic, social, and cultural rights are one of two classes of internationally recognized human rights. They guarantee individuals socially provided goods and services (such as food, health care, social insurance, and education) and certain protections against the state (especially in family matters). They are codified in the International Covenant on Economic, Social, and Cultural Rights and in Articles 16–17 and 22–27 of the Universal Declaration of Human Rights (see Table 1.1).

Ethnic cleansing is the genocidal "purification" of the population of a territory through murder and forced migration. The term entered international political vocabularies to describe the strategy and practices of Serbian separatists in the former Yugoslavian republic of Bosnia-Herzegovina during the civil war of 1992–1995.

Genocide, in the narrow, technical sense of the term, involves systematic killing and similar methods aimed at destroying, in whole or in part, a people (*genos*) or ethnic or religious group. In a looser sense of the term, it involves targeted mass political killing—"politicide"—directed against a group that may not be defined by common descent.

Humanitarian intervention is **intervention** (see below), almost always involving the use of force, for humanitarian purposes, typically in situations of genocide, armed conflict, or severe humanitarian crisis (especially massive famine).

Human rights, the rights that one has simply because one is a human being, are held equally and inalienably by all human beings. They are the social and political guarantees necessary to protect individuals from the standard threats to human dignity posed by the modern state and modern markets.

The **Human Rights Committee** is a body of eighteen independent experts created by the International Covenant on Civil and Political Rights. Its principal activities are reviewing periodic state reports on compliance with the Covenant and reviewing individual complaints of violations. Compare **treaty bodies.**

An **intergovernmental organization**—often referred to as an international organization—is a treaty-based organization of states. Prominent global examples include the United Nations and the World Health Organization. The European Union is the most prominent regional example. Compare **nongovernmental organization.**

The **International Bill of Human Rights** is the informal name for the Universal Declaration of Human Rights and the International Human Rights Covenants, considered collectively as a set of authoritative international human rights standards. This title underscores the substantive interrelations of these three documents.

The **International Human Rights Covenants** comprise the International Covenant on Economic, Social, and Cultural Rights and the International Covenant on Civil and Political Rights, which were opened for signature in 1966 and entered into force in 1976. Along with the Universal Declaration of Human Rights, these are the central normative documents in the field of international human rights.

Internationalist and **internationalism** refer to a conception of international relations that stresses both the centrality of the state and the existence of social relations among those states. See also **society of states.**

An **international regime** is a set of principles, norms, rules, and decision-making procedures accepted by states (and other relevant international actors) as binding in an issue area. The notion of a regime points to patterns of international governance that are not necessarily limited to a single treaty or organization.

Intervention, as the term is used in international law and relations, means coercive interference, usually involving the threat or use of force, against the sovereignty, territorial integrity, or political independence, or any matters essentially within the domestic jurisdiction, of a state.

The **like-minded countries** are a group of about a dozen small and medium-size Western countries, including Canada, the Netherlands, and the Nordic countries. They often act in concert in international organizations and generally pursue foreign policies that are more "liberal" than those of the United States, Japan, or the larger western European countries. The like-minded countries particularly emphasize development issues, and they have tried to play an intermediary role between the countries of the South and the larger northern countries.

A **nongovernmental organization** is a private association of individuals or groups that engages in political activity. International NGOs (INGOs) carry on their activities across state boundaries. The most prominent human rights INGOs include Amnesty International, Human Rights Watch, and the Minority Rights Group. In some areas, especially international relief, NGOs are frequently referred to as private voluntary organizations.

Nonintervention is the international obligation not to interfere in matters that are essentially within the domestic jurisdiction of a sovereign state. This duty is correlative to the right of sovereignty and expresses the principal practical implications of sovereignty, viewed from the perspective of other states.

Peacekeeping involves the use of lightly armed multilateral forces to separate previously warring parties. Peacekeeping is distinguished from collective security enforcement by a limited mandate, an effort to maintain neutrality, and reliance on the consent of the parties in whose territory peacekeepers are placed.

Quiet diplomacy is the pursuit of foreign policy objectives through official channels, without recourse to public statements or actions. A standard mechanism for pursuing virtually all foreign policy goals, it became a political issue in the United States in the late 1970s and 1980s, when conservative critics of the policy of the Carter administration and defenders of the policy of the Reagan administration argued that US international human rights policy toward "friendly" (anticommunist) regimes should in most cases be restricted *solely* to quiet diplomacy.

Realism (realpolitik) is a theory of international relations that stresses the absence of international government (that is, the presence of international **anarchy**) and the centrality of egoism in human motivation, thus requiring states to give priority to power and security in international relations and to exclude considerations of morality from foreign policy.

A **relativist** believes that values are not universal but are a function of contingent circumstances. **Cultural relativism** holds that morality is significantly determined by culture and history. Marxism is another form of **ethical relativism,** holding that values are reflections of the interests of the ruling class. **Radical cultural relativism** sees culture as the source of all values.

The **society of states** conceptualizes "the international community" as a largely contractual community whose principal members are states. See also **internationalism.**

To be **sovereign** is to be subject to no higher authority. International relations over the past three centuries have been structured around the principle of the **sovereignty** of territorial states.

Statist and **statism** refer to a theory of international relations that stresses the centrality of sovereign states. Realism is usually associated with a statist theory of international relations.

Thomism is the philosophy of Thomas Aquinas, which continues to play a central role in Catholic moral and ethical theory.

A **treaty** is an agreement between states that creates obligations on those states. Treaties are one of the two principal sources of international law, along with custom (regularized patterns of action that through repeated practice have created expectations and thus acquired an obligatory character). The two most important international human rights treaties are the International Covenant on Economic, Social, and Cultural Rights and the International Covenant on Civil and Political Rights.

Treaty bodies is the term of art used for the various committees created under the International Human Rights Covenants and other international human rights treaties to monitor state compliance. Compare **Human Rights Committee.**

The **Universal Declaration of Human Rights** is a 1948 UN General Assembly resolution that provides the most authoritative statement of international human rights norms. Together with the **International Human Rights Covenants,** it is sometimes referred to as the **International Bill of Human Rights.**

Universalism is the belief that moral values such as human rights are fundamentally the same at all times, in all places, or across some particular "universe" of application. It is the opposite of **relativism.**

Utilitarianism is a moral theory (most closely associated with Bentham and Mill) that holds that the right course of action is that which maximizes the balance of pleasure over pain. This is the most common form of consequentialist ethics, which focus on the consequences of acts rather than their inherent character.

Index